Top Guns

TOP GUNS

Arsenal in the 1990's

Jon Spurling

Aureus

First Published 2001

©2001 Jon Spurling

Jon Spurling has asserted the Author's right under the Copyright, Designs and Patents Act 1988 to be identified as Author of this Work.

Front cover: Tony Adams lifts the Premiership Trophy aloft in May 1998. ©Professional Sport
Back cover: Lee Dixon helps Ian Wright celebrate after Wright became Arsenal's all-time record goal scorer in September 1997. ©Professional Sport
All photographs: ©Professional Sport

ISBN 1 899750 23 1

Printed in Great Britain.

A catalogue record for this book is available from the British Library.

Aureus Publishing Limited, 24 Mafeking Road, Cardiff, CF23 5DQ, UK.
Tel: (029) 2045 5200 Fax: (029) 2045 5200
Int. tel: +44 29 2045 5200 Int. fax: +44 29 2045 5200
E-mail: sales@aureus.co.uk
          meuryn.hughes@aureus.co.uk
Web site: www.aureus.co.uk

Contents

This book is for my Mum and Dad

I also dedicate this book to the memory of David Rocastle -
tragically gone
but always a true Gunner

Acknowledgments

I would like to thank the following for their assistance in the preparation of this book:

The large number of Arsenal fans who wrote in with their '90s memories; Ian McPherson, Rob Kemp, Jo Selby, Mickey James, Roy Jones, Richie Montague, Chris Baines, Johnny Franks, Dave Noble, Dave Ritchie, Alex Marks, Colin Arthur, Matt Allgood, Barry Ferst, Chris Athanasi, Chris Driver, Robbie King.

The ex-players and manager who spoke to me: Paul Davis, Alan Smith, Anders Limpar and Bruce Rioch.

Kev and Dave on the fanzine stall for all their help and encouragement, and Ian Trevett at *Highbury High* for his help.

Richard Lewis at Sportspages and Angela Painter and Toby Spencer at the Bookcentre, Hoddesdon.

Linda Durkin for typing the book.

Iain Cook at Arsenal Football Club.

Meuryn Hughes of Aureus Publishing for publishing the book.

Helen, Murray and Stuart.

John Booker, for his lifts to the games and for his sterling work as co-ordinator of the unofficial Ray Parlour fan-club.

To all my mates, whom I continue to bore with tales about Arsenal; Barry, Phil, Seb, Marnie, Jo, Gareth, Louise, Nuno, Adam, Brummie, Geordie, Tim, Lucy, Edsie, Andy, Si Williams, Si Barrick, Steve, Lucy and the Langton posse (Louise, Charlie, Sam and Becky). My apologies to you all.

Thanks to Collins Willow for allowing me to quote from *Mr Wright* - Ian Wright's autobiography and *Addicted* - written by Tony Adams with Ian Ridley. Thanks to Andre Deutsch for allowing me to use quotes from *The Glory and The Grief* - George Graham. Thanks also to *The Sun*, *The Mirror*, the *Daily Telegraph*, the *Evening Standard* and *The Times* for allowing me to use various quotes. And finally, to Ian Trevett at *Highbury High* and Kev and Mike at *The Gooner* for allowing me to use several quotes from fanzines.

And finally to Helen, who, on a daily basis, puts up with my unhealthy obsession for Arsenal. I promise that one day, I'll get into gardening, instead.

Introduction

Top Guns focuses on Arsenal's fortunes in the 1990s, and the developments, games, players and personalities which shaped the decade. Those ten years were the most thrilling and turbulent in the club's history. Fans were treated to a cascade of silverware, and watched the scoring exploits of the club's most prolific striker - Ian Wright. The Gunners' greatest post war talent - Dennis Bergkamp, helped to push the team's style of play onto a higher plane and captain Tony Adams marshalled a defence whose longevity defies belief. But as Arsenal charged headlong into the digital age, so the Taylor report, the Graham affair, the Bond Scheme and the impact of Sky T.V. strained many fans' relationship with the club. Heroic deeds on the pitch combined with upheaval behind the scenes; it was to be the story of Arsenal in the '90s.

The summer of 1990 provided clear evidence that old orders and beliefs were about to be swept away. Out of touch Eastern European dictators were toppled weekly, the Iron Lady was clearly suffering from battle fatigue and Presidents Bush and Gorbachev declared the end of the Cold War. Nelson Mandela's release from prison signalled the dismantling of apartheid, which pleased everyone, it seemed, except stressed out University Chancellors who had to rename their Student Union bars pretty bloody sharpish.

The hype surrounding Italia '90 provided broad hints that football was also changing irrevocably and was set to become 'cool'. Gazza's antics (you remember - tears, tantrums and plastic tits) ensured that a generation of children were kitted out with Gazza lunchboxes, Gazza duvets *ad nauseum*. And programmes like *Panorama* question why so many teenagers are hyperactive and badly behaved. Having Gazza as your role model when you're barely out of nappies may provide the answer. Though the lard-arsed Geordie's face was the enduring image of the World Cup, the team's anthem spoke volumes for football's new found status.

For years footie songs had been garbage but when New Order's *World In Motion*, including the John Barnes rap, was thrust on the nation's youth in pubs and clubs it was an instant hit. This was no mean achievement, considering that the summer was so rich musically. The Creation label spawned the likes of Ride, whose shoe-gazing antics and hazy guitar sounds made them hits among the student population. The Charlatans and Stone Roses showered us with mournful, moody and psychedelic echoes and the Happy Mondays' dance inspired anthems and general bagginess meant that 'Madchester', apparently, was the place to be that Summer (unless you didn't like flairs or Mancunians). A Ska revival was also in full swing - but most footie fans will maintain that *World in Motion* was the most memorable sound of the summer. It was a watershed moment in English football. Quite simply, the football and music industries were entering into a marriage that would last well into the millennium, although the signs had been there for a while; The Wedding Present's *George Best* album for instance.

In the '89/90 season, Arsenal seemed reluctant to take the bullet train ride into football's Promised Land. Early cup exits against QPR and Oldham, together with fourth place in the league, amounted to a 'treading water' season in Tony Adams' words. Not a single Gunner represented his country at Italia '90. So, having failed to capitalise on the 'Anfield experience', Arsenal players also missed the chance to participate in the most high profile World Cup of the era. But showbiz, music, T.V. and wadges of cash penetrated even Highbury's marble halls by the end of the decade. Ian Wright would cut a record and present a chat show. Tony Adams dated super model Caprice and Paul Merson became hooked on the recreational drug of the rich and famous. Staggeringly, King George himself would eventually be swept away on a tidal wave of financial scandal. Clear proof therefore, that outside influences sculpted AFC's profile throughout the 90s.

In a sense, this book also focuses on two vastly different playing styles. George's earthy, blue-collar sides swept up a Championship and assorted Cups in the first part of the decade but by '95 major internal surgery was urgently needed to restore the team to former glories. When David Dein summoned Arsène Wenger to fumigate the lingering stench of scandal after the Rioch fiasco, he ushered in a new era. The Wenger-inspired passing game, blended with George's defensive legacy, brought the Double to Highbury in his first full season. It suggested that all the blood letting and horror of the mid '90s was actually beneficial in the long-term. After all, the later '90s really did represent a French revolution, and *le Marseillaise* would truly have been a fitting tribute to the '98 side.

Some reckoned that by winning the Double so early in his Arsenal career, Arsène had immediately exorcised George's ghost. Subsequent events suggested that may not be the case and, with the passing years, George's achievements appear more and more remarkable. Allied to a proposed move away from Highbury and the gradual disintegration of the side's defensive core, the very late '90s were bizarre times for true Arsenal fans. The quality of football on show was the best in living memory but many feared that the soul of the club was in danger of ebbing away.

All of this, however, is some way off in a story which begins in the summer of 1990. Highbury buzzed with transfer activity and George's 'best of British' side was about to take the league by storm.

I

Awesome Arsenal

With Saddam's tanks rolling into Kuwait, London N.5's dictator plotted some tactical manoeuvres of his own. George Graham, with scalpel and chequebook at the ready, set about empire building - Highbury style. Single minded in every way, G.G. eschewed the delights of *Nessun Dorma* and stuck to an old favourite of his - Frank Sinatra's *My Way*. Graham was at the height of his powers during the Italia '90 afterglow. Sprinkling his pre-season interviews with phrases like 'hunger' and 'fighting spirit', he was clearly psyching the team up for another assault on the summit some twelve months after the Anfield experience. Tellingly, he also spoke about 'battling against the odds to achieve goals'. Maybe George had a premonition; after all, this was to be a season stuffed with adversity and obstacles.

The boss raided Highbury's coffers in order to rejuvenate his jaded ex-Champions, although his first purchase was a controversial choice. David Seaman had long been earmarked as a transfer target by the boss. To that end on deadline day of the '89/90 season, Graham attempted to nab him and send John Lukic in the opposite direction. It backfired and Johnny refused to go. We all knew that Lukic's cards were marked though, and in the last few games of the season, he was granted full martyr status. Chants of *'we hate Seaman'* had been audible during our game at Norwich; bizarre but true. By June though, Seaman was ours for £1.3m (a record for a goalie) and Lukic was bombed out to Leeds. George's mastery of unpopular but correct decisions was unparalleled, as Dave's towering performances would show.

Fans over the age of twenty quickly realised the importance of Seaman's arrival. With Kevin Richardson's imminent departure, Arsenal would have been a 'tache-less side, and all successful Gunners teams in the modern era have had at least one 'tache-face in the team. To be honest, we never took to Richardson's rather weedy effort under his nose, and Seaman's privet hedge was the best top lip growth seen at Highbury since the days of Alan Sunderland.

Shoring up central defence was Andy Linighan, whose £1.25m signing from Norwich seemed a tad unnecessary. Indeed, George was gaining a burgeoning reputation for suffering from Imelda Marcos syndrome in his attitude towards collecting towering stoppers. With O'Leary, Adams, Bould and Pates already at Highbury, Linighan would spend much of his first season on the bench, but a combination of injuries and the law meant that he would play a crucial role later in the campaign. If ever a signing reflected George's Midas quality in his first four years as manager, it was the arrival of £1.1m Anders Limpar from Italian club Cremonese. Desperate for creativity on the wing, which had been lacking during the previous season, Graham snapped up the Swedish wideman after he had shown promise in their otherwise disastrous Italia '90 tournament. Anders turned out to be the spark which lit the blue touch paper. From the start, though, he would cause George as many headaches as he did opposition defenders.

Graham continued to adopt a hard-line stance in public. In the *Daily Mirror*, he threatened to get rid of players who 'stepped out of line'. Perhaps that phrase needs clarification, because by demolishing a wall and writing off his Ford Sierra while three times over the legal limit, Tony Adams could be said to have broken several rules. So could Paul Merson, who'd been involved in a well-publicised poolroom brawl. Both men's hedonistic lifestyles had caused concern for some time. Indeed, the conventional view held that Merse had already got pissed in the 'last chance saloon' several times already. Graham was always far more concerned with those who stepped verbally out of line. His shabby treatment of David O'Leary simply lengthened the list of those who felt the steel tipped end of his jackboot. After his World Cup exertions with Eire, O'Leary (the model pro) requested an extra few days break before returning to pre-season training. Graham's tactful response was to make him train with the reserves. It wasn't a surprise, Brian Marwood once told me that 'George didn't care about international football. He didn't even care about Scotland, let alone anyone else'. The O'Leary situation should have been a warning to new signing Anders Limpar about putting country before club.

Marwood hastened his own departure by making a few barbed comments about Graham in his book, *The Life Of Brian*. Admittedly, Limpar's arrival meant that the PFA activist would have been keeping the subs' bench warm, but he deserved better than to be given George's 'cold shoulder' treatment. There was always the lingering suspicion that Graham saw

Marwood as a troublesome barrack room lawyer. For his pains he was flogged to Sheffield United. Kevin Richardson, also renowned for 'speaking his mind', was sold to Real Sociedad for £1m. He was never able, in his final season, to shrug off the boo-boys who sneered at his lack of finesse. Poor old 'whoops-a-daisy' Martin Hayesie staggeringly became Celtic's record signing for £650,000. He'd escaped his Highbury nightmare, but talk about stepping out of the frying pan and into the fire... Only Jason Donovan can compete with him as far as rapid '90s declines go. Within five years, Hayes was flogging cars at Highbury Corner's Ford Garage. Nice suit though, Martin.

George had bought three players and sold four. Most experts reckoned that our squad was perilously thin and that Liverpool were light years ahead of us in terms of title winning potential. Emlyn Hughes, who'd recently been sacked from *A Question of Sport* on the grounds of talking too much crap, had been given his own column in *The Sun*, where spouting pro-red Scouse rubbish was considered a virtue. His opinion on the forthcoming Championship race was: 'Kenny's boys will run away with the title as usual. No doubt. No contest. It's all over before the first ball has been kicked'. Old Emlyn wasn't the only one who'd be scraping egg off his face come May.

George's line-up for the first game of the season was : Seaman, Dixon, Winterburn, Adams, Bould, Davis, Thomas, Rocastle, Limpar, Smith, Merson. It was the sleekest of all George's line-ups, and when the engine purred properly, it proved to be the best. On a scorching August day, 10,000 Gooners annexed Plough Lane, ready to see the team face the flying elbows and stiletto blades of Wimbledon's hatchet men. The half melted wagon wheels, stale cheese and onion crisps in the catering vans and the terrible view from the away end couldn't dampen our enthusiasm for the prospect of seeing Seaman and Limpar make their competitive debuts. In the second half, Arsenal clicked into breathtaking form. Anders skipped away from his marker and curled over two glorious crosses which Paul Merson and Alan Smith dispatched with relish. A contemporary writer reckoned that the Davis, Rocastle and Thomas combination was a 'dream midfield'. Davis' repertoire of deadly flicks, together with Rocky's forward bursts and Mickey's endeavour outfoxed their butchers and hod-carriers. Late sub Perry Groves cracked in a third shortly before the end and Gunners' fans streamed away in the sunshine, delighted with the rejuvenated freshness of Arsenal's counter attacking.

Clock End regulars were in for an unpleasant shock on the night of the first home match of the season against Luton. Walking in and discovering that the South East corner had been torn out over the Summer and replaced by a police room was bad enough. The capacity was now slashed to 47,000 and great chunks of history would be ripped out over the next three or four years. Even worse was being told by the draconian stadium announcer to 'stop jumping up and down', in the aftermath of Merson's onion bag ripper and Thomas' half volley that gave us a scrambled 2-1 win. The stadium announcement was one of the first signs of the purging of terrace culture from English grounds. The middle class code of sensible behaviour and political correctness had well and truly arrived and talk of banning away fans from all games and ejecting supporters for swearing became commonplace. Who said that watching football was supposed to be fun?

The Gazza bandwagon spluttered into town on the following Saturday when Spurs paid us a visit. The riffraff from down Seven Sisters Road provided us with unrivalled piss-taking opportunities during August 1990. How many Arsenal fans had misguided Spurs supporters come up to them and claim that with Gary Lineker and Gazza, they would finally be crowned champions? It didn't take long to realise that another 'transitional' season was upon them (*de rigeur* since 1961) and that the club was financially being flushed down the U-bend. Those who expected to witness a Fatboy masterclass went away sorely disappointed. He was subbed early in the second half after being taught a few lessons on how to run a midfield by Paul Davis. It was a grim fight. Spurs blanket defended with nine men, and only a diabolical refereeing performance by Joe Worral, who missed a blatant foul on Davis allowed Spurs to leave with a point. *The Independent* reckoned that Davis was the 'visionary in the land of the blind'. He had been loaned to a Swedish second division side in order to get his fitness and touch back over the Summer. His renewed enthusiasm was one of our most potent weapons during the season.

The first sign of Arsenal's ability to blow away teams in half-hour lightning bursts emerged during the clash with perennial dark horses Chelsea at Highbury. Tipped as a good outside bet for the title in August, their odds considerably lengthened after Arsenal's second half maelstrom blew them away. Anders Limpar tormented them on the wings and volleyed in his first Arsenal league goal. Paul Merson's clever runs pulled Monkou and Dorigo all over the place and he added another before Rocky and Lee Dixon got in on the act in a spectacular 4-1 win. Andy Townsend, Chelsea's new captain, thumped the ground in rage and wondered why he'd chosen to sign for them and not us. Poor Chelsea; for all their delusions of grandeur and King's Road style, they'll always be the club of Kerry Dixon and David Speedie at heart.

Two routine 2-0 victories over Forest and Norwich put us second in the table and further elevated Limpar and Davis' status. Limpar and Rocastle destroyed Des Walker at the City Ground and Davis' unexpected double at home to the Canaries seemed to surprise everyone, including the scorer. He recalls that George was none too happy - telling him that 'you should-n't be pushing so far forward like that'. So far, so good though; five wins and two draws.

Things still weren't quite right though. As yet there was no real intensity to the season. We'd started well, although we knew that epic battles against Manc and Scouse enemies were just around the corner. Indeed, Liverpool still blazed a trail out in front, despite Arsenal's best efforts. Certain players seemed to be going through the motions; Mickey Thomas, unquestionably our coolest player, was accused of being over casual by many fans and Alan Smith still had not shaken off his sluggish form of the previous year. George's mailbag was apparently bulging with letters advising him to drop Smudger and introduce raging bull Kevin Campbell, who'd looked a decent prospect at the end of the previous season. Luckily for us, George didn't give a toss what fans thought - though Smith and Campbell would link up in the New Year.

The wake up call to players and fans soon arrived. In a season crammed with turning points and omens, the vicious match at Old Trafford was by far the most important of all. After the seismic events of October 20th, the Gunners' season would change course entirely. Eight thousand Arsenal fans that travelled North on an infamous afternoon could not believe what they were about to see.

Manchester at 3.00 p.m. on a Saturday afternoon. It was grey, dark and drizzly. With weather like that all year round, no wonder Mancunians are always moaning. Their Scoreboard End was heaving and swaying with travelling Gooners and the damp air crackled with hatred. After half an hour, Arsenal were comfortably containing United's underachievers. Mickey Thomas, in his last truly great performance for the club snuffed out the threat of Robson and Ince and Adams dealt with Mark Hughes. Just before half time, Davis' short corner found Limpar, whose quick thinking and snap shot caught Sealey napping and was over the line before he had a chance to claw it back. There was bedlam at the Scoreboard End when the ref signalled that the goal stood. What could be more amusing than a furious United at Old Trafford, becoming more spiteful by the minute because they were losing? Just after David Seaman had made a blinding double save from Ince and Robson, tempers exploded.

Rob Kemp, an Arsenal fan from Harlow recalls events: 'The game at Old Trafford is my main memory of that season. Anders' goal must have really pissed them off. Both sides were full of feisty sods weren't they? It was never going to take much to light the blue touch paper. Nigel Winterburn and Brian McClair had been niggling each other all game, they really hated each other didn't they? In every game during the last three years between the two sides, they'd tried to kill each other. The fans' chants, I noticed, were getting more unpleasant - at the bottom of it was the fact that United still couldn't win the league.

The game exploded when Anders tackled Irwin and left his foot in. Nigel Winterburn charged in and tried to break Irwin's leg. Irwin booted him when he was on the floor and then all the guys piled in, Davis, Rocky and Mickey Thomas all got involved. It was staggering to watch. Rocastle and Mickey went for McClair, Tony Adams screamed at Webb and Alex Ferguson. The scrap seemed to go on for ages, though in hindsight it was all over in thirty seconds. The noise that was going on was unbelievable. It really was a savage atmosphere.

The thing was that I think Arsenal came out of it a stronger side. Rocky mentioned in Amy Lawrence's book *Proud To Say That Name* that that team would fight and die for each other and that's what they did really, so I think this incident improved team spirit. And of course the FA and the tabloids got really pompous about it all. We were branded a disgrace - and Arsenal quite enjoyed being the outsiders - with something to prove. I'm convinced that this event gave an added focus to our season and spurred us on after the points deduction.

Looking back, it was all hugely amusing anyway. For all the talk of a brawl, I don't think that a single punch was thrown. But it did intensify the feelings of dislike between us and United, which got worse and worse in the '90s. So I think it's a really historic match. The other thing was, that despite all the controversy, we actually won the match, which showed just what a great side we were.'

Rob Kemp, Arsenal fan from Harlow

Two weeks later, Arsenal were fined £50,000 and deducted two points. United were deducted one point. The main perpetrators - Winterburn, Limpar, Davis, Thomas and Rocastle were each fined £5,000 and George himself £9,000. A twenty-two man brawl (where punches were thrown) involving Derby and Manchester City on the same day barely even made the press, and no punishments were handed out. It was the first time in modern English football history that a team had been docked points for bad behaviour. Of course, the tabloids screamed hysterically about the whole thing; the *Daily Mirror* pompously blasted that 'six should have been sent off on soccer's day of shame' (but thanks for helping us sell a few hundred thousand extra copies, lads).

More importantly, Arsenal were now eight points behind the Scousers, prompting David O'Leary to say: 'They might as well have handed Liverpool the title on a plate'. Others agreed that the title race was now over, but as Rob Kemp suggested, more complex forces were at work. Anders Limpar recalls that in many ways, the deduction worked in our favour. He recalls: 'Old Trafford was the turning point of our season. We knew that we were a good side, and the win at Old Trafford showed that we were and that we could be combative when we needed to be. When the news about the ban came out, it bonded us together as a group. We were all furious - why should we be docked two points and they only one? It made us feel hard done by and hungry to prove people wrong. It made us feel that we were written off and we had to show them.

I have to say that Graham was excellent in the way that he turned all the bad press on its head and used it to inspire us. He rightly pointed out that we were still second top, we had a huge match with Liverpool coming up at home and we could still win the league. He was a master of using negative press to the team's advantage. He said that we must now go out and prove everyone wrong. He'd use this approach later in the season and it was one of the key reasons for our success that year'.

From now on, Arsenal's matches were closely scrutinised for further evidence of indiscipline. The sneerers scoffed at George's claims that we could still win the league. Fans were furious about the points deduction. Some wrote to the FA to complain about it (which inevitably fell on deaf ears). Most of us decided to inject our energy into shouting on our team. As we would eventually discover, revenge is a dish best served cold. By the end of November, Arsenal had strung together a run of results which hauled Liverpool back within range. The team was playing superbly as a unit; Smudger's form miraculously returned to its '89 Golden Boot winning best, Paul Davis maintained his majestic early season excellence and

Tony Adams marshalled the division's tightest defence. Goals were being shared democratically around the side. Example: a week after the Battle of Old Trafford, Lee Dixon dispatched the winning penalty in a scrappy 1-0 win over Sunderland after ex-Gunner John Kay had chopped down Limpar. Looking back, it seems strange that a full back should be our penalty king, rather than one of our strikers, but as George said, the '91 team was primarily about the collective.

Paul Merson and Siggi Jonsson (in for the crocked Mickey Thomas) set up Limpar for two lightning strikes at Elland Road to grab us a draw at newly promoted Leeds. The tall and elegant Jonsson 'retired' soon afterwards due to chronic back injuries. Strangely, he made a comeback and earned rave reviews as Dundee United's captain by the end of the decade. What does that say about Scottish football? On the day that our points deduction was announced, Paul Davis was the orchestrator behind the destruction of Southampton. It helped that the obliging Saints had assigned Neil Ruddock to mark Limpar ('like a carthorse chasing Red-Rum' my neighbour that day reckoned). Anders scored one himself after Davis' pass bisected their defence, Merson scrambled in another and then he helped Smith smack in his first since the opening day of the season. Perry Groves, on as a late sub, curled over a cross which Smudger dispatched with a glorious header for his second. Smith, who'd been dropped a week earlier, was elated. The 4-0 win had been a superb spectacle and the message to the FA rang out loud and clear: *'You can stick your fucking two points up your arse.'* Alan Smith later told me that that became the players' mantra for the rest of the season as well.

Both of November's London derbies showed that a defensive fortress was equally as important as attacking flair. The season was liberally sprinkled with ten life threatening clashes against our cousins from the capital. Crystal Palace and QPR, both decent sides in the early '90s, before they were asset stripped by their chairmen, were keen to derail our challenge. Anders came closest to breaking down title chasing Palace (the very concept reminds you just how times have changed) and their offside trap at Selhurst Park. Our stars were Seaman and the criminally underrated Steve Bould, who thwarted the Wright 'n' Bright combo on three heart stopping occasions.

Rangers' fans at Loftus Road seemed intent on giving Seaman and Adams an afternoon of unparalleled abuse. Even the Lukic lovers had by now accepted that Dave was a superior model, so when QPR supporters started goading him, we told them precisely what we thought of their, ahem, 'compact ground'. Mortally wounded, they turned their attentions to

Tony Adams. Donkey chants had been considered retro for a year or so, but what can you expect from fans who worshipped Gerry Francis, 70's fashion victim and a devout mullet man? With 75 minutes gone, QPR, frankly were pulverising us. Paul Davis reckons that our astounding comeback from being 0-1 down was one of the 'key moments of the season'. Paul Merson rammed in the equaliser and Adams flicked a few V-signs around the ground for good measure. Sixty seconds later Smudger gave us the lead. When Kevin Campbell banged in a third just before the end, Rangers fans had long since slinked away, stunned by the ferocity of our comeback. Yet again, group mentality and togetherness had proved decisive.

One player, though, continued to earn the ravest of reviews. At the end of November, the astonishing match winning ability of Anders Limpar was by far the most rampantly destructive force in the old first division. At Coventry, the team had been under the cosh for an hour. Only Seaman's spectacular point blank saves kept them out, before Anders scuttled towards goal. His two quicksilver sprints and devastating shooting gave us an undeserved 2-0 win. Those Arsenal fans at Highfield Road will always remember Anders' sorcery and impish celebrations. George Graham had already dubbed him 'my new match winner'. Behind the scenes though, their relationship had hit choppy seas.

Here's a paradox for you; in George's eyes, Limpar's unpredictability and maverick genius was his greatest strength (in terms of match winning ability) and at the same time, his Achilles heel (he found Anders hard to fathom). It was a bizarre situation, which led Graham to admit in his book that 'Anders and I could never get on the same wavelength'. A criticism of Limpar, or an ironic admission of George's inability to man-manage true flair players?

When George signed Limpar, he had secured the services of a star player - complete with a stubborn streak and mesmeric skills. If you'll pardon me for lapsing into racial stereotypes, Limpar, who was an unpredictable mixture of Swedish and Hungarian blood, combined East European feistiness with Scandinavian logic and coolness. Case in point: rather than play against Chester in the Rumbelows Cup, he defied managerial orders and skipped off to play for Sweden against Germany. His contract stated that Arsenal had to release him for internationals, but Anders recalls that Graham was never happy about the situation: 'Do you *have* to go Anders? It's Arsenal who pays your wages, not Sweden', Graham would say. Perhaps a less strong willed player would have backed down, but Limpar exercised his right to go. Some would argue that Anders had made a foolish move. Certainly his decision to shoot from the hip to any Scandinavian journalist on the trip who cared to listen, was less than shrewd. The Swedish press reported on alleged bust ups at Highbury. George Graham, apparently, was always shouting at players and Mickey Thomas was alleged to be fuming about the limitations of his midfield role in the team.

Limpar later apologised for his actions and claimed that he'd been mis-quoted. Of course, George had to continue picking him but perhaps by the end of November 1990, Limpar had already sown the seeds of his own destruction in George's mind. From now on, GG classics on Limpar such as 'he needs to impose himself more on the game' became *de rigeur*. The number of substitutions also told their own story (all these fates later befell Ginola at Spurs). The situation would become far more unpleasant over the next three seasons, and Anders was on the route to a Highbury nightmare with GG as chief tormentor. The small band still loyal to George, maintain that he had a point and Anders did sometimes go missing from now on. But we worshipped him and his pure genius set up a bounty of chances for Merson, Smith and company throughout the rest of the season.

No matter which way one approaches it, the first weeks of December were truly memorable. You could argue that during that month three mighty edifices crumbled to dust. Margaret Thatcher's term in office came to an abrupt halt when, midway through a European summit, her position as leader was shown to be untenable. Rather amusingly, she reckoned that 'treachery with a smile' from her cabinet members had forced her out. At almost the same time as her departure, East German pickaxes got to work on the Berlin Wall; at long last the final vestige of Communism in Eastern Europe was taken down, brick by brick. The final sign that the old order was being summarily dismantled was Arsenal's humiliation of Liverpool in front of a stunned T.V. audience. Horrified by the 6-2 thrashing, which Manchester United had inflicted on us in the Rumbelows Cup, George decided to revamp the side and go for a 5-3-2 formation. He ended O'Leary's exile in the reserves and opted to play him as sweeper in order to combat Ian Rush.

Right from the start, Anders Limpar and Paul Merson destroyed Hysen and Gillespie. After a desperate goal mouth scramble, Merson's headed effort was judged to have crossed the line much to the chagrin of Barry Venison and his crap haircut. Merse roared away to the Arsenal fans, show-ing just how much he was relishing his role as Smudger's striking partner.

In the second half Limpar shredded the cowering Scouse defence and was tripped by Gary Gillespie. Lee Dixon hammered home the penalty. 'Limpar is a cheat' sobbed the inept Liverpool defenders in the press next day.

The final denouement was delivered with ten minutes to go. Merse, displaying outrageous skill, back-heeled the ball at speed into the path of the onrushing Alan Smith. Smudger paused before drilling his shot to Grobbelaar's right. Arsenal had trashed Liverpool 3-0, an event not seen at Highbury since 1984. The win was delivered courtesy of razor sharp attacking football - to which Liverpool had no answer. Even though Liverpool stayed top until the end of January, the Gunners had delivered a mortal blow to the superstructure. Doubtless, Kenny's bags were almost packed by the end of the match.

Essex is the county around which so many urban myths revolve; of white stilettos, sparkly handbags, of Sharons and Traceys visiting the tackiest of nightclubs and drowning themselves in gallons of Aussie lager. Crucially for Arsenal in December 1990, Essex is also the county where judges have a reputation for demonstrating the ruthlessness of Judge Jeffries in the Bloody Assizes when it comes to dealing with drunk drivers at Christmas. The barbecue which Tony Adams had attended in May before crashing his Sierra had been turned by the press into a full scale orgy, the like of which hadn't been seen since the days of hedonistic Roman Emperors. The news that guests enjoyed sausages in baps took on a whole different meaning. It hardly helped Adams' case in his forthcoming trial that barbecue host Mick Hynes claimed in *The Sun* that 'There were couples bonking all over the house'. Tone apparently was too drunk to participate though, contenting himself instead with playing drunken cricket in the garden. Our captain's chances of being let off in his forthcoming trial with a slapped wrist were thin indeed.

With public interest in the trial reaching its height, Arsenal's famed team spirit had never been so necessary. After thrashing the Scousers, there followed two hard fought draws where tin hats and helmets were very much the order of the day. At home to Wimbledon we seemed to be cruising after Merson's opening goal and Adams' thumping header (a sort of Christmas cum 'see you in February' gift to the fans) before their aerial bombardments caught us napping in the last minute. Fashanu scrabbled a jammy point for them in the 2-2 draw. Hugely unloved Luton also pegged us back on a day of Arctic weather. The Arse slipped and slithered on the drastic plastic, cheered on by a couple of thousand fans that had defied the Hatters' poxy away fan ban. Alan Smith gave us the lead, before Adams' clumsy tackle on Dowie gave them a penalty. They scored, naturally. Adams' red card for the tackle, a cretinously over the top reaction by a cretinous ref did not exactly bode well for his day of reckoning in the following week. He had been dismissed for the lightest of nudges on Dowie and was also under investigation for V-signs made to QPR fans who had done nothing but hurl abuse at him at Loftus Road earlier that month. Such was the lot of a high profile Arsenal captain.

Judge and jury sentenced Tony Adams to jail for three months. Representatives from the 'don't drink and drive' lobby made a reference, which referred as much to Arsenal in the '90/'91 season as it did to Adams: 'We had to make an example of him'. No one doubted that Tone's actions had been inexcusable but few journos did themselves any credit in their coverage of the trial or its aftermath. Most focussed on the ghoulish aspects of his likely treatment inside and dredged up old stories about ex Arsenal con Peter Storey to sell a few more copies. Patrick Barclay was one of the more sane voices, pointing out coolly that it was now of greater importance to see how Adams handled the situation.

Those who foamed at the mouth and hoped that this would be the end for Tone and Arsenal got it seriously wrong. Immediately GG and Managing Director Ken Friar voiced support for him. To win the title now and overhaul Liverpool would take a monumental effort. Every time Arsenal drew closer, another obstacle was placed in the way; a bit like telling Hercules that after he'd finished his ten labours, he had to complete a triathlon. Paul Davis recalls that: 'While it wouldn't strictly be true to say that now we were 'doing it for Tony', he was always in the back of our minds. It was another example of adversity making us strong'.

With Tone doing his Porridge, George's fetish for centre backs paid dividends. At Villa Park, Andy Linighan entered the fray to partner Steve Bould at the back. He played well and acted out the 'stopper' role perfectly. In a season of crap decisions the ref's blindness meant that Comyn's trip on Perry Groves went unpunished. Arsenal had now gone three matches without a win and desperately needed more incisiveness from midfield. David Rocastle, who'd been dropped by George and then undergone a knee operation, re-entered the fray on Boxing Day, much to the relief of the pitifully small 26,000 crowd.

It wasn't that the delights of Noel Edmonds or Hyacinth Bucket on T.V. kept people at home, more a combination of mitigating circumstances. It was pissing down with rain and BR decided not to run any trains on the 26th (making it almost impossible for visiting fans to come). Of course festive London derbies were now a thing of the past. It was too demanding on police resources, apparently. F.A. Cup replays now also needed ten days notice which would soon make marathon ties *passé*. Strange how police have had a hand in every decision to make football less enjoyable, isn't it? The drowned rats who did turn up were cheered by a 3-0 win, courtesy of Smith's aerial majesty and Merson's opportunist third goal. Three days later newly promoted Sheffield United came to Highbury and shockingly took the lead. Masquerading as highlighter pens in their luminous yellow away tops they were finally blown away by another Smith double, a Dixon penalty and Thomas' tap in. Those fans that dared to brave the Moss Side slums on New year's Day yelped when Smudger's thunderous roof smasher finally saw off Manchester City. Still unbeaten in the league that season, and with Liverpool's lead over us down to just two points, even getting hopelessly lost in the maze of danger-filled streets outside the ground didn't seem so bad.

If there were lingering doubts about Graham's wisdom in signing David Seaman, his displays in January destroyed any dissension. It wasn't that Spunky hadn't played well previously; his unflappability, coolness and athleticism were already apparent. It was just that in early New Year, his displays reached a level, which showed the importance of having a top class goalie. After we'd seen off Sunderland in the FA Cup 3rd round, we drew Leeds in the 4th round at Highbury. On paper, it was a tasty clash, but it turned into a tedious scrap, which meandered aimlessly towards a 0-0 draw. In the last minute, Gary McAllister cracked in a goal bound blockbuster, which looked destined to rip open the net. Clock Enders braced themselves for a Cup exit, until Seaman hurled himself to his right and clawed the shot over the bar and away. McAllister simply stood dumfounded and Sergeant Wilko booted an advertising hoarding in frustration.

If that Seaman save had been astonishing, what followed in the North London derby defied belief. Spurs, aided by incompetent ref Alf Buksch were pulverising us. Three times, Lineker had one on ones with Seaman; each time Seaman miraculously smothered his efforts. Even golden-boy Gary let slip a few f-words in Seaman's direction. Paul Allen then had a gilt edged chance to win it for them in the last minute. Bould and Linighan prepared themselves for the worst, but Dave risked life and limb to keep it goalless. Our sad North London cousins' howls of frustrations told us everything; we can't beat Seaman and the Arsenal.

While Desert Storm raged against Saddam's forces in the Gulf, Arsenal prepared for the twice-yearly barrage from Everton. The Toffees' bombing of our backline pegged us back and, in truth, we struggled to get out of our own half, but carrot topped Perry Groves, our very own super sub, sprinted up the right wing early in the second half, and swept in a cross which Merson toe-poked in. Finally, we'd overhauled Liverpool and hit top spot.

The Everton match; a patchy and disjointed game, had shown just how draining the chase for the league had become. Ironically, having reached the summit, the team was visibly wilting. Anders was going through a quiet spell and as the forward thrust spluttered, the defence came under greater pressure to hold out. The inevitable finally happened against Chelsea at Stamford Bridge on February 2nd. Andy Linighan and Steve Bould looked nervous all afternoon and Seaman was temporarily transformed into a ponderous bag of nerves. Stuart and Dixon put them 2-0 up; Smudge's last minute consolation was too late. To think that bloody Kerry Dixon was the man responsible for inflicting upon us our only league defeat of the season. Has anyone less deserved a place in history? It was almost enough to make you want to give up football - but that was never an option once Leeds' Lee Chapman began to make grandiose predictions in the press about our 'imminent' FA Cup exit. 'Arsenal are not up to much', reckoned our ex-striking disaster. Old 'firkincant' would soon discover that we were no pushovers.

The epic FA Cup saga with Leeds dragged on well into February. By the time the third replay arrived at Elland Road, we'd again seen Anders' supreme skills on show. On the previous Wednesday, he'd darted into their area, slipped past Whyte and Fairclough and cracked in a blistering shot past Lukic for the equaliser in the 2nd replay. After 270 minutes of intense Cup action between the teams, only a touch of the unexpected would enable either team to break through. The game was effectively over by half time. Paul Merson's rampaging run and shot and Lee Dixon's sharp finish after a sumptuous one-two put us 2-0 up. Chapman's late strike made for a frenzied final few minutes, but we'd made it into the fifth round.

George was not fooled by this win into believing that the team had miraculously rediscovered its old zest. After forty games, fatigue was still the biggest fear factor. Wafer thin on midfield cover after Rocky's broken toe and Thomas' loss of form, Paul Merson had been repeatedly hauled back from his favoured striking role, giving the team a rather unbalanced look. Desperate for reinforcements, George looked no further than the two newest items from the Arsenal production line; Kevin Campbell and David Hillier.

Hillier's willingness to get stuck in was useful in the do or die clashes we would face during the rest of the season. He acted as an effective foil for Paul Davis and certainly played his part. Spookily, though, his league debut was almost ten years to the day after Peter Nicholas reared his ugly head in an Arsenal shirt. Hillier, over the next few years, would become even less popular than his much-unloved prototype. In Alan Smith's opinion, Kevin Campbell's impact after February was akin to that of 'a new signing'. With searing pace and brute force emanating from his bulging thighs, Campbell was in many ways the x-factor in the final leg of the title challenge. Neatly contrasting with Limpar's dazzling skills and Merse's intelligent running, Kev was to demonstrate irresistible form.

Also thrust back into the action by early March was Tony Adams, recently released from prison after three months. The rapturous 'welcome home' messages he received from the 7,000 fans that turned up to the Reading reserve match spoke volumes for the support he had among fans. Naturally Fleet Street vultures had their own angles on the situation. Tabloids focused on the titillation titbits - discussing at length his role in the 'Porridge' football team, and the letter he'd received from Reggie Kray. Simon Barnes' sobering 'perils of alcohol' article in *The Times* was perhaps the most perceptive article of all, pointing out forcefully the pitfalls of alcohol and the dangers it posed for young footballers. Such stark warnings would again become grim reality for Adams by the mid '90s.

As Tone breathed the sweet smell of freedom, and the new impetus provided by Hillier and Campbell, the games with Palace and Liverpool could not have come at a better time. Palace, staggeringly, would have hit top spot if they'd managed to beat us at Highbury in early March. Their fans, who'd travelled from strange outposts like Norwood Junction arrived in their thousands, kitted out with balloons and confetti, and bellowed their tedious mantra: *'Eagles, Eagles'*. Wrighty threatened us early on, but George's employment of a back five shackled him. When David O'Leary bundled in a corner and Eric Young's hilarious slip let in Paul Merson for a second, it was clearly our day. In the second half, Alan Smith's astonishing dummy and curling shot swirled past Martyn before Campbell tidied up a penalty box mess to give us a 4-0 win. Poor Palace were never taken seriously again.

What better moment could there have been for Tone to return than at Anfield in yer archetypal blood 'n' guts six pointer? In effect, it was the title decider, and the Scousers were in turmoil. Dalglish had already decided to desert the sinking ship, citing stress as the reason. His parting present to the Kop had been Jimmy Carter, the kind of shitty gift that managers who are losing their touch bestow on their clubs, as we'd soon find out. Graeme Souness, their new boss, still talked a good fight in the press but as we'd see throughout the season, wild predictions of Scouse success and rebirth counted for nowt.

The game began with wave upon wave of Scouse attacks raining down upon Seaman. Beardsley and Rush tormented our back line and hit crisp drives, which Dave tipped away. By the end of the first half, David Hillier had man marked the lard arsed Jan Molby out of the game, and cut off the supply route to their strikers. At the start of the second half, Arsenal were pumped up and ready for another 'smash and grab' Anfield raid. Adams bellowed, Merson probed and Smith hustled the inept Glenn Hysen. Liverpool finally cracked when Merson picked up Peter Beardsley's mis-placed pass. He played a delicious one-two with Smith and galloped forward. As Thomas had in '89, Merson waited for Grobbelaar to commit himself and gently nudged the ball into Liverpool's net. Once he'd checked that the linesman hadn't ruled him offside, he galloped to the Arsenal fans and broke into that trademark grin of his. The sight of away fans and players going ballistic with joy after the 1-0 win at Anfield in '91 was one of the enduring images of the decade. And just think - if the Old Etonians on the Arsenal board had had their way, Merse would have been plying his trade for Rangers in the wastelands of the Scottish Premier league.

With a three-point cushion in the title race, and the later rounds of the FA Cup competition looming, the southern press naturally began to hype up talk of the Double. Indeed, with the dramatic conclusion to the '79 final now just a fading memory, the Cup assumed an importance of Holy Grail proportions. We played dismally at Shrewsbury in the fifth round, but Mickey Thomas won us the game; just about a fair result in the circumstances. Sixth round opponents Cambridge United were the ultimate purveyors of the long ball game. Manager John Beck slapped, punched and threw iced water over his players as a way of 'psyching' them up before games. I wonder what the watching master of Total Football, Johan Cruyff, made of Beck's team from the stands that day. Considering that Cambridge have no real history with regards to football, the fact that they brought 8,000 screaming fans to Highbury for the Quarter Final was staggering. Equally as shocking was Dion Dublin's equaliser for them after Kevin Campbell headed us into the lead. With Tone still a bit nervy on his return to the side, their long punts threatened to cause a sensational giant killing. Just when an uncomfortable looking replay at the Abbey Stadium seemed a distinct possibility, Adams himself bundled in our late winner.

With a blistering Semi-Final against Tottenham looming in mid April, we were happy to shamelessly rip off The Righteous Brothers' hit *'We've Lost That Loving Feeling'* and boom out *'We've got that Double Feeling'* over the next few weeks at Highbury. It sounded excremental and glorious all at once - if you get my drift. After a stuttering period in early March, Arsenal's stupendous league form over the next few weeks ensured that the mantra became more ear splitting by the minute.

Kevin Campbell's raw power was Arsenal's inspiration during those games. He smacked in a late brace of goals to send Leeds packing, thundered in another to grab us a point at home to Forest and tested the strength of Norwich City's stanchion in a goalless draw at Carrow Road. While we struggled away in East Anglia, Liverpool pulverised Derby 7-1 at the Baseball Ground. Once again, our championship lead temporarily narrowed and Souness claimed Arsenal were 'worn out'. Considering that this was the man who would soon replace Beardsley with Paul Stewart, Mr Souness' judgements should never be taken too seriously.

Three straight wins in three crunch games stuffed words back down Scouse throats. At Derby, Shilton again did his best to wreck our title dreams with a superhuman display. Soon to be relegated Derby couldn't cope with Arsenal's carbon copy set pieces though - Bould's flick-ons and Smith's powerful headers giving us a 2-0 win. Sheffield United's Bob Booker and Vinnie Jones masqueraded as the Blades' twin hatchet men and did their best to hack our limbs to pieces at a rain sodden Bramall Lane a week later; Campbell gave his most effective Arsenal performance yet. Linking up superbly with Alan Smith, he thumped us into the lead and set up the marauding Smudger for a second.

But the best Highbury performance of the season was the destruction of Aston Villa on April 3rd. Jo Selby takes up the story: 'As the season got near the end, the atmosphere at Highbury got more and more intense. I remember that season's end for the chants which were going around. Before the Villa game I remember us in the Clock End just bouncing up and down to *'we're gonna win the football league again'.* What I still recall to this day was the feeling that we were about to do the Double. My Dad used to go on about Charlie George and Bob Wilson, but I really thought that we were going to match that achievement in '91.

The Villa match was practically a procession. We just annihilated them in an unbelievable half-hour blitz. I can remember the goals even now. Limpar was in brilliant form and he slipped Campbell in for his first. At that time, Kev was one of the best strikers in the country. Alan Smith got two really good goals. But the best of all was from Paul Davis. He was having his best ever season for us, and he got the ball on the edge of the area. He sort of flipped it over his head and back volleyed it into the roof of Spink's net. It was unbelievable. He was a player who you sort of knew was bright, intelligent and alert and that goal showed amazing vision and skill. You had to be in Avenell Road after the game to appreciate the atmosphere. Everyone was singing *'We've got that double feeling'.* The Highbury Barn rocked to it!! We'd stuffed Villa 5-0. We were cruising in the league and we had the Spurs match coming. We just felt invincible. I know that Arsenal fans get criticised a lot for not making as much noise as we used to, but those final games of '90/'91, all of which seemed to be evening games, were just amazing. I didn't think we could fail to do the Double'.

Jo Selby - Arsenal fan from Nazeing

With only five league games left, and the team exuding so much confidence, the bookies were giving good odds on Arsenal becoming the first team to complete the Double Double. Poor old Liverpool; as Souness doubted our bottle and stamina, he forgot to tell his team to keep theirs. They blew it against QPR and Southampton. Still, the FA Cup semi-final did provide the sneerers and the Arsenal haters with one memorable moment of *schaden freude.*

April 14th 1991 - Wembley. Our worst nightmare is unfolding before our eyes. Paul Gascoigne, ably assisted by the goal hanging Gary Lineker, is destroying our Double dreams. His mortar shell free kick and Lineker's first goal, set up by Gazza, have put us 2-0 down after only ten minutes. Smudger's header is never going to be enough and David Seaman's slippery handed display lets in Lineker to give them a 3-1 win which, let's be honest, they deserved. It is the worst possible scenario; Spurs fans shouting at us *'You've lost that double feeling'* and their '90s mantra *'We beat the Scum 3-1'.* Anders Limpar recalls that after the game, George Graham let rip at the team: 'You've let me down, I can't believe it'. Paul Davis reckons that Graham made a tactical error by assigning Thomas to mark Gascoigne, rather than letting Mickey pelt forward, but somehow it felt as though it would always be their day. Streaming away from the stadium, it seemed like the pain of such an embarrassing defeat would never leave us. A defeat by Spurs had cost us the Double.

With hindsight, that game sums up the North London rivalry quite neatly. It later emerged that Spurs simply had to win that game in order to secure their financial future. If they had failed to do so, rumour has it that they may have ceased to exist. Of course, such dire forecasts rarely come to fruition, but the irony is irresistible; even in a Spurs victory there lies farce and pseudo-tragedy. To take this a step further, Spurs went on to win the Cup in '91 but the only thing people now remember of that game is Gazza smashing up his knee. Even their Worthington Cup victory in '99 came in a competition which no big club gives a toss about anymore. Everybody, it seems, has long since figured out that Spurs are condemned to an eternity of second class status in North London.

God looked kindly on them once in a decade (when the year ended in a 1) and this was one of their few moments of redemption in an otherwise miserable existence. Indeed, their chant of *'We beat the scum 3-1'* which they belted out at derby matches, took on a mournful quality. By the end of the '90s, they were reduced to harking back to a victory from almost ten years before, and shouting about ex-Spurs players scoring against us in big matches. 'Tis the lot of the wretched to shout about the misfortune of others, whilst having nothing to crow about themselves. We must therefore allow that generation of Spurs fans to enjoy the memory of Wembley '91 and smile graciously when they mention it. (Although you could remind them that we won the biggest prize that year and won five trophies after that). No doubt they'll end up gibbering about Wembley '91, Nayim and Popescu and the 'glory game' in their retirement homes for the terminally sad. We'll be gibbering as well, but at least we'll bore people with heroic deeds of Double Doubles, of Tony Adams, Ian Wright and Dennis Bergkamp. May Spurs fans rest in peace at their White Hart Lane graveyard.

Inevitably, the vultures from the press circled, waiting for Arsenal to collapse in the league. Crapping on about 'creeping doubts' and 'the jitters', they almost got the crisis story they wanted after our home game with Manchester City. A late first half collapse gave City a 2-2 draw, after Merson and Campbell put us 2-0 up. Coming only four days after the Wembley defeat, our players seemed shell shocked and traumatised. Mickey Thomas' error, which let in David White for their first, wasn't lost on George, who axed him from the side for the rest of the season.

Despite the capitulation against Manchester's bluenoses, Arsenal could still virtually smell the title with just four games left. Twenty four hours earlier, Liverpool beat Palace 3-0 to keep them in touch, but the season's biggest crowd at Highbury - 42,393, turned up expecting us to hammer QPR. With an hour gone though, Rangers' defence held firm (what else would you expect with Don Howe as boss?). Nerves were being shredded until Paul Davis was scythed down; Lee Dixon's penalty gave us the lead. That goal acted as a release for the banks of fans at both ends of the ground and from now on, Highbury almost boiled over. Kevin Campbell's venomous drive virtually decapitated their goalie and Paul Merson's lightning reactions secured a 2-0 win.

Up at Roker Park three days later, George decided to axe Anders from the team and play a cautious line up. In a terrible game, Sunderland chucked everything at Seaman. With a minute left, Gary Owers curled in a seemingly unstoppable thirty yarder. Dave miraculously tipped away the shot, tweaked his moustache and grinned at the relegation haunted Sunderland fans behind his goal. When the final whistle went a few seconds later, their stadium announcer filtered through the good news; Chelsea had hammered Liverpool at the Bridge. After that, it didn't really matter that most of us who'd travelled by train were being forced to spend the night up in the North East.

The incompetent old codgers from the Football League had bowed to the power of T.V. and allowed the kick-off to be delayed to 5.00. Even us fans, who've learned to be adaptable over the years, couldn't stretch to catching the last train back to London at 6.00. Still, it gave us a chance to sample the gorgeously cheap beer on offer and gorge ourselves in the city centre's curry houses. Suitably refuelled, we hared back down South on the Sunday to prepare for the May day carnival game with Man United.

Showing just how fickle we fans can be, none of us whinged when ITV suddenly decided to bring Liverpool's game with Forest forward by two hours. The Scousers simply had to win in order to keep alive their title dreams. How apt, in this season of turmoil and perverse logic, that Ian Woan, a Liverpool fan and more Scouse than a purple shell suit, should provide the *coup de grace* with Forest's winner in their 2-1 victory. Arsenal had been crowned champions, two hours before a potentially tricky home match with the Mancs.

After all the trauma of the season the champagne could finally flow. It was a unique experience for most of us who'd been reared on pants-filling endings to seasons and Cup Finals - like '79 or '89. The landlords around Highbury have never done such good business before a game. It's a wonder that any Gunners fans can actually remember what happened that night, given the joyous alcoholic state most of us were in. Arsenal turned on the style against the under achieving Mancs. The chilled out Gunners tore them apart; Alan Smith thumped in a hat trick to secure the Golden Boot award and just for good measure, Anders took out Bryan Robson with a lunging tackle - divine retribution for some of the maulings he'd given us over the years. The defence, with Adams and Bould majestic, easily repelled Hughes and Robins. Only the tight arsed spoilers from the Football League sullied the occasion, keeping the Championship trophy locked away in their cabinet at Lytham St Annes until the following Saturday. Still, on that memorable May night in 1991, trophy lifting wasn't needed to confirm that Arsenal, two years after the Anfield triumph, were once more the best in the land.

The final game of the season at home to Coventry was, in truth, nothing more than a Championship parade, with the match itself a mere side-show. Yet it attracted several exiled fans from around the globe. Mickey James, who'd moved out to Boston, U.S.A., from Finsbury Park in 1983 takes up the story: 'When I heard that Arsenal had won the league, I went straight to a pub in Boston which is really popular with British expats. There were a couple of other Arsenal fans in there and we had a fantastic night. I remember getting really plastered - and the three of us walked home past the Cheers bar shouting *'Champions, Champions'* at top volume. But even in my inebriated state I knew what I had to do. I had to be at Highbury on the Saturday to see the Arsenal play Coventry.

I hadn't seen a game for two years - when we'd beaten Boro 3-0 at Highbury. But once I told my girlfriend what was happening she knew I had to go. I frantically made some 'phone calls - to my boss to book a few days off work, to my mates in London to fix me up with a ticket and a place to crash when I got there. The flight to Gatwick on the Wednesday seemed to take an eternity and my mate was there to pick me up when I arrived. We spent the next couple of days inside pubs and various curry houses, making sure we were ready for Saturday.

Highbury looked packed and magnificent that afternoon. My mate had got me a ticket on the North Bank and, as it turned out, it was the last time I'd stand at Highbury. Coventry were really just 'lambs to the slaughter', weren't they? I'd heard and seen on T.V. lots about Anders Limpar and he turned on a brilliant show for me. He scored a superb hat trick and tormented his marker all afternoon. Alan Smith and Perry Groves scored too. The final score was 6-1. We just totally destroyed them in awesome fashion. In a way, I was a bit annoyed that I'd been abroad for the whole season. But

I'll never forget Tony Adams lifting the trophy about five yards in front of me and posing for a picture. I've still got it at home. I just call it 'The Class of '91 which is apt isn't it?

It's always amazing to think that the team won the title that season with all those tribulations. Most sides would have folded under all the pressure. But then that Arsenal side wasn't just any old team, was it? Now, I have every video from each game sent out to me by my mate. It's expensive, but who cares?'

Mickey James - Arsenal fan from Boston, USA

The '91 Arsenal side, labelled by John Roberts in *The Independent* as 'masters of adversity' had been defeated just once in the league that season. Only Preston's 'invincibles', back in the days of Queen Victoria, had matched our feat. Such a monumental achievement is unlikely, ever, to be beaten or equalled again. Another fact worth remembering is that the side consisted of ten Englishmen and one Super-Swede. That alone shows just how much football became globalised by the end of the '90s. Many predicted that an Arsenal dynasty would stretch through the decade. In our euphoria, we were happy to believe them. Who would have guessed at the time that the team and its manager had already reached their zenith?

In the midst of record breaking triumph, a large black cloud hove into view. It was announced in the souvenir Coventry City programme that the club had decided to finance the cost of making Highbury all seater (around £22.5 m) through a bond or debenture scheme. The club, eventually, hoped to sell £16.5 m worth of bonds to fans, while the rest would come from within the club's not unsubstantial coffers. Rangers redeveloped Ibrox through such a scheme, as had several clubs in America. Doubtless this was from where David Dein got the idea. It was announced that, for an outlay of either £1200 or £1500, buying a bond would entitle a fan to 'exclusive rights' to a season ticket for up to 150 years (Christ, even the Queen Mother would be struggling there) and a Bond Certificate signed by Pete and Georgie.

The battle to save terracing had long since been lost. Clubs were informed that if they refused to comply with the findings of the Taylor Report, their safety licences (i.e. rights to stage footie matches) would be revoked by season '94/'95. It was a *coup de grace*; over a century of tradition was all but over. Fans were annoyed about that, but what rankled most of all was the high handed manner in which AFC went about the whole 'all-seater' process.

Dein, Friar and co. were extremely adept at quoting bits from the Taylor report to protesting fans, but, unsurprisingly, they demurred from trotting out the part which recommended that clubs should involve and 'consult' fans on any pending decisions. In his report, Taylor said: 'As for the clubs, in some instances, it is legitimate to wonder whether the directors are genuinely interested in the welfare of their grass-root supporters'.

Rumours about the bond had already leaked out in the *Evening Standard* but the 'consultation process', which Taylor advocated, consisted of a few vague public meetings and a dim witted questionnaire in the Arsenal V Leeds programme. The half baked questions were unlikely to gauge public opinion on the 'all-seater' debate. In truth the most important information the club received through the survey was contained in the box after the word 'Address'. Those who responded (an estimated 15,000) were sent a glossy brochure on the merits of the scheme. As for the findings of the questionnaire, they were never made public. Strange eh?

Immediately, it became clear that if pursued, the Bond scheme would have a major impact upon the social makeup of the Highbury crowd, due to the necessary outlay in instalments (around £100 a month for a year or more) or as a lump sum of over one thousand pounds. This was *on top* of the price of a season ticket. One band of Arsenal fans spent the Summer establishing the Independent Arsenal Supporters Association (IASA). In the words of one of its founders, Ian McPherson: 'We were incensed that the club thought that they could push through these proposals at the last minute, unchallenged, and hope that everyone would forget it over the summer. It was unforgivably arrogant on the board's part'. Thus the Board would spend much of the following season embroiled in a damaging public slanging match, where Dein and co. were almost universally condemned for their lack of public relations skills. So at the end of the first full season of the decade, success on the pitch seemed to go hand-in-hand, off it, with alienation of fans. Welcome to the '90s, on both counts.

Anders Limpar - The 'Super-Swede'

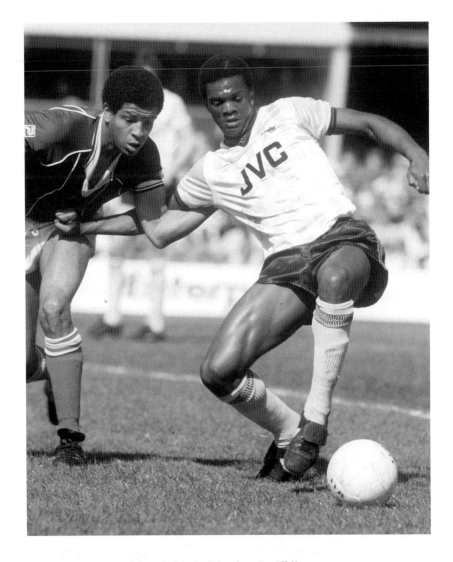

Paul Davis - Style and grace in midfield

2

Down The Wright Path

Close seasons in the early '90s had a reassuring predictability about them; they were always sun drenched from mid May right through to mid August (remember those days?) and Paul Merson would inevitably try and fool us in tabloid questionnaires. He would claim that his favourite drink/food was Perrier water/salad and that he only put the 'occasional' £20 on the gee-gees. The Summer of '91 was the most joyous of all. Most of us drifted through it in a beatific state, convinced that George Graham's Arsenal would dominate the '90s. Our confidence was buoyed, in part at least, by tabloid headlines. After the siege mentality of the Championship year, most hacks seemed keen to give us serious respect.

Having previously blasted our players for being a bunch of donkeys, drunks and brawlers, they suddenly poured forth a torrent of praise. Even John Sadler in *The Sun* wrote that 'George Graham has created an organisation in North London that looks set to dominate English football for the next FIVE years'. Such a bizarre show of good will was totally unexpected. Most staggering of all was that Alex Ferguson got in on the act, admitting that we were 'awesome' and that we 'fully deserved' the title. Georgie and Alex then posed for a couple of lovey-dovey publicity shots - GG with the title trophy and Fergie with the Cup Winners Cup. It probably had more to do with the fact that they are both Scottish, but the whole thing was sick making. Whatever next, Nigel Winterburn and Brian McClair eloping to Gretna Green, perhaps?

The pre-season friendlies added to the 'feel-good' factor hanging over Highbury. Our ex-hero, Charlie Nicholas, returned with Celtic for Paul Davis' testimonial; he was given a rapturous reception and scored a cracker in the rip-roaring 2-2 draw. Young striker Andrew Cole nearly won the Charity Shield for us against Spurs. The latest product from our youth academy looked a good prospect and we reckoned that George had unearthed another gem. Little did we know that we wouldn't see him again in an Arsenal shirt. And David Rocastle scored and played a commanding role in the Makita Tournament. We finally lost on penalties, but the team coped well against Italian heavyweights Sampdoria, and the thought of a fit again Rocky tanking forward every week was mouth watering. Temperatures in Europe soared during that golden Summer. T.V. images showed even Muscovites and Yugoslavs suffering from heat stroke. Not even month-long sun drenchings would prevent both countries descending into civil chaos before the clocks were turned back, though. If Arsenal fans hadn't been so light headed from all that Championship champagne, we would probably have realised that problems were on our horizon, too.

Most of us overlooked the fact that George had failed to add any player of note to his squad over the summer and shore up our increasingly flimsy looking midfield. All teams, no matter how awesome, need the 'cattle prod up the jacksie' effect of a new signing at the start of a season. Obligatory Summer target Andy Townsend once more decided that life at Stamford Bridge was preferable to life with the Champions. That was quite an amusing joke in July, but it ceased to be funny by Christmas. The midfield issue was about to become the Gunners' Achilles heel.

The grapevine had long buzzed with rumours that Mickey Thomas was unsettled. Clearly pissed off with George's tactics, he'd stalled over signing a new contract and had several blazing rows with the boss. Mickey believed that George's increasing emphasis on a defensive, deep lying midfield meant that his own attacking instincts were being suffocated. It is alleged that one of their biggest tiffs came when they disagreed over whether or not Mickey could go to the toilet - and George wonders why players called him Gadaffi. After a couple of months, injuries and arguments would also cost Paul Davis his place, leaving only David Rocastle as a midfielder with any forward thrust. As for David Hillier, who'd done a decent job in the Championship season from March onwards, Jasper Rees' ironic comment in *The Independent* summed up his situation perfectly: 'Hillier..... is one of those footballers who plays best when you hardly notice he's there'. The North Bank soon 'noticed' Hillier with increasing regularity. By Christmas we realised that we had a '90s Peter Nicholas in our midst. Still, a winter of discontent was the last thing on the minds of the 38,000 who piled into Highbury for the first game of the season against QPR.

Arsenal's cloak of invincibility disappeared after the three terrible opening performances of the season. Only Paul Merson's undeserved, last minute equaliser against Rangers ground out a point. Then at Villa Park and Goodison, both home sides took the piss for ninety minutes, comfortably gaining 3-1 wins against the reigning champions. Against Everton, not even Nigel Winterburn's thundering half volley could stop the team being booed off by travelling fans. The reasons for these embarrassments were multicausal; Steve Bould's thigh injury which kept him out for the start of the season and disrupted the centre of defence, Graham preferring to play Hillier rather than the more adventurous Mickey Thomas in a two man midfield, and a general 'after the lord mayor's show' feeling shown by some players. Some even blamed our vomit inducing new away kit for our display, which apparently affected our player's co-ordination. Maybe it was the reason for Lee Dixon's ridiculous thirty yard lobbed own goal over David Seaman against Coventry. The shirt was a sickly combination of yellow, blue and green - surely a tribute to early '90s acid house culture. Anders Limpar recalls that Everton's Dave Watson told him: 'you lot look like a bunch of pricks in those shirts'. Nice to see that Scouse wit continues to thrive, isn't it? Our friends in the press suddenly turned, quoting any old fitful under achiever like Tony Daley who blasted: 'Most of the teams have now worked out the best way to stop Arsenal from playing. The answer is close them down.... Arsenal are becoming a bit predictable'.

Fans' moods were not improved with the news of a 33% price hike in match-day tickets around the ground. In the final season of the old North Bank, each goal should have been greeted with added intensity. It was a crying shame that some crowds slumped beneath the 30,000 mark, reduced due to inflation busting ticket prices and discontent over the Bond scheme. David Dein, now majority shareholder with his 42% stake in the club, was unquestionably the driving force behind the new initiatives. The day before the season began, the first division Chairmen, with Dein at the forefront, announced that in the following season, they would form a breakaway Premiership. This, together with his relentless pursuit of the Bond Scheme showed that the legacy of Thatcherite principles was alive and kicking in North London. Anyone who saw the normally ultra smooth Dein ruffled at forthcoming Bond meetings half expected to be decapitated by killer swinging handbags.

Two home victories in a week quickly steadied the ship and sent us shooting up the table in late August. Luton were easily seen off by two sharp strikes from Smith and Merson. Anders got himself sent off after clouting some pedestrian defender who'd been trying to rip his shirt off all evening; George was not best pleased, of course. Manchester City arrived on a boiling Saturday, all puffed up with false confidence after three straight wins had put them top of the table. After another stuttering first half defensive display, with Winterburn's obscene one footedness exposing him to David White's pace, we got it together in the second half. Alan Smith bundled in an equaliser before Limpar cracked in our onion bag ripping winner from an amazingly acute angle after Mickey Thomas, briefly restored to the team one final time, fired his shot against the bar. The North Bank went mad, marvelling at Limpar's genius. With the blazing heat running on into September, Arsenal goal fests were about to become commonplace.

The Gunners' 4-1 win at Selhurst Park utterly humiliated Crystal Palace. Kevin Campbell marked his return from injury with two of the most venomous strikes you'll ever see, but it was Mickey Thomas' brilliant one-two and finish which lives long in the mind. This was partly due to the fact that we'd seen Mickey's trademark jig of delight after scoring for the final time in a Gunners' shirt. By the time Sheffield United were destroyed 5-2 by Smith's glorious double, Perry Groves' crackling half volley and Campbell's mortar shell, all of us were once more enthusing about the differing qualities within our strike force; the raw pace of Campbell, Smith's elegant line-leading qualities and the sheer unpredictability of Limpar and Merson. If a total of nine goals on consecutive Saturdays was glorious enough, then the filling in the sandwich, our 6-1 slaughter of Austria Vienna, was simply delicious. It was Arsenal's first match in the European Cup for nineteen years and Paul Merson turned in a dazzling performance. Marauding through their defence at will, he wreaked havoc on the left and his sumptuous cross with the outside of his right foot let in Alan Smith for the second of his four goal haul. Smudger's poaching skills that night were awesome, and the performance was topped off by Limpar's silky finish. Conventional wisdom held that Arsenal's attack was by far the most potent in the old first division and, populated as it was by youngsters (Smudger was the oldest at 27), George wouldn't need to tinker with it for years. Things didn't quite go according to plan.

If, strictly speaking, Arsenal had already stepped into football's modern era, then September 23rd, 1991 is the date on which the Gunners' modern history changed course entirely. David Dein casually enquired of Palace's chairman, Ron Noades, if Mark Bright was available for transfer. Noades said that he was not, but within two minutes the conversation had been turned on its head, and a bemused Palace chairman agreed to sell Bright's striking partner, Ian Wright. Arsenal shattered its transfer record, signing him for £2.5 m. There were some initial doubts when he first arrived. Some said that capturing him was unnecessary and that he mightn't even get a place in the side. Other 'tactical experts' claimed that rather than playing up front, he might function in midfield or even on the wing. Spectacularly wrong on all counts, as it turned out.

The reasons why Wrighty wanted to leave Palace are fairly clear. The press highlighted the fact that Noades said in a T.V. documentary that black players lacked 'bottle' and didn't 'like the cold'. This ignorant outburst probably made up his mind for him, but Wrighty had long since realised that his genetic makeup 'required a larger stage'. We already had an affinity for him after his single handed attempt to derail Manchester United in the 1990 Cup Final. The bewildering speed with which he dispatched his goals, his emotional celebrations and his rampaging ego were laid bare in front of a goggling T.V. audience. But the maelstrom that was Ian Wright was all too much for Palace - a club whose limited fan base often meant that Selhurst Park was semi-deserted, despite Noades' protestations that they were about to become a big club. Thus we had signed a star who felt, as he later commented: 'that I was born for the really big occasions - Arsenal gave me that stage'.

In order to fully understand the extent of Wright's burning desire when he arrived at Highbury, one only needs to look at his background. Originally considered too lightweight and flimsy to make it as a pro, he seemed to be headed on a road to nowhere. Jailed for seven days in Chelmsford for non-payment of car fines, and burnin' rubber in London without MOTs, tax or car insurance, he was in with a 'bad crowd'. By age 21, he was certainly no over-nannied and cosseted young star; he was up to his knees in filth repairing and constructing tunnels for Greenwich Borough Council, struggling to make ends meet in order to support his young family. He drifted around the non-league circuit, playing for Greenwich and all black side Ten Em Bee. He finally turned professional at 22 with Palace, quickly turning himself into their cult hero. When he arrived at Highbury, he was 28 years old and, realising that his shelf life was limited, he knew he had to make up for lost time. We instantly fell under Ian Wright's spell because he fitted in perfectly with our perceptions of what being a Gunner is all about, and a great deal more besides.

He made his debut in September away at Leicester after Alan Smith's injury gave him an early first team chance. It was a fairly bog standard type of Rumbelows Cup game against Second Division opposition on a grey night.

Away fans amused themselves by shrieking 'ACIEEED' each time a Gunner received the ball. Just before half time though, Wright scored his first goal in an Arsenal shirt. He got the ball just outside the area, steadied himself after slipping slightly and curled a skimming twenty yarder into the right hand corner. Steve Walsh's late equaliser hardly mattered, we'd already seen the breathtaking potential of the Wright effect. This was tame compared to the match at the Dell on the following Saturday. Inside Southampton's tiny ground, the 5,000 travelling Gooners crammed the away end and waited for a glimpse of the new striking superstar. It was a totally unforgettable occasion.

Roy Jones, an Arsenal fan from Luton recalls: 'We've won Cups and trophies in the nineties, but I honestly believe that Ian Wright's debut was the most amazing game I've ever seen. Most people hated going down to the Dell, but I've always really enjoyed going there because the atmosphere is quite unlike any other ground in the country. You're so close to the action that you can hear everything that's said on the pitch in front of you.

When Arsenal ran out, the players came to warm up right in front of the crowd. I just looked at our forward line and thought 'Christ, that is one awesome line up'. You had Alan Smith, who'd won two Golden Boots, Anders Limpar, who could do anything with a ball, Paul Merson who wasn't far behind and of course Ian Wright. Straight away, you could see that he was a unique player, a one off. He knew exactly how to milk the crowd. He'd kiss the canon on his shirt, grin at us and, as we'd see, celebrate a goal like it was his last one ever.

We were lucky that day because Southampton gave us space to play. David Rocastle set him up for the first. He got the ball and slammed it in. We went ballistic of course but I remember his second goal even more clearly. Limpar played him in and he beat the goalie from a tight angle. His celebration was unbelievable. He climbed up on the metal fence near where we were standing, lent over and hugged the bloke in front of me, screaming '*I love you all*' in that drawl of his. His hat trick goal, like, exploded into the net and again he just came over and screamed at us. He just went mad, I've never seen anything like it. The rest of the team quickly piled in. I have never seen anyone score goals like he did or celebrate goals like he did. I loved him straight away and I bet if you ask the Arsenal crowd to name their favourite ever Arsenal player, over fifty per cent will say Ian Wright. He's certainly mine'.

Roy Jones, Arsenal fan from Luton

Wrighty had already become an Arsenal hero after those ninety minutes. His three spectacular goals, all carved out after intricate passing between himself, Limpar, Davis and Rocastle and his infectious enthusiasm never failed to inspire during his Arsenal career. A week later, he scored his first Highbury goal in a sensational 3-2 win over Chelsea. The West London boys got so cocky when they went 2-0 up that they forgot to defend and allowed the inspired Kevin Campbell to thrash in our ferocious winner after Wrighty had squeezed in an equaliser. Yet again, though, it was the latter who grabbed the headlines. Wright immediately tapped into many Arsenal fans' psyche. The guy I stood next to for the Chelsea match turned to me and said 'That's how I'd want to play for Arsenal if I got the chance - just like Wrighty.' He was an in yer face raging inferno of speed, skill, anger and aggression. There was a rawness to his game which hadn't been seen at Highbury since the days of Charlie George.

Being honest, how many of us, if we got to play for the Gunners, wouldn't launch a torrent of abuse at Roy Keane, go screaming straight to the Arsenal fans if we scored, or try to maim Peter Schmeichel? Of course we would, and that is half the reason we idolised him. It's not politically correct to say so of course and I'm sure that Michael Parkinson wouldn't like it but Ian Wright, like Vieira, was red-bloodedly loved by us because there was a dangerous edge to him. Boiling passion occasionally spilling over is something the majority of us like to see at games. Don't let the politically correct lobby tell you otherwise. We were privileged to witness Ian Wright's unique brand of passion for the next seven years.

Apart from the Wright factor, one of the reasons for Arsenal's sensational Autumn form was David Rocastle's move back into central midfield. Dogged by the cruellest of luck over the last two years, he began to motor again within the engine room of the team. His knee once more 'felt right'. Rocky's rejuvenation was evident at Old Trafford, where his slithering run left Robson and Ince crawling around on the floor. Looking up, he saw Schmeichel off his line and chipped him superbly. Rocky was well and truly back, although Steve Bruce's header scrambled a point for the Mancs. After a routine 2-0 win at home to Notts County, Arsenal lay in fourth position. Early season jitters were behind us, it seemed. The defence had tightened up, Rocky was purring along and Wright was in superlative form, ably assisted by Smith and Limpar. All of our pre-season cockiness returned, particularly after the supremely confident and assured 1-1 draw away against Benfica, in the European Cup second round first leg. Atmospheres simply don't come any more intimidating than a packed Stadium Of Light. Eighty thousand Portuguese fans roared and screamed their players onto the pitch, releasing Roman candles and fire crackers which belched out red, orange and purple smoke.

Richie Montague, a Gunners fan from Finchley, couldn't resist the lure of travelling to see Arsenal play in one of Europe's glamour grounds. He remembers: 'When Arsenal were drawn against Benfica in the Cup, I knew that I had to go to the game. I was too young to have gone to the game in Turin in 1980, so I knew that I had to be inside the Stadium Of Light. The problem was, I had no money and my boss would never let me take two days holiday to go. At the time, I was working in a seriously iffy Turkish warehouse in London which I'd better not name, otherwise the boss would probably come looking for me. Suffice it to say that packing rugs into boxes was just a cover for a more lucrative business, shall we say. And the police still haven't rumbled him!

My mate found a cheap deal which meant that our flight plus the ticket for the match would cost about £150, which I could just about stretch to. I took two sickies and went to the game. It was electrifying and frightening. So much noise and colour and the size of the stadium! One corner was empty, but still there were over 80,000 there. We played really well after a shaky opening. Kevin Campbell's goal after David Rocastle slipped him through was excellent - we went mad, all 2,000 of us! But when Benfica scored through Isaias, it was as if a volcano had erupted. Suddenly all their fire crackers exploded, and my ear drums nearly split. What shocked me even more was that the stadium literally shook. In unison, their fans started to jump up and down together, shouting *'Benfica, Benfica'*. And then, all the stories about Latin fans came true. Over came bottles, food, wood - whatever they had to hand. It was wild, and it's so different from our own football culture - which seems tame in comparison. Anyway, we were well pleased with our 1-1 draw. We spent a couple of days looking around Lisbon, and then flew back on the Friday. I got home, checked my answer phone and got a message saying: 'Don't bother coming into work on Monday - I know where you've been'. Someone in work had obviously grassed me up - but in the end I didn't really care. I'd seen a great match in an unforgettable atmosphere. That makes it worth getting sacked from a shitty job doesn't it?'

Richie Montague - Arsenal fan from Finchley

Back in the second leg on a night of incredible intensity, shark-nosed Colin Pates got his five minutes of Highbury fame - swivelling and crashing in our only goal. It could and should have been more. Campbell almost shattered the goal frame with an explosive shot and Alan Smith fired inches wide. Then Isaias, our torturer in Lisbon, got into gear and thumped in an equaliser. Extra time kicked in and, frankly, Arsenal panicked. In Tony Adams' words, we employed 'helter-skelter' tactics. Alan Smith skied his shot into the despairing North Bank when only a touch was needed. Tony Adams shinned his shot against a post and we resorted to desperate punts forward to the heads of Smith and Campbell. Twice, though, arch ball snaffler Stefan Schwarz fed Isaias and Kulkov killer balls, and Arsenal were out, beaten 4-2 on aggregate.

The fall out from the defeat was far reaching. Smith, Davis and Limpar all agreed that this reverse impacted massively upon Graham's future tactics; Anders says that: 'He withdrew more and more into his defensive shell after this'. Never mind that on the night, we were by far the better side, having had three times as many shots as them. The whole thing was made worse by the fact that Benfica would be by far the most inept team in the group stages of the inaugural Champions League. But their skilled power play had taught us an arse-stinging lesson; an ultra organised defence and sharp counter attacking were the keys to European success.

The team's progress was disrupted for some time. Within a week, we were beaten at home by West Ham in the league, a team destined for the drop, and Coventry knocked us out of the Rumbelows Cup at Highfield Road. Destabilising too, was the effect on squad morale. Mickey Thomas continued to rant in *The Sun* about his 'Highbury hell'. His relationship with George was beyond repair, reflected in a wretched performance in his final Arsenal match against the Hammers. Mickey did have sympathy from the Hillier-haters in the crowd. After all, Graham's tactical straitjacket clearly ground down Thomas' confidence and effectiveness.

In truth though, his half hearted displays on the pitch had already alienated him from many fans and the oasis of surging runs had practically run dry by early 1990 anyway. By December '91, Arsenal's coolest player was, shockingly, appearing in a Scouse red shirt. Souness splashed out £1.5m to take him to Liverpool. Seeing him turn out weekly for the Scousers was as jarring a sight as seeing Gail Porter with her clothes *on*. Years later, he confessed in *Four Four Two* magazine that he felt let down over his wages at Highbury. By 1991, he and other stalwarts from the '89 side remained on

£800 a week - scant reward when Chelsea's captain of the time was alleged to earn five times that amount. With hindsight, Thomas' grumbling over money and Graham's tactics proved to be the thin end of a growing wedge of discontent at Highbury. Mickey also admitted that scoring the most memorable goal in Arsenal's history acted as a millstone around his neck. After all, how could a rising 22 year old midfielder ever top that moment during the rest of his playing days? If only we could all damage our careers in such memorable style.

Equally as concerning was George's cold shouldering of Paul Davis. This was a classic case of cutting off one's nose to spite one's face. Davis' innate ability to split open a defence with a measured pass and to dictate the pace of play in frenzied '90s games was considered to be an unnecessary luxury by George. Asked to play more of a harrying, chasing game, he and George quickly fell out. Davis recalls: 'I had been asked to chase and track back more by George, particularly in the Benfica game. I didn't think it was my strength, and I told him that. So we argued about it and I was dropped. The fact is that when you argue with George, you have to be prepared to accept the consequences.' The 'consequences' for Davis and the team were dire. Over the next eighteen months, he'd appear just twice in the first team. Arsenal were left with a midfield consisting of an over burdened David Rocastle and David Hillier. It was hardly rich pickings and looked even worse when compared with the talent oozing up front.

Winter was turning into a grim fight, in more ways than one. The boys were lucky to grab a point at Hillsborough and, up at Oldham's Siberian outpost, Ian Wright was subjected to the full monkey chant treatment from home fans. As those with cars parked near the ground discovered, doing ape impressions and putting through car windows constitutes youth entertainment in those parts of darkest Lancashire. It seemed that neither sunlight nor information on other cultures had reached that far North by late '91. How typical of the FA that Wright and Merson were made to apologise for flicking Vs at their taunting fans, while no mention was made of the racist abuse. Some things never change.

As you would expect, though, there were some moments of pure genius from the likes of Wright and Limpar. In the most one-sided North London derby for years, Wrighty and Kev Campbell clinically finished off a meek Spurs team. However, not even Paul Merson's majestic chip could save us away at Forest a week later. Three down with half an hour to go, Arsenal's late onslaught wasn't quite enough to gain us a point in a 2-3 defeat. More baffling was the arrival of the Highbury pantomime season against Everton. A mad 4-2 game, complete with relentless attacking and suicidal defending made for a superb spectacle. Unquestionably, Winterburn and Dixon were the ugly sisters - gift wrapping two easy tap ins for Beardsley and Johnston. Anders, no doubt fired up by George's jibes about him in the press, was the genie in our ranks. His magic unlocked the Toffees' defence four times for Ian Wright to grab a brilliant quadruple haul, all dispatched via his chest, knee and foot.

The riotous delight against Everton was as unreliable an indicator of Christmas that year as possible. Santa, it seemed, had only turds to deposit in our stockings during the festive period. The trip to Luton's drastic plastic on Boxing Day, where Arsenal played abysmally and lost 1-0, immediately followed by an identical scoreline at Maine Road, finally wrecked any change of retaining the title. With Adams and Bould still not fully fit, we endured the ghastly duo of Pates and Linighan at the centre of defence, surely the most gruesome pairing in those days before Christine and Neil Hamilton were on the scene. When the team then drew two mind numbingly awful games at home to Villa and Wimbledon, confidence seemed to be visibly disappearing by the week. While playing the Dons, Nigel Winterburn had a heated *tête-à-tête* with a fan, and by now, the team had crashed to eighth in the league. At least it appeared that the fates were being kind to us in the FA Cup. By now it was our only hope of salvaging a frustrating season. A third round trip to Wrexham, who'd finished bottom of division four in the previous season seemed to be just the tonic.

It's strange how the mind plays tricks. Although he'd arrived from Liverpool in October of the previous year, the week leading up to the Wrexham game was the first time I'd become aware of George's most recent acquisition. Jimmy Carter; a £500,000 '90s nightmare. Be afraid, be very afraid. The *Blair Witch Project* has nothing on the ghastly image of Jimbo on the wing in George's later years at Arsenal. Even his name made people snigger, when they remembered his namesake US President counterpart as a bungling clown. His arrival alarmed us straight away. After all, even Graeme Souness realised that Jimbo was useless. This was a damning indictment on George's judgement indeed.

Carter was an accident waiting to happen in every sense of the word. Statistically, he was a curse on the team, eventually playing in thirty games and appearing on the winning side just five times. Astonishingly, George saw fit to drop Limpar and replace him with Carter in early January. Is it any wonder that we slumped so badly just after Christmas and the New Year? Simply speaking, the Wrexham match was the biggest giant-killing of the decade. Alan Smith scored just before half time and we seemed to be cruising with three minutes to go. The team was at full strength save for Limpar and Wright, but in the second half inexplicably seized up. Every schoolboy now knows that Mickey Thomas (about to be banged up for distributing dud fivers to their apprentices, and not to be confused with our '89 hero) levelled the scores, before Steve Watkin prodded them into a 2-1 lead with one minute to go.

That game summed up Carter's fortunes perfectly. We tore up field in a desperate bid to salvage the tie and he slammed in an injury time equaliser only to see an idiotic linesman raise his flag for no good reason. Neither we, nor Jimmy, could believe our bad luck. If that goal had stood, we would at least have been grateful to him and given him a place in our hearts. As it was, he symbolised the start of George's failing antenna in the transfer market and this game, according to Tony Adams in *Addicted*, symbolised the start of the slow decline of George's Arsenal. Limpar and Davis reckon the Benfica defeat started the rot, Captain Tone reckons it was the Wrexham debacle. Either way, George Graham's reign was never quite the same again after that grim day in Wales. And it was all because of Jimmy Carter. Only kidding, Jimbo.

For the first time since George arrived back in '86, serious questions were asked about the 'hunger' of certain players. He said in *The Independent* 'that we've forgotten the spirit we had last season and how we fought for each other'. Unquestionably, key players lost form at the same time. Lee Dixon and Nigel Winterburn had had poor seasons; Dixon in particular seemed to have forgotten how to defend at key moments. Merson's and Limpar's goals temporarily dried up due to, ahem, 'inconsistent' performances. Alan Smith's form was cause for the greatest concern though. With hindsight, Smudger was the first casualty of 'the Wright affect'.

Smith explained the phenomenon to me in 2000: 'When Ian arrived, he became the life and soul of the dressing room. He was a really funny lad, with a strong personality on the pitch too. He wanted the ball all the time and, to be honest, we started to play to his strengths too much. We seemed just to give it to him all the time which made us far too one dimensional and too focussed on him. The affect on my game was immediate. I'd always scored lots of goals, but they dried up almost immediately. My strength was holding up the ball, and allowing others to come into the game. But with Ian, he wanted the ball immediately, and so I saw less and less of the ball. Subconsciously, I think that some players thought 'if we give it to Ian, he'll do the business for us' which I don't think is too healthy for a team. The effect didn't really kick in on the others until the following season. After all, towards the end of the season the team played some of the best attacking football I ever saw'.

Smudger was right. In February, the gathering storm clouds miraculously began to lift. Desperate, at least, to salvage a UEFA Cup place, Arsenal embarked upon a goal laden, unbeaten gallop to the end of the season. Ironically, the renaissance was ushered in by the defensive reunion of Tony Adams and Steve Bould. As we know, Adams was by now gaining an almost talismanic status. The fact was that when he was absent or semi-fit Arsenal's foundations were much more insecure. Bouldy also won over the early sceptics who doubted his positional sense and distribution. His form rarely dipped beneath the rating 'excellent' for the rest of the season. The final three months of the season was a last hurrah before George changed tack and plotted the raging Cup battles which would characterise the final years of his reign. We would be given one last chance to surge, dance, and jump around on the North Bank in homage to our front players and their golden strikes, before we were literally and metaphorically told to 'sit down' (or 'get out').

If our faith in some of the players was shaken, then many fans' trust in the Board of Directors had long since been shattered. After deciding to press on with the Bond Scheme, the Board stood accused, by its own fans, of two heinous crimes; namely social engineering, and total high handedness in dealing with supporters. The anti-bond Independent Arsenal Supporters' Association (IASA), which was formed in June of '91, had already achieved notable success. Early that month, a *Time Out* article publicised the movement, which prompted David Dein to threaten legal action against the group. Dein had obviously calmed down a few days later, because the movement's leader, Dyll Davies, and *One Nil Down's* editor Tony Willis were invited into the inner sanctum to meet with Dein and Friar and discuss their differences.

The meeting was heated but fairly good natured. The transcript from the meeting was reproduced in *One Nil Down* some weeks later. One question/answer in particular summed up the gulf between fans and the board. They were asked the question; 'What provisions are being made for loyal fans who cannot afford a bond?' (namely the majority of teenagers, students, OAPs and the core of the North Bank). Friar and Dein apologised for the chaos that was likely to occur but said that 'the club is not run as a charitable institution'. A fair point, but in a nutshell, they'd admitted that no provision was being made for lower income fans. 'The people's game', if football ever was that, was dead in London N.5.

Dein and Friar's responses at the meeting were terse and sharp. The reason for this was that out of 16,000 bonds up for sale, only an estimated 5,000 (£5m worth) were sold by Christmas '91. The IASA's campaigning was proving to be a serious pain for the club and they were about to discover the true strength of fan power.

Ian McPherson wrote several articles for *One Nil Down* and helped put together the IASA newsletter. He recalls the prevailing attitude amongst many fans at the time: 'I don't think that the club ever *really* understood what our grievance was. The North Bank had always been the traditional stronghold of our support. In general, it was populated by the lower income, sections of our support. It was, therefore, of real symbolic importance. The Bond Scheme was an exclusive, elitist scheme, which asked those people to shell out a large sum of money. It was money which many did not have. In effect, the club was telling people on the North Bank that money was more important than loyalty. They were constructing a new kind of football audience; a well heeled, middle class audience who would then be able to spend a fair proportion of their cash on club merchandise. In effect, it was a form of social engineering. I remember that Tom Watt said at the time that the club was afraid of its own supporters. Look at the way the club dealt with the whole issue. In effect, they used threats all the time. They said that if they were forced to take the money from the club's coffers, then they wouldn't be able to afford any decent players. Then they said that in order to attend games, you had to have a season ticket and in order to get one of those you needed to have a bond. Someone told me that the club, allegedly, used to call us the 'intelligentsia' - which kind of hints that they found the IASA intimidating. That's actually quite amusing, but it just goes to show that for all their claims of being a 'progressive club', it was actually being led by an archaic elite, with no PR skills at all.

We saw it as our responsibility to come up with an alternative plan for financing the conversion of Highbury into an all seater stadium. We proposed that, firstly, a debenture scheme should guarantee season tickets at a reduced rate, which meant that fans would get a real return on their investment. We suggested issuing a maximum 6,000 of these. Secondly, we suggested setting up a membership scheme which, for £20 a season, would enable fans to obtain an option on buying a ticket for every home match. Thirdly, we put forward the idea of a limited share issue-raising between £2m and £4.5m. Added together, this would have brought in between £12m and £14m. The membership card scheme mysteriously appeared in the following year. This was the *club's* idea, of course!!!'

Ian McPherson, Arsenal fan and IASA founder

It soon filtered through that over the next two years, when the capacity was to be slashed to around 28,000, the club hoped to sell all 16,000 bonds. They also hoped to make 'up to' 12,000 tickets available to fans on match days. We knew what this meant - by the time the away side had received their share and the touts had got their grubby hands on some of them, closer to 6,000 tickets would be available to non-bond holders for each game. It would, in effect, turn Highbury into Fort Knox, with sufficient cash to buy a bond seemingly being a pre-requisite for regular entry to the ground. Once fans comprehended this news, letters of support and cash donations flooded into IASA headquarters. Ian McPherson allowed me to see the wodges of letters they received. They all express similar emotions; namely a sense of betrayal at the club's willingness to 'liquidate' them, and a fear that Saturday pilgrimages to Highbury would soon become a thing of the past. I reproduce extracts from two of the letters:

'I'm not against making Arsenal the best in the land but not all people can afford such a sum to pay for a bond. And the sad thing is I have already had the sad duty of telling my son (12) that this is probably the last season for some time that we can attend all matches, if any. My son and I love this club with all our hearts. I don't think the club's as loyal to us, just our money'.

'As the father of two children who are devoted to Arsenal, I'm appalled at our exclusion from any thinking into restructuring plans. It is simply way beyond my means to pay for bonds for the children. Will we ever be back after this season?'

(names withheld from both letters)

Steve Beauchampe commented in the *Daily Star* that a tragic novel could have been written about the Bond Scheme. Perhaps *'Fear and Loathing In Highbury'* would have been a good title. The saga raged on into the following season, when we'd see for ourselves the real cost of turning Highbury all-seater. In the film *'Falling Down',* Michael Douglas' character goes on the rampage when he realises that he is no longer 'economically viable'. Is it any wonder that furious fans who felt that they were about to be liquidated crusaded against the Bond? Ian McPherson recalled that 'for every bond that wasn't sold, it meant that a loyal fan who couldn't afford the bond could get into games over the next two years'. We realised that the word 'fan' meant little in '90s football speak. Perhaps 'expendable unit' would have been a more appropriate term.

The carefree end of season fun began with a gritty 1-1 draw at home to Manchester United. Rocky's last ever Arsenal strike equalised McClair's effort. Once Alan Smith's excellent goal beat Notts County away (our first win in seven), the goal fests began. Chief providers, Anders Limpar and Paul Merson, hit golden form at the same time, ready to wreak havoc in opposition penalty areas. Kevin Campbell and Ian Wright were ready to resume their goal exploits after the early New Year lull. The home match with Sheffield Wednesday in early February seemed to be drifting into obscurity. The half time score was 1-1 in front of a sleepy crowd. Some Yorkshire wags were even shouting *'Champions, Champions'* at half time because an away win would have put them in top position. Forty five minutes later, they couldn't get to Kings Cross station quickly enough after being hit by six second half goals. Our forwards fired on all cylinders and blew holes in the Wednesday defence. Campbell's blistering shooting gave him a brace and Limpar's drive and endeavour brought him a majestic double. Pick of the bunch, though, was Paul Merson's lazy, arrogant chip over Chris Woods. Torturing Sheffield Wednesday proved to be a joyous pass-time for a couple of years, even though they did finish above us in '91/'92.

Two scrappy away wins at Norwich and Coventry rocketed us back up the table. Under the cosh at Highfield Road, Kev bulldozed through and smacked in a winner before Norwich were ridiculously unlucky to be hit by a couple of Wright breakaways on a Wednesday night. Lucky escapes were par for the course in that bizarre week, though. John Major, who, opinion polls reckoned, was about to be unceremoniously booted out of Number 10, miraculously escaped the executioner's axe and, of course, won the bloody election. It was a victory that even Graham's Arsenal would have been proud to achieve.

Wrighty's thunderous double at Upton Park hammered the East End boys. It was another nail in the coffin for the West Ham fans. We'd even protested with them before the game about the injustices of our Bond Schemes but, unfortunately for them, whingeing about directors was about all we had in common. The goals and thrills continued unabated at Highbury. There was a mad 3-3 frenzy with Forest; two late strikes from Merson and an injury time saver from Tony Adams grabbed us a point.

Anders' display that night was perhaps his greatest ever in an Arsenal shirt. Stuart Pearce and Des Walker actually tripped over each other on three occasions in their vain attempts to stop his marauding.

Visiting Palace fans forced Wrighty to endure the *'Ian shite, shite, shite'* cries for the full ninety minutes. His embittered former worshippers had the small satisfaction of seeing him fail to score, but Paul Merson grabbed a spectacular hat-trick in our crushing 4-1 win. Kevin Campbell's scorching volley was delicious enough, but Merson's sumptuous arcing lob over Nigel Martyn topped the lot. The Merse had again proved that he was a genius, but, as Frank McLintock said at the time: 'Being a genius only takes you so far. It needs application too'. The next two years proved that our Double winning captain knew exactly what he was talking about.

If Arsenal's Christmas had been the worst for many years, then Easter more than made up for it. Top of the list was a stupendous 4-0 whipping of Liverpool. Ian Wright's performance that afternoon was breathtaking, but Anders' display was not of this earth. His jinking, weaving and roaming pulled Liverpool all over the park. When David Hillier belted in his first ever Arsenal goal, you knew it was our day. Limpar then bisected the Scousers' defence to find the galloping Ian Wright. At full tilt he didn't even break his stride as he curled the ball past Hooper. The goal was greeted with the surging ferocity it deserved. The scorer jumped straight into the North Bank to celebrate. Wrighty's strike was tame compared with Anders Limpar's goal just before half time though.

He received the ball just inside his own half and cut through Molby's flimsy challenge. Seeing Hooper wandering off his line, he launched a fifty yard lob straight over him. Limpar describes the goal: 'I looked to pass to Ian Wright but he was offside so there was really nothing else on. I looked up and thought I'd give it a go. It was an amazing sight as it hit the back of the net. It's a once in a career moment - it's still a great memory for me'. Anders was hoisted up into the air by Kevin Campbell and the Swede clutched his hands together in mock prayer. The North Bank paid its own homage to the Swedish God, while Liverpool skulked back to Merseyside, well aware they were now merely a second rate force in English football.

With the season nearing its climax, Arsenal's dramatic assault on a UEFA Cup place finally fell after a messy 1-1 draw at Stamford Bridge. Not even Lee Dixon's last minute curler, which salvaged a point, could help us overhaul Wednesday. The final game of the season against Southampton was the last rites for the North Bank. On an emotion packed afternoon the fans flocked in to pay homage to the end of an era. It was a game which demanded drama, and with Ian Wright aiming to win the Golden Boot award, the match lived up to its billing.

Of all Wrighty's achievements in an Arsenal shirt, we'll always be eternally grateful to him for his display on that afternoon. Save for several choruses of *'You'll never take the North Bank',* the cries were for *'Ian Wright, Wright, Wright'* and his whirlwind display. The media hyped up Wright's and Lineker's contest for the golden boot. With five minutes to go in the Southampton game, it looked as if Saint Gary had won after his strike at Old Trafford. We'd made heavy weather of beating the Saints with scrambled goals from Smith and Campbell, and Wright's penalty. Ever the showman, Wrighty had tapped his boot at the crowd after his successful spot kick, probably knowing full well that the sequence would be shown on the lucrative Nike ads that he'd agreed to make.

With five minutes to go, the crowd prepared to sing a mournful tribute to the old terrace, feeling slightly deflated about the whole day. Then Wright struck. Furious at the thought of losing the race for the Golden Boot, Wright dropped back into his own half and Seaman threw the ball out to him. Wright galloped at full pelt deep into Saints' territory, brushed past Terry Hurlock and slammed the ball past Tim Flowers. If the scenes that goal produced were chaotic, then what came thirty seconds later was simply orgasmic. Campbell squared a ball to Wright. He shinned in his hat-trick and was hoisted high in front of the maelstrom that was now the North Bank. Our Golden Boot winner beamed with delight and the crowd celebrated with him. It just showed that Wright always picked the right event on which to rise to the occasion, and on that May weekend he gave us memories we'll always remember. The old terrace couldn't have had a better send off. The North Bank; gone but not forgotten.

It was the end of an era in more ways than one. George had been making some rather unusual comments towards the end of the season. He'd mentioned his desire that Arsenal should 'always play attacking football' and that he hoped to be 'entertained in a similar way next season'. As we'd suspected, these were the rantings of a man who was indulging in self-delusion. George was probably going home at night, booting the cat and sticking forks in his legs to punish himself for the goal frenzies which punctuated the end of the season. By the time we reassembled in August, 3-3 and 5-2 thrillers were a thing of the past. Friar George clearly spent the closed season repenting and cleansing himself and the team of any such self-indulgent gluttony. Titanic wars of attrition were about to become the order of the day.

David Rocastle - 'Rocky' - in action

3

Cup Kings

When the bulldozers tore down the North Bank in the Summer of '92, they not only ripped a gigantic hole in the stadium, they also surgically removed the beating heart from Highbury. For a while it seemed as if the old terrace would actually receive a year's reprieve. Islington Council blocked the club's original plans for the new stand, almost out of sheer bloody mindedness, commenting that 'David Dein will have to reduce the size of his ego'. Local residents were also unhappy about the plans for the new stand, claiming that it was too high and obtrusive. GAAS (Group For the Alternative Arsenal Stand) was vocal in its protests, but eventually the club's second proposal was approved, and work on the £16m stand began, although the 'wrap around' effect the club originally promised was not forthcoming. We were told that the second version would fit in better with the art-deco East and West stands. So we terrace boys were forced to migrate to the Clock End for our 'last stand', and the songs and chants, instead of reverberating around the ground, simply disappeared upwards into the North London mist.

What made things worse was the decision taken by Arsenal and the council to erect the mural. It was designed to act as a surgical dressing for the bleeding stump that was now the North End of the ground. In principal, it wasn't a bad idea, because it did enclose the ground and keep it 'intimate'. Actually, it was akin to rubbing salt into gaping wounds, rather than soothing them. The mural saga left the club open to merciless piss taking by other fans. Jibes were bandied around that the 'painted persons' had more passion than the reduced Highbury crowd. The crowning denouement arrived when the politically correct posse in North London realised that ethnic minorities were not represented on the mural.

The whole issue received a great deal of publicity, made all the more ridiculous when Cypriots and Afro-Carribeans wrote to local papers admitting that they weren't offended at all and didn't actually give a toss about the issue. The necessary daubs of paint were added with all due haste, though. 'Clearly these do-gooders needed to get out and socialise a bit more', a Cypriot Arsenal fan recently said to me. By the end of the season, most of us would far rather have looked at pylons, scaffolding and workmen's fat arse cracks over the previous nine months. It was small wonder, that we'd have to trek to Wembley for our finest moments of the season.

Over the Summer, all of us realised that the team desperately required midfield reinforcements. It was hoped that George would acquire a thrusting box to box dynamo akin to a young Mickey Thomas, and possibly a more cerebral presence to either compliment Rocky's skills or supplement Paul Davis'. Wrong, on both counts. In early June, George decided to sell David Rocastle to champions Leeds for £2m. It was a truly grim and inexplicable day in our history. Rocky was a Highbury legend, who had come back stronger and fitter than ever after two years of injuries and was virtually always present in the previous season. Indeed, he'd pushed Ian Wright very close for the supporters' player of the season award. George later hinted that Rocastle's knee was permanently damaged - a fact that Rocky always vehemently denied.

His spells at Leeds, Chelsea and Manchester City told a meandering tale of under achievement and, shockingly, he wound his career down in Malaysia, when less talented players of his age were still bossing Premiership midfields. It is a sobering thought that Rocastle, along with Mickey Thomas and Stewart Robson, was tipped to be a future England captain when he was a teenager. All three were bombed out by George before they reached their 25th birthdays. Rocastle later suggested that it may have been due to burn out, brought on by the relentless running which George insisted his midfielders undertook. Of course, like Lambeth born Mickey, Rocky was London born and bred. My Dad reckons that all Arsenal teams should be stuffed with only *bona-fide* London boys and Rocky's departure left Wright and Merson as the only two regular first teamers who hailed from the capital.

Times were changing fast in top grade football and, crucially, another 'one of ours' had flown the nest. It is well known that Rocky loved Arsenal as passionately as the fans, having worked his way up from our youth team. Along with Tony Adams he was arguably the best and most committed of the starlets who rose to prominence in the mid to late '80s. Rocky confessed to sobbing his heart out when George told him he could leave in August '92. He wasn't the only one, and his shocking and untimely death from cancer in

2001 meant that more tears were shed by his fans. He'll always be a true son of Highbury though.

In place of our departed hero, arrived the Dane, John Jensen, who seemed to have fooled the press into believing that he was Rocky mark II. His thumping finish against Germany in the final of Euro '92 made us dream that we'd captured a gritty, box-to-box sharp shooter. In fact JJ would soon become the least welcome Danish visitor to these shores since the Vikings pillaged and murdered their way around the North of England some 1500 years earlier. Even they, at least, livened things up a bit, whereas Jensen's limpet like close marking and short passing game made him a David Hillier clone. Two peas in a pod, one might say, or two cretins in the same area of the park. When George eventually stuck Steve Morrow and poor Martin Keown in midfield as well, you realised why we were starting to mutter about Graham's judgement. Only Ray Parlour's occasional flourishes and Paul Davis' late season entry could save our midfield from an entirely moribund nine months.

The first game of the season was laden with omens for our league campaign. To celebrate the dawn of the Premiership era, a team of parachutists descended on Highbury. How fitting that one of them made a prize burke of himself by landing on the building site behind the mural. The game also ended up like the proverbial lead balloon. After Campbell and Bould put us two up, we caved in during 45 humbling second half minutes. The Canaries' silky midfield of Phillips, Goss and Bowen swamped Hillier and Jensen, and Ruel Fox and Mark Robins savaged Arsenal with four late goals. Warning signs were there for all to see; the midfield clones were destroyed and even the attack looked lightweight without the unfit Wrighty.

Visiting newly promoted Blackburn three days later provided an excellent chance to see exactly what the new Premiership was really about. Here was a club whose glories were long past, whose crowds had previously been around the 7,000 mark and whose stadium was a slum. They were in the process of being brought out of stasis by Jack Walker, a disciple of Thatcherism and a steel magnate who was now a multi-millionaire. Walker was the first of the '90s sugar daddies, whose pumping into the game of 'new money' millions contrived to produce hyper inflation in transfer fees. This in turn led to us fans being fleeced in order to maintain players' lifestyles. Walker's aim was to take short cuts to success; to buy a team rather than nurture it. In short, it was a case of wealth and ostentatiousness above substance and reality. Surely all true fans rejoiced when they crashed back into Division One at the end of the decade.

By August '92 Dalglish had signed Alan Shearer, whose surliness and ability to get away with murder on the pitch annoyed even then. He won the game for Blackburn in the last minute, after the ref failed to notice his blatant shove on Jimmy Carter. Arsenal had suffered two defeats in two games. It didn't seem to be the best time to pay a visit to Anfield, even if it was our first ever live Sky Super Sunday.

Into the breach was thrown Ray Parlour, the curly haired mop top who'd first surfaced against Wimbledon the season before. Immediately, he provided more balance in midfield; a pacy runner rather than a workhorse. Parlour played like a superstar that afternoon, tormenting roly-poly Molby with his fleet-footed ventures into enemy territory. Early in the second half, he got to the by-line and delivered a curling cross. Limpar instantly controlled it and smacked it past David James. Ten minutes later, Parlour squeezed past his marker and threaded the ball through to Ian Wright, who dispatched the chance with customary aplomb. His fervent celebrations incited a near riot among away fans. We'd have celebrated all the harder if we'd known that this would be our last win of the Millennium at Anfield. Parlour also showed his usual verbal skills in early interviews, admitting 'I'm well pleased', and that Wright's goal was 'well impressive'.

The press once again seemed convinced that we were back on the 'Championship trail'. Two efficient home wins against Oldham and Sheffield Wednesday rocketed us back up to fourth place. There was one slight concern, though. These successes hinged on the inconsistent talents of Parlour and Limpar. The reality was that Anders was about to be axed again - which was baffling and yet predictable at the same time, as was Ray Parlour, who George seemed to enjoy making the scapegoat for other's deficiencies. Mind you, Ray's occasional excellence could give way to awfulness at any time, as we'd soon discover.

Wintry problems were not far off but September and October proved to be the most productive of months. Admittedly, the incompatible midfield line-ups of Hillier, Jensen, Campbell and Merson fooled no-one into believing that all was well, but six straight league wins seemed to justify our pre-season billing as title favourites. Ladbrokes had installed us as 5-1 favourites - the same odds you could have had on Kinnock's Labour Party winning the '92 election, incidentally. There's nothing like misplaced confidence, is there? Merson and Campbell admitted in the press that they were not wide midfielders - but George still insisted on making Kev fire in crosses each week. They tended to end up in the same place as Jensen's shots; in Row Z of the stand. Yet George continued to berate Kev for not scoring enough goals - which had echoes of the Cruyff-Lineker catch 22 situation. Who said that Ian Wright was responsible for draining Kev's confidence?

Smith's and Wright's sudden glut of goals temporarily dispelled the growing feeling that they could not effectively play alongside each other. Two goals of stunning quality destroyed Chelsea. Paul Merson's chip levelled the scores before George brought on Anders in a late attempt to win the game. With his first touch, he delivered a ball which Ian Wright smacked in, right under the noses of Blues' fans. Considering they believe themselves to be the hardest fans in London, their reaction to Wrighty's winner was positively girlish. Some of them decided to inform the police that he'd made 'inflammatory gestures' at them. Diddums!! It was all a bit rich considering the level of abuse the Shed gave to visiting fans and players over the years.

Two more comfortable Highbury wins followed. Wright's acrobatic header at the mural end from Campbell's excellent cross beat Manchester City. Reread that last sentence; there are two events mentioned which seemed virtually impossible. For over six hours of play, the Gunners hadn't scored at that end, and a decent cross was an even rarer event that season. Another Wright header would have been good enough to beat Everton, but late sub Limpar's gliding finish for our second added real polish to the performance.

Aesthetically speaking, Arsenal's 2-1 away win at Crystal Palace was the pick of the bunch. Brian Scovell later commented in the *Daily Mail* that Arsenal produced 'some of the finest one-touch attacking football seen this season, away from a Channel 4 television match from Italy'. Alan Smith's delicious flick set up Merson for a first; away fans could hear the thump when his shot crashed into Martyn's net. Ian Wright's winner was outstanding. High speed, mazy passing between Dixon, Wright and Campbell left Wright free to crack home a beautiful goal with his left foot. It was sweet revenge for a man who'd ridden the gauntlet from bitter Palace fans all evening. Alan Smith also got his reward for the goals he'd set up. His beautifully executed volley won us the game at Forest and his headed goal at home to Coventry not only helped us beat the Sky Blues 3-0, but was also his hundredth Arsenal goal. Top of the table Gunners once again peered imperiously down on 'the pack', which included Norwich and Manchester United. We'd soon be caught and torn to pieces, though.

If there were any danger signs lurking in mid November, it was the fact that George Graham seemed intent on shifting massive black clouds over Anders Limpar's head. One can assume that by November '92, GG decided that the Swede was an unpredictable luxury we could do without. His dazzling skills were still there, as was the adoration from the Highbury crowd. But his swerves and jinks were becoming an increasingly rare sight. Brought on with six minutes to go against Chelsea, he'd set up Wright's winner and his performance against Everton, after coming on as sub in the 36th minute, raised the game to a higher plane. George remained unconvinced, though.

Anders was probably guilty, once again, of pushing his manager too far in the club v country debate. Turning up crocked on the eve of the Blackburn match was not the most sensible course of action - but George's double standards were immediately apparent. On Jensen's excursions with Denmark, GG commented 'We knew what would happen with John', whereas Limpar's foreign jaunts were 'difficult to cater for'. Do you see a pattern developing here, readers? George said of Limpar's skills to the *Daily Mirror's* Harry Harris: 'When they come off they're breathtaking; when they don't it can be a nuisance'. The Super Swede would now be reduced to the periphery at Highbury for the next fifteen months, during which time he became more and more disconsolate. It is a jarring thought that his goal against Everton was his last in an Arsenal shirt.

The Gunners' league form collapsed in November and December amidst a string of grisly defeats against old foes. Leeds' McAllister, Strachan and Speed - all midfielders we'd been linked with, destroyed us at Elland Road, Mark Hughes' goal for Manchester United beat us at Highbury and an Alf Buksch - aided Tottenham won the North London derby. The ref's cretinous incompetence led him to refuse two blatant Arsenal penalties. No wonder George blew his top afterwards. Christmas matches were little better; the draws at home to Middlesbrough and Ipswich were truly excremental. Ray Parlour was occasionally reintroduced to replace Campbell and he did well in the circumstances, given the fact that David Hillier was his midfield partner. 'Leave the boot on; take him off' yelled the Clock End when John Wark's meaty challenge tore off Dave's footwear. By New Year's Day, the team had secured only two points from a possible twenty-one, with one solitary goal to comfort us during the bleakest of Winters.

The problem was that key personnel all lost form at the same time;

Adams and Dixon looked particularly tired, due to the lack of midfield protection. Alan Smith was injured, meaning a move back up front for Campbell, whose confidence was 'shot' after his spell 'out-wide'. Justifiably, he felt 'messed about' by George, but our impatience didn't exactly help him. Nor, it has to be said, did Ian Wright's listless form alongside him. The team was having difficulty in gaining league points but Wrighty was having few problems in accumulating disciplinary ones.

Back in September, he'd thumped kung-fu black belt John Fashanu and broken his own fingers. Wright had actually managed to score twice that day in our 2-3 defeat. It's a miracle that he had time to do so in between dust ups with Jones and Sanchez. His right hook on David Howells in the North London derby brought him a hefty fine and a three month ban - followed a week later by a running battle with Ken Monkou at the Dell. Crucially, his goal supply temporarily dried up by the end of the year. He later confessed that he felt as if he was 'living in a goldfish bowl'. Wright was an early example of the *Big Brother* culture under which top players now live, and, apart from trying to spot Sarah Ferguson giving various men toe-jobs, tabloids seemed anxious to publicise each one of Wrighty's misdemeanours. Frankly, though, a publicity craver like Wright couldn't really complain about the exposure he received.

By now, he'd overtaken 100 metre Olympic Champion Linford Christie as the most marketable black sportsman in the country; quite a turnaround for a player who had been plying his trade for Palace only a year before. One of the spin off effects of being a hot-shot striker is that a host of boot companies line up to help you become seriously rich. Once Nike snapped him up, and presumably gave him a cheque which paid for a gob full of gold teeth, their publicity men set about turning him into football's anti-hero figure. He appeared in ads to the backdrop of Lou Reed's *Walk On The Wild Side*, pointing to his boot and goading fans. But it was the arrogant image he presented in the 'Gary Who?' commercial which really shifted public opinion against him. Turnip Head Taylor discovered that only the Queen Mother was more sacred than Gary Lineker in the early '90s and, when Wright won the Golden Boot, he'd pipped Saint Gary to the prize, just before he moved to Japan. Wright was portrayed as a dangerous and divisive figure. Even in Japan, Lineker remained the whiter-than-white, Luke Skywalker of English football; Ian Wright was being portrayed as its Darth Vader.

Wright later commented in his book *Mr Wright* that Nike's campaign was a public relations disaster for him, but his wild behaviour on the pitch that Winter was his real downfall. Anders Limpar later commented: 'Off the pitch

Ian was a lovely guy. But on the pitch he was an animal. He was so desperate to score goals - it was an anger inside him. He did some terrible things on the pitch in order to get them. Some of these incidents were caught on camera, some weren't. You had to be near him to hear his language on the pitch, which was certainly industrial! I don't excuse his behaviour but by that time, Ian was the only player likely to score for us. That's a lot of pressure for anyone to bear, even someone like him'. Anders has a point. It's a worrying thought that Wright's behaviour could have deteriorated further if the thrills of Cup football hadn't focussed his mind once more.

This Arsenal side was able to kick and scrap better than any team in the country. Such an ethos could not win us the title, but in stirring Cup battles, brick wall defending and Rottweiler midfield play would weaken the enemy before an opportunist Wright or Merson strike killed them off. In particular, Andy Linighan and Steve Morrow had gained respect, if not adoration from the Highbury crowd. Linighan replaced Steve Bould in central defence after Bouldy's thigh injury and his positional sense and distribution improved massively. Morrow's bustling midfield style certainly made him more popular than David Hillier, who was losing confidence and support by the day. As we'd see, it wasn't just glitzy front players who were keys to salvation that season. Every drop of sweat and blood would be needed in the wars of attrition that were to come.

Early rounds of the Coca-Cola Cup provided an indication of the type of battles which lay ahead, and Millwall's old Den was the first stern cup test. Keith 'psycho' Stevens roughed up Wrighty all night. The cold night air was filled with racist abuse aimed at our front two, flying coins directed at Seaman, and the kind of hatred that only our much unloved East London cousins can provide. Kevin Campbell silenced the racist element; his excellent goal the kind of payback which Jesse Owens would have been proud of. The game still went to penalties and, despite the variety of missiles being thrown at him, Seaman made three top-drawer saves to put us through. Not too many of us celebrated openly down Cold Blow Lane that night though. We preferred our skulls to be intact, ta very much.

Third division Scarborough awaited us in the fourth round and on an archetypal lower division marsh, set about kicking lumps out of our players. Referee Hacket seemed blind to the violence, partly because of the thick fog that rolled across the ground. With the game seemingly set for a late abandonment, Nigel Winterburn's thirty yarder flew through the mist to put us into the Quarter Finals.

Early in the New year, the press swarmed around Yeovil's ground in dark-est Somerset, prematurely ejaculating at the thought of the Goliath that was the Arse being slain by gallant minnows in the FA Cup 3rd round. Excitement was fuelled, of course, because it was almost a year to the day since the Wrexham disaster. To be fair, the game was fairly even, except that the meanest striker who'd ever stomped the land was in a class of his own. Ian Wright's classic hat-trick - a combination of top quality poaching and precision shooting silenced the feisty home crowd in a 3-1 win. All Gunners' fans realised the importance of the victory. With the cup min-nows brushed aside, the team could concentrate on knocking out Premiership big-guns.

9.00 p.m. on Monday January 25th. Arsenal's season appeared to be vir-tually over. Speed and Chapman had put Leeds 2-0 up at half time in the FA Cup fourth round at Highbury. Outfought and outplayed, we faced the grim prospect of just a Coca-Cola Cup run to take our minds off this sea-son of under achievement. Amidst deafening boos from the Clock End, the Arsenal players slunk off the pitch for their half time cuppa. God only knows what the catering staff put in the tea, but in the second half, the fans and players were miraculously transformed into a rampant machine. After all, how could we lie down with scarcely a whimper, in what could be the last Highbury FA Cup match played in front of the terraces?

When Tony Adams started roaring on the troops at the start of the sec-ond half, it was infectious. The ripples spread to the Clock End and the chant of *'Georgie Graham and his red and white army'* spread until the terrace shook. With 51 minutes gone, Leeds began to crumble. Ray Parlour, trans-formed from the anonymous figure he'd been in the first half, glided through Leeds' defence to slam in the first. Leeds hung onto their lead until the 82nd minute. Paul Merson, loitering with intent inside their half, received the ball from Parlour's pass. He cruised towards their area, defend-ers backing off in fear, and cracked in a 30 yard drive which screamed past Lukic. Out of jail, Arsenal pressed for a last gasp winner. Campbell was denied by a flailing Lukic hand, but we travelled to Elland Road for the replay, reputations intact and ready for the most thrilling game of the sea-son.

Chris Baines, an Arsenal fan from Luton recalls the game: 'Leeds' away end at that time was horrible. It was open to the elements and really exposed in the Winter months. It didn't help that we'd had a walk through the North side of Leeds to get into Elland Road - a bit like taking a Sunday afternoon stroll in the Bronx. My mate likened it to that part in The

Magnificent Seven where Yul Bryner and his friend rode up the street expecting to be shot at any minute. We got a police escort going in and with the Leeds thugs shouting *'You'll never get out alive'*, we certainly needed one.

My memories of the game are cameo images. The lads performing in those horrible early '90s away kits. Alan Smith volleying us into the lead and bounding towards us with joy. Gary McAllister's free kick and the Leeds apes chanting *'Leeds, Leeds, Leeds'* for ten minutes - such imagination. Then they took the lead and with a minute to go, they're all chanting *'Que sera sera, we're going to Wembley'.*

Ian Wright's equaliser came with about 30 seconds to go and all of us were bouncing up and down to *'Georgie Graham and his yellow and blue army'.* Extra time was knackering and thrilling. Words can't describe Ian Wright's winner which squeezed through John Lukic's hand. Wrighty flew over to us and shaped to shoot in a mock pose. No interpretation needed - he was the Top Gun. All the players coming across to applaud us. So close you could hear Wright cackling like a mad man. We'd won 3-2. The long trip back down South with the minibus rocking to *'She wore a yellow ribbon'*; all superb memories, which make you proud, as ever, to be a Gooner. We were on our way to Wembley'.

Chris Baines - Arsenal fan from Luton

It seemed that the greater Arsenal's heroics were in the Cups, the worse our Premiership form became. By January and early February, we'd reached the 'down the toilet and around the U-bend stage'. After Liverpool beat us at home, the Gunners slipped to within four points of the drop zone. Being honest, it wouldn't have been surprising if we'd slid into the pit judging by a 0-1 home defeat by Wimbledon. So disenchanted was the Clock End, that it watched the match against the Dons in morbid silence. My appalled neighbour said to me: 'It'd be easier to get shit out of a rocking horse than get a goal from Arsenal tonight'. Indeed, but thankfully this was as grim as it got in the inaugural Premiership season.

In reality the Premiership's cheap gimmicks, new inventions and media intrusion failed to bowl us over in astonishment. We weren't particularly impressed with refs in purple or green, by ridiculous sights like Jimmy Carter in a number 25 shirt (surely number 13 was the appropriate number for 'unlucky Jim'), or by the abysmal pre-match Sky entertainment. We were mighty pissed off with the fact that, on a whim, Sky could tinker with the fixture list. Gone was the guarantee of twenty home league games on a Saturday. In '92/'93 only eleven home matches were played on the football sabbath. We got the message that TV now commanded and demanded, and not even the old farts at the FA could stop the process.

In a way, the 'eyes and ears' that was satellite TV had its compensations. With its obsession for sticking cameras and microphones up every orifice, Wrighty's industrial language and Tone's clattering tackles reverberated around living rooms. On the other hand, these rogue cameras now picked up every sly punch and two fingered salute at opposition fans, which cost Wrighty a few bob. The bottom line was that, in terms of skill and entertainment, nothing had really changed. In the days before silky foreign midfielders roamed the land, the Premiership was jammed with honest journeymen and some ruthless cloggers. With the exception of Manchester United and Norwich, few sides had yet embraced the concept of a 'passing game'. The Gunners would eventually become one of the prime exponents of this culture but, for now, fighting and scrapping was the order of the day circa '93.

Martin Keown was brave enough to want to step back into the morass. He became a Gunner again after signing from Everton for £2m. Originally flogged by George because he wanted an extra £50 a week, he now cost ten times the amount for which he was sold. A case of George cutting off his nose to spite his face, perhaps? Poor Martin. With his red boots and his pace, he would become a star under Wenger. But for now, he seemed to be nervous and unsteady; an unnecessary addition to a team screaming out for a creative midfielder. Cup-tied in both knock out competitions, he was forced to play occasionally in the whimper that was passed off as our league campaign. Keown missed out on the Cup thrills that season, and it took him some time before he won over the boo-boys.

Nottingham Forest now blocked our path in both Cup competitions. Previously the masters of lightning counter attacking, Forest had fallen into terminal decline, and became hooked on hoofing and spoiling tactics. Brian Clough, of course, was about to bow out of football management in the most ignominious of circumstances. The Coca Cola Cup Quarter Final was settled by two poachers' strikes from Ian Wright but, in truth, the sensational midfield battle between Jensen and Keane overshadowed the evening's events.

The team's over reliance on Ian Wright was becoming more and more obvious. The chant booming around Highbury at that time was *'And it's Ian Wright FC'*. It was deadly serious too. George's successor was smart enough to realise that the team's dependency on him to score was a huge flaw, but such doubters were shouted down at Highbury in the early '90s. And no-one could really complain about the man himself, could they? Was it really his fault that Smith or Merson or Campbell didn't score enough goals? Or that the midfield ceased to chip in with strikes at all?

The guilty party in this situation was Graham and the board, who were unwilling to stump up the cash to pay for fresh new talent. Being honest, Wrighty's exploits were the main reason for turning up to some of the games in the later part of Graham's reign. Case in point; Forest at home in the FA Cup fifth round. Two stellar strikes from Wright shone like a beacon in our 2-0 win. The first was a blistering half volley which flashed into the net after young Ian Selley's excellent work in midfield. The second was a twisting, dribbling run finished off by a net-busting smash. His aura was irresistible. No wonder a journalist said at the time: 'When you watch Ian Wright play, you might just be watching the best football you'll see in your whole life'.

Finally, Arsenal's fighting spirit in the killing fields of the Cups was reflected in league performances. Up at Oldham's Arctic outpost, Linighan and Keown successfully kept the defence tight, before Andy stormed forward to head the winner. Jimmy Carter's performance against Southampton proved that Andy Warhol's comment 'everyone will be famous for fifteen minutes', wasn't total spaced out '60s bollocks. Perhaps it would be more accurate to think of this game as evidence that every dog (no matter how lame) has its day. Just as his namesake's finest hour came at the Camp David agreement in '78, Jimbo's moment arrived against the Saints on a blazing, surreal afternoon. There was, arguably, more incident packed into these ninety minutes than in the rest of the league campaign. Le Tissier's ball juggling and box of tricks gave the visitors the lead twice, before Jimbo, the white knight, rode to the rescue. Cracking in the equaliser to make it 3-3, he then scored a superb winner. Jinking inside the full back, he cut inside and with the outside of his left foot, curled in an excellent goal. 4-3 to the Arsenal, and Jimbo was the star. For once, anyway.

The Southampton win and the previous week's 2-0 victory at Coventry finally ushered away the relegation storm clouds. If you'd gone to either of these matches, you'd wonder why Arsenal were stuck in the bottom half of the league. Cool, calculating and incisive, the team cavorted freely in the spring sunshine. The main reason for the transformation was simple. Paul Davis - placed under house arrest for a year by George, was finally allowed some fresh air. Emerging from 'the most depressing period of my career - George had made his point', his elegant through ball set up Campbell's first goal at Highfield Road.

His performance was an aesthetic delight, bearing in mind that we were now heartily sick of JJ's leathery endeavour and offensive little moustache. Davis' reinstatement and subsequent key role in the Cup clashes proved one thing. George was willing to punish and dump the likes of Sansom and Nicholas against fans' wishes, knowing that they could be replaced. But Davis was different; he was brought back in from the cold. Graham knew that no-one else at the club, or any other player who cost less than £3m, could dictate the pace of a game like he could. Davis was a unique player, in that George tortured him for nigh on two years, but demurred from delivering the fatal blow.

Arsenal's relish for the Cup 'combat zone' was never better illustrated than at Selhurst Park for the Coca Cola Cup semi-final clash with Crystal Palace. The howling wind and sheeting rain blinded the Gunners' fans banked on the open away end - god knows what effect it had on the players. Ian Wright incurred the wrath of his ex-worshippers from start to finish. Noades and Coppell had murmured smugly all week about their 'secret weapon' - a destructive force which would bring about Arsenal's downfall. The weapon turned out to be Eddie McGoldrick who'd been given the task of stifling Ian Wright. 'Eddie's my jack of all trades' boasted Coppell to guffawing reporters just before the game.

Eddie made his mark after just five minutes. Wright surged free from his 'man marker' and McGoldrick chopped him down. Wrighty belted in the penalty. Ten minutes later, Wright's pace left Eddie for dead and Alan Smith grabbed our second. Smudger finally added another to his tally to give us a 3-1 first leg lead. Coppell later admitted that he'd got his tactics 'completely wrong'. We'd seen that McGoldrick was a joke figure - even at Palace; he was unable to perform competently in any position. The joke would be on us by August though. Wright and Linighan sent us to Wembley with their goals in our routine 2-0 win in the return leg at Highbury.

By the time Ipswich were clobbered 4-2 in a mad FA Cup Quarter Final, complete with own goals, penalties and ridiculous goal line scrambles, the club's Cup fortunes were boiling over in a frenzy of excitement. The victory at Portman Road guaranteed the prospect of another Wembley Semi-Final with Spurs. Tony Adams' performance at Ipswich, capped by a thudding header, was simply astonishing, bearing in mind that he was probably suffering from the mother of all headaches. Fully bevied up and ready to party ten days earlier, he'd crashed down a flight of concrete steps in a nightclub.

The head wound he sustained needed twenty five stitches to seal it up. The season's sternest tests were now upon us. Indeed, the phrase 'judgement day' hardly did the forthcoming semi-final clash justice, such was the hype surrounding the game. Arsenal's bruised and grizzled warriors were certainly up for the fight. Could they lay the ghost of '91?

April 4th 1993. The left hand side of Wembley Way was lined with smug Spurs fans chanting their obligatory mantra: *'We beat the scum 3-1'.* Deep down, the ditty still hurt but two years after that grim day, the taunt had taken on an almost mournful quality. It was a poignant remembrance chant for their long since departed stars - Lineker and Gascoigne. Sad Spurs fans had discovered that Gordon Durie and Steve Sedgely were hardly up-market replacements. Most amusing of all was that '93 was the Chinese year of the cockerel, which further fuelled Spurs' belief that victory would once again be theirs. I guess the wretched have to seek solace in oriental superstition.

The game was a brutal struggle, not helped for those of us in the Paddock area by stewards and cameramen standing in front of us and blocking our view. Most Gunners' fans in that area of Wembley were forced to stand on the sawn off plastic bucket seats, craning necks to see the crunching struggle on the pitch. The likes of Peter Storey would have loved it; adept as he was at kicking the crap out of anyone who ventured near the Arsenal box. Vendettas raged between fans and players. Dixon and Edinburgh scrapped like a couple of tetchy velociraptors and the barracking Tony Adams received from the Spurs fans made the roof shake.

Ian Selley probably had the best early chance of all. His flying volley was tipped away by Thorsvedt but Wright and Merson, who usually upped the tempo on such high octane occasions, were very quiet. Verbally abusing Neil Ruddock was fun - but that alone wasn't going to win us the match. The moment arrived in the 79th minute. Ray Parlour, who had been the only incisive midfielder of the game wriggled clear and was cut down. When Merson prepared to float the free kick into their area, Tony Adams trotted forward amidst a cacophony of boos and donkey braying. He met the free kick perfectly with his head to power it past Thorsvedt and roared away in celebration.

The ref's stopwatch kept ticking up to 96 minutes. Venables, who'd helpfully left out Nick Barmby from the starting line-up, sent him on in a vain attempt to salvage the match. The last ten minutes saw us put virtually the whole team behind the ball (which was down to ten men after Dixon hacked down Edinburgh). When the final whistle blew, most of us fell off our chairs in sheer relief that we'd got revenge. I didn't hear any Spurs taunts on the way to Wembley Park underground, more an ear piercing *'Two years, we only waited two years, we only waited two years, and now the Scum are in tears'.* It was payback day in every way. Not only had Tony Adams stuffed the donkey braying down Spurs' throats, we'd also destroyed the urban myth that they had some divine right to win FA Cup Semi Finals. Their position as a 'big club' also died that day. Never again have Spurs even threatened to win a major trophy. Local rivalry aside, the jubilant red and white army had seen Arsenal roar to Wembley for a double header with Sheffield Wednesday in the Coca Cola and FA Cup Finals.

The countdown to the Coca Cola Final seemed almost anticlimactic compared to the hype surrounding the Spurs match. The media, obviously unhappy that both finals would be contested by the same teams, harped on about Wednesday's unfashionable image and Arsenal's attritional approach. Conventional wisdom had it that the Yorkshire side was no match for the Gunners. This ignored the fact that Wednesday had finished above us in the league for the last two years. On paper, they were also a better balanced team than us, with John Sheridan directing the midfield and Chris Waddle in the best form of his life. Paul Warhurst had also made a spectacular transformation from defender to attacker. There was certainly no danger of Arsenal fans suffering from complacency. We remembered all too clearly some of the Wembley disasters we'd suffered over the last twenty years.

ITV decided that the Rugby World Sevens were a more worthy spectacle and delayed the kick-off to 5 p.m. on the Sunday, not exactly the optimum time for football. It didn't stop 40,000 supporters of both sides cramming Wembley. Many of those Arsenal fans had been locked out of Highbury all season - no wonder that the atmosphere at Wembley that day was the best of the season. It's ironic that the FA Cup Final, supposed to be the season's showpiece event, is a total nightmare for many fans who have to pay massively over the odds to spivs, or rely on corporate hospitality, to gain a golden ticket. The much-derided league cup, in its various guises, is rightly dubbed the 'fans' final'.

The rip-roaring atmosphere in the stands transformed itself to both sets of players who played some dazzling football. Wednesday began at breakneck speed. Warhurst smacked his shot against the post before John Harkes thumped them into the lead. Stunned, but not downhearted, Arsenal fought back. At last, Kevin Campbell showed his stirring form of old, turning sharply and hitting the post. Parlour and Davis ran and twisted around in midfield before Ray was clobbered just before half time. From the free kick Paul Merson struck a swirling volley which stunned Chris Woods and brought the roof down at our end. After four replays, Kevin Keegan still maintained that the shot must have been deflected. Reassuring to know that the future England boss recognised what true skill is, isn't it?

The second half was a never-ending Arsenal assault on their goal. Ian Wright, laughably written off in some quarters as 'a small man in big games' had a superb lob struck off for a non-existent push on Viv Anderson. Late on Steve Morrow, who'd kept Sheridan subdued all afternoon, ventured forward and thundered in the winner. We chanted *'there's only one Stevie Morrow'* at top volume for the rest of the game, pausing only to ask *'Are you watching Tottenham?'* at odd intervals. Stevie and the red and white hordes behind Woods' goal screamed their heads off in celebration when the final whistle went. It's good to know that he enjoyed his moment. He was about to discover that, in Vic Reeves' words, 'pleasure is always followed by pain'.

In a turbulent season crammed with uncertainty, it was fitting that the images after the final whistle lived longer in the mind than the memory of Stevie's winner. Man of the match Paul Merson indulged in his 'let's all do the Merse' routine, simulating the knocking back of beers in front of jubilant Arsenal fans. It summed up how we all felt at the time, but we'd soon discover that the gesture had a more sinister undercurrent. And of course, there was the sight of Morrow himself, lying in agony on the turf with a broken arm after being dropped by Tony Adams. Bitter Spurs fans boasted that he'd suffered the injury after 'falling off a donkey'. Since when have donkeys gone around lifting silver cups? Whatever strange forces were at work that day, they couldn't disguise the fact that Arsenal were already half way towards an unprecedented cup double.

Sandwiching the two finals was the tail-end of our league campaign. George's decision to employ the squad rotation system meant there were few highlights. Paul Merson's majestic free kick at Portman Road beat Ipswich and Paul Dickov's debut goal began the 3-0 rout of Crystal Palace. David O'Leary's farewell match gave us the chance to pay homage to two departing institutions. Our record appearance holder had been given a free transfer to Leeds and Highbury was full to see the Gunners take on Champions Manchester United in a 'friendly'. In the final piece of goodwill ever demonstrated between the two sides, Bruce and Pallister parted to allow Dave to score at the Clock End. For many fans it was the last time that they celebrated a goal on a terrace. 'It's been a privilege to play for you all', O'Leary told us after the game. There was barely a dry eye left inside the ground at the end. Truly the end of an era.

For all the ceremonials surrounding O'Leary's imminent departure, Arsenal's performances in some of those end of season encounters said much about the state of Graham's realm, circa 1993. The players remained tight lipped at the time, but in years to come many of them admitted their growing unease with his tactics. Limpar, Smith, Davis and Adams have since commented that they felt staleness creeping in and that playing for Arsenal simply wasn't as enjoyable as it used to be. For black humour lovers in the crowd though, those end of season games provided an oasis of jokes for years to come.

With his bubble perm and fluffy moustache, there had been allegations flying around that John Jensen was actually a Scouser sent to destroy us from the inside. At Goodison Park JJ proved he was innocent of these accusations by pole-axing a member of the Merseyside constabulary and almost decapitating an Everton ball-girl with his wayward shooting. Martin Keown quickly became known as George's odd job man - playing, as he did, in six different positions between April and May. It was poor Andy Linighan who was made to look the biggest chump of all, though. Brought on as a sub against Villa to replace Wrighty in the 60th minute, he spent the last half hour of the match tiptoeing around, trying to kid us that he knew what he was doing. At least it gave him the chance to practice his heading routine at corners. When Pal Lydersen, Neil Heaney, Mark Flatts and Jimmy Carter appeared in the same team in the home defeat against Spurs, one can understand why even George admitted 'I'm glad I didn't pay to watch'. Lydersen, thankfully, was about to disappear back to Norway, taking his white towelling socks and flared jeans with him. Paying £500,000 for him did not exactly represent the best piece of business ever done at Highbury. Still, it seems that George had other reasons for signing him, doesn't it?

Although the euphoria of the '89 and '91 title triumphs was disappearing rapidly, Arsenal needed no psyching up for the FA Cup Final. Morrow, Jensen, Linighan and Hillier and the like proved themselves to be supreme battlers along the Wembley trail. Somehow, you just knew that blood 'n' guts would be telling qualities in the FA Cup Final. Arsenal fans blocked out the horrors of the league campaign and got behind the team. The Supporters Club ensured that the Gunners' end would be a sea of red and white on the day, and the red and white army marched on Wembley yet again to try and complete the cup double.

Not even the magnificent sights and sounds emanating from the cauldron of 20,000 Gooners, complete with balloons and cards could detract from the fact that the final lacked real energy. It was a tit-for-tat encounter, with both defences holding firm and David Hirst and Wright the best players on the pitch. It was no surprise when Wrighty scored to give us the lead, or that Hirst grabbed a late equaliser for Wednesday. A draw was a fair result, although Andy Linighan should have won it for us with his golden chance to head past Woods. No matter, Andy was simply saving himself for the replay.

On Thursday May 20th, with most Premiership footballers busy sunning themselves in the Med or the Caribbean, Arsenal and Sheffield Wednesday did battle one last time. Bryon Butler would later describe the game as 'muscular chess' - certainly the two sides had virtually reached a stalemate on the pitch.

Johnny Franks attended the Wembley replay. He describes Arsenal's 59th game of the season and its monumental climax: 'It was like the game and the season was never going to end. We got to Wembley really early and had a few drinks in a pub only to find that the kick off had been delayed 'til 8.30. It became clear that no-one was gonna get much shut-eye that night. It was a drizzly, warm evening and when we eventually got inside, there was steam coming off the pitch. It was kind of mystical, if you know what I mean!!

Arsenal fans seemed much more 'up' for this game than they'd been on Saturday and when the boys warmed up, Ian Wright came over and waved his arms around as if to say 'sing up you lot'. We bloody well did and virtually lifted the roof off with our songs. The first half was knackering. You could tell that both sides were running on an empty tank. All except for Ian Wright. The vision of him chipping the ball over Chris Woods to give us the lead - I still remember it today, as he ran off screaming to the heavens with steam drifting around him.

Wednesday were filthy bastards that night. Mark Bright splattered Linighan's nose all over his face and Waddle was even more despicable; diving to try and get Winterburn sent off. We all reckoned that, after Waddle equalised, it would go to penalties. We'd just seen the worst examples of finishing in a game from Bright and Merson, hadn't we? It didn't seem *possible* that anyone else could score. Those players were shagged.

The ref had the whistle in his mouth when Merson swung over the corner. Time went into slow motion and Andy Linighan's head connected with the ball. When it went in, no-one could believe it - we all pogoed around for about five minutes!! It's the most intense feeling I've ever had at a game. People around me were making noises I didn't think humans could make! For some reason, I thought it right that he should get the winner. He'd been booed by most of us when he first arrived. His nose was bent to the side - he looked terrible!! But there he was, soaring to win us the Cup double. He was the unlikeliest of heroes in a strange season. It was also brilliant that David O'Leary came on as sub in his last Arsenal game, wasn't it? No-one deserved a winner's medal more. I remember thinking that it had been a weird season. It was almost as if the boys thought 'well Highbury is just a building site this year so lets really go for it in the Cups'. And they did, didn't they??

John Franks, Arsenal fan from Holloway

Fans hung around late into the night to savour the atmosphere of a first FA Cup win since '79, when Alan Sunderland had also performed last minute heroics. Behind the joy of being the first team to achieve a cup double, it was impossible not to notice how much George's Arsenal had changed since his first triumph at Wembley in '87. The team was: Seaman, Dixon, Winterburn, Linighan, Adams, Campbell, Wright, Smith, Merson, Davis, Jensen (Sub O'Leary). Only Paul Davis and Tony Adams had survived from that Liverpool final, with O'Leary about to disappear into the sunset.

It was the post match chant of *'No-one likes us, we don't care'* from sections of fans which was most revealing of all. Here was proof that we'd mutated into a rich and successful version of Millwall. How different it had been six years earlier after Charlie's goals beat the Scousers at Wembley; that victory in the blazing sun seemed to belong to a dreamy, bygone era. This double Cup victory ushered in a harsher and more brutal era in the Gunners' history. It was strangely befitting that both Morrow and Linighan should end up with broken bones in their glory games - it had been an attritional season after all. George's team had delivered again though, and he said prophetically after the game: 'There's only Europe left for us to conquer now'.

Andy Linighan celebrates his last minute FA Cup Final winner with Ian Wright

Steve Morrow scored the winning goal in the 1993 Coca-Cola Cup Final

4

One Nil To The Arsenal

With two cups glittering in the Highbury trophy cabinet, George retreated into his bunker over the Summer to ponder Arsenal's Cup Winners Cup offensive. He later admitted in *The Glory and The Grief* that he felt like a 'field marshal' during the '93/94 season. The war analogy soon proved to be apt. We'd not got the respect we deserved for the double cup win, a slight which George later admitted he found hurtful, but at least the boys had a chance to prove themselves against continental opposition and rectify the Benfica '92 nightmare. The sneerers looked at the developing Champions League and scoffed at Arsenal taking part in what was considered the weakest of the three European competitions. This year was different though - Ajax, Athletico Madrid and heavyweights from Italy and France blocked our path. We'd soon put some aristocratic noses out of joint.

As well as dreaming of more trophy winning, George spent the close season thinking hard about Arsenal's image. He let slip that he'd consulted a P.R. firm in an attempt to rectify his dour public image. It wasn't a surprise - politicians and football clubs were becoming ridiculously media conscious. Bill Clinton delayed take off in his private jet while he spent $200 on a haircut and Tony Blair would soon plug his 'friendship' with Alex Ferguson to show just how 'right on' he was. In the mid '90s, perhaps we were lucky that Kate Hoey, who actually attends Arsenal games, was the only politician who professes love for the Gunners. Better than having the likes of David Mellor crawling all over you, isn't it?

The advice George received from the P.R. firm couldn't have been too good. Apart from a rather sickly interview with 'lifelong Gooner' Melvyn Bragg, he now came across as even more stubborn, slagging off 'prima donnas' and repeating the fact that he mistrusted star players. Most tellingly, he told Joe Lovejoy that Eric Cantona 'would always let you down at the highest level'. With a manager sending out these signals, were we ever going to sign the star midfielder which George supposedly craved?

Rumour had it that Graham introduced a swear box to the London Colney training ground in the Summer of 1993. After a couple of hours, it was apparently overflowing with 50p pieces, which were soon dispatched to North London's grateful charities. No doubt Ian Wright, who'd long been afflicted with pseudo-Tourette's syndrome contributed most of all, and maybe Anders Limpar, who also has a sound knowledge of English expletives, directed a few in George's direction. Mind you, the boss' transfer activity caused us fans to launch a torrent of colourful language, too.

The country's hottest midfield property, Roy Keane, chose to sign for Manchester United ahead of us. It was hardly a surprise. According to the press, Keane's wage demands were double the going rate Arsenal were prepared to pay. *90 Minutes* also leaked the news that we'd turned down Andrei Kanchelskis a couple of years before. The sight of him weaving through defences like an exocet missile over the next few years for United was even more galling after that particular revelation. We needed the complete goal-scoring, creative midfielder. Instead, George signed Eddie McGoldrick for £1m, a cut price utility man from Crystal Palace. Nicknamed Eddie the Eagle, the parallels with his hapless ski-jumping namesake didn't stop there...

By now, the club's tightness on the purse strings, and George's insistence that he was searching for a creative midfielder was starting to annoy. Considering the money we'd raked in from two cup runs and the £1,500 some fans had lashed out on a bond, we'd every right to question the club's transfer policy. Admittedly, the board had to meet the cost of turning Highbury all seater, but they'd categorically stated two years earlier that it would 'not hinder George's attempts to purchase new players'.

We realised that Arsenal circa '93 didn't have the flair of the '91 team and was unlikely to win the Premiership. Cup kings we may have been, but for many of us this was no longer enough. In *The Gooner*, Mike Francis tersely pointed out that George's successes were the best return we'd had for sixty years. He was right, but with hindsight, the Scot was now becoming a victim of his own success.

Gunners' fans expected the team to challenge for the league and the cups and, crucially, we now wanted flair as well. It was a message which George, seemingly, never comprehended. Tony Francis wrote in *The Sunday Times* that Graham's Arsenal should have been copying Manchester United and Norwich in style, to justify their crown as the South's premier club. He wrote 'he (Graham) says he wants expressive football - it's time for him to put his money where his mouth is'. How refreshing that a journalist should be able to encapsulate fans' feelings in a newspaper. It's a pity G.G. didn't read it - maybe he was strictly a *Guardian* man. Little did we know that this season would be Graham's last crusade. With trusted lieutenants like Adams, Winterburn and Wright by his side, his team would deliver one last time amidst scenes of chaotic joy.

The hi-tech, all singing, all food dispensing North Bank Stand was unveiled for the opening game of the season, against Coventry. It wasn't quite finished and with the Clock End a mass of concrete slabs and cement, Highbury remained more of a construction site than a football stadium. Still - the all seater era was here and even some sceptics were won over. One fan sought out David Dein and admitted: 'If I have to sit, then this stand is the business. It's the dog's bollocks.' Those who didn't keel over from vertigo after clambering all the way up to the new Upper Tier would have had a bird's eye view of the lard-arsed Mick Quinn belting an unbelievable hat-trick past Seaman in Coventry's 3-0 win.

The line-up against the Sky Blues was: Seaman, Dixon, Winterburn, Davis, Linighan, Adams, Jensen, Wright, Campbell, Merson, Limpar. The worrying point was that this team was most fans' favoured line-up. Ex-Gunner Stewart Robson shackled Davis and Jensen in his last ever competitive game and the strikers didn't have a shot on target all afternoon. All those present agreed that Anders Limpar's excellent display was some consolation but, inevitably, he was axed after this calamity. Perhaps we should have now nicknamed him the 'can-carrier' rather that the 'Super Swede'. Paul Merson was dropped as well but somehow you knew that he'd be back soon. Fans were delighted when Limpar's proposed move to Monaco fell through but George's executioner's axe hurtled ever close to his neck. There was no time for sulking after the opening day debacle though - not when a North London derby approached.

The early season encounter at The Lane was the most one sided match you'll ever see. Tony Adams' struck off effort was so far over the line it was virtually in the back of the stand before Calderwood knocked it away. Merson's replacement, Ray Parlour tormented Calderwood all evening. Eddie McGoldrick also had a decent full debut, darting down Spurs' left flank and Paul Davis' raking passing stretched them all evening. For all our efforts, it looked like we'd drawn a blank. With five minutes left, we forced a corner and Andy Linighan rose to head the ball goalwards. In our poxy Paxton Road seats, we saw that the ball was flying wide, until Wrighty leapt to flick the ball into the top corner of the net. Such glorious moments demand riotous celebrating and he didn't disappoint. Already touted as a future media star, he executed his high speed 'boggle' and ran the full length of the pitch to scream '1-0' at us. Choke back the vomit, Spurs fans.

Our main man and most explosive personality had just released his first single; *Do the Wright Thing*. It was a sure sign that he was on the road to becoming a showbiz celeb. In a dance number, produced with Pet Shop Boys' Chris Lowe, Wrighty announced to a bemused world: 'If you've nothing good to say, just keep the peace'. It was around this time that Tony Willis questioned the 'Wright effect' in *One Nil Down*, and its impact on the rest of the team. In *Addicted*, Tony Adams admitted that some players were getting 'lazy' and relied on Wright to poach the goals. Kevin Campbell's goal supply had dried up and he seemed to have developed an inferiority complex. Far removed from the bullish powerhouse he'd been in '91 alongside the more selfless Smudger, Kev frequently looked hesitant and unsure.

A classic case of this came at Hillsborough in the third game of the season, where even our players seemed amused by the fact that Wednesday's new boy, Andy Sinton, had chosen to sign for the Owls ahead of us; a decision as misjudged as Napoleon's opting to invade Russia during the skiing season. Campbell's excellent approach play set up Wrighty for our winner but in the goal celebrations, Kev pointed admiringly at Wright, as if to say 'he's the main man'. Rioch and Wenger quickly surmised that in some ways Wright's overwhelming presence came at the expense of a successful team. Not that it was wise to bandy such an opinion around Highbury in George's day. Brave souls like Willis who voiced their doubts about Wright being at the centre of our universe, were treated with the same kind of contempt that early heliocentrics were given. And to be fair to the man himself, he couldn't be criticised for the quality of his displays.

His genius was there for all to see against Everton on a boiling August afternoon. The double he knocked past Southall in our 2-0 win had to be seen to be believed; the first was cracked in with utmost savagery, the second was a juggling, dazzling delight. Wright twisted Matt Jackson inside out with his mid air gymnastics before leaving Southall stranded with a delicate chip. His celebration again stole the limelight. Gold tooth glinting in *The Sun*, he crossed the divide between fans and players to lean over the advertisement hoardings and shake hands with us. Kevin Campbell's confidence also received a boost. His thunderous half volley away at Blackburn grabbed us a deserved point and his clinically taken hat trick at home to Ipswich gave us a 4-0 win. The Campbell of old had briefly returned; powerful headers, strong running and ruthless opportunism. George proclaimed him man of the match, doubtless hoping to restore the self esteem to our 'confidence player'.

We'd rocketed to second place, only trailing Manchester United on goal difference. By the time Leeds had been seen off, even with Strachan running us ragged for an hour, Arsenal had won five on the trot. Paul Merson had played well in that game, poking in our second, but he still looked bloated. Merse pleaded with George to play him up front with Wright rather than wide on the left, but the boss simply commented that he needed to be more 'consistent'. Judging by the amount of booze he admitted to drinking at that time in *Rock Bottom*, it's a wonder Merson got onto the pitch at all.

United easily saw us off at Old Trafford in the clash between the division's top two. Cantona's explosive free kick settled it but, frankly, the Champions murdered us. Ince and Keane must have been delighted at the prospect of facing our midfield of JJ and David Hillier. It was hardly a prospect to worry the two Manc rottweilers was it? Paul Davis was rested and the game was really all about damage limitation. That result knocked the stuffing out of our league campaign.

The Gunners suffered a dire October, drawing four consecutive blanks against the likes of Oldham and Norwich. These disasters were not helped by the fact that George rested some players for Europe. Of course we were furious - how dare he give up the ghost so early in the Premiership campaign? After a month, he let slip that he considered a routine home league game to be 'less important' than the Cup Winners game with Odense. His obsession for European success was admirable, but what about us poor sods who were forking out £15 per game for a seat at Highbury? George's tactlessness suggested that he needed less a p.r. firm, more a decent spin doctor. Maybe New Labour's rising bright young thing could have given him a couple of contacts. A clump of fans unfurled a cryptic banner at home to Norwich in an appalling goalless draw: 'Give the suckers their money back'. Was this an unsubtle reference to the Bond (Peter Hillwood's *faux pas* led him to call Bond holders 'suckers'. I think that's what they call Old Etonian humour), or the poor fayre on show?

The calls for Anders' return reached a crescendo in the game at home to Manchester City. Even the East Stand boomed out the chant of *'We want Anders'*. George turned around and gave them an admonishing shake of the head. The clouds hanging over our league campaign dispersed only occasionally in that difficult Autumn; Merse's spectacular overhead kick beat Southampton and, best of all, fit again Alan Smith and ruthless Ian

Wright combined to beat newly promoted Newcastle 2-1. Andy Cole had mouthed off in the press before the game about what he'd do to his old club. Such a boast is never a wise move when coming to Highbury.

Given the whole of the now all-seated Clock End, Newcastle's fans helped prove that all seater stadia can occasionally produce an electric atmosphere. Cunning old tricks did for the Geordies and their fanatical travelling support. Steve Bould shoved Paul Bracewell in the back twice at corners, to flick on headers which Smith and Wright latched onto. Limpar was reintroduced at home to Aston Villa. His dodging down the left flank opened up a couple of chances for Wrighty, one of which he put away. We still lost 1-2, with the Brummies striking twice in the last two minutes. Anders proved his point - yet again, and the newspapers described his contributions as 'superb'. But he would feature just five more times in an Arsenal shirt and not once in Europe. It was lucky for George, then, that the team excelled themselves in the Cup Winners Cup.

It's hard to overestimate the disappointment George felt after the Benfica defeat in '91. The second leg at Highbury was a match of furious intensity - 'gung ho' football as Alan Smith later described it. George came to realise, after the Portuguese side's victory, that patience, tight defence and phenomenal resilience were the keys to European success; qualities this side had in abundance. The Cup Winners Cup draw pitted us against Odense in the first round of the Cup Winner's Cup. Those fans who travelled to Denmark were impressed with the Gunners' comeback, after Lee Dixon scored an early own goal. Luckily Paul Merson was on top form. He charged through to give us the winner after Wright had equalised. The second leg was turgid - although it gave Kevin Campbell a chance to shine and he scored our goal in a 1-1 draw. We were through, but George wasn't impressed. He forced the entire squad to sit through a video of the match, saying to them: 'If I have to sit through it, so should you'. A guy in the Highbury Barn, charming bloke that he was, told me he reckoned that it must have been the equivalent of being forced to eat one's own diarrhoea.

The Odense struggle meant that the glamour puss managers of more stylish rivals labelled us 'cloggers' and 'journeymen'. Arie Haan, manager of next opponents Standard Liege, predicted that the Belgian's svelte playmakers would destroy Arsenal. Haan, a star of Holland's '70s total football team remarked that Jensen and Hillier were certainly no Rep and Cruyff. So Haan was adept at stating the bleedin' obvious, but he proved to be a lousy tipster.

Hammered 3-0 at Highbury in the first leg, he had nothing to say about

Liege's performance at the post match press conference. Ian Wright's form was scorching. His stealthy header, crafty chip and non-stop running destroyed them. Paul Merson's masterful curling free kick was a fitting moment in an electrifying display. Three thousand Gooners made the trip to the away leg, a match for which Wrighty was rested. Dave Noble clearly recalls a memorable visit to Belgium: 'I've travelled all over Europe with Arsenal. I've seen them play in Rome, Amsterdam, Turin - even Moscow. The combination of sight-seeing, boozing and watching the boys play abroad is something I've always enjoyed. When I found out we were playing in Liege, I bought a tourist guide to the place. It talked about 'quaint old restaurants' and 'cobbled streets', which sounded pretty good.

When we got to Liege, I swear that most of us thought we'd ended up in Chernobyl. The place was a dump. All you could see for miles was coal and steel plants pumping out industrial fumes and, worryingly, there was a sort of hanging yellow mist which mixed with the fog rolling in from the North Sea. It was spooky - I'm half expecting to get some horrible lung disease in later life - all because of that day in Belgium!!

Inside the stadium, they had an 'oompah band' going, really loudly. I remember Alan Smith volleying in a goal after about a minute, and that basically killed the tie and shut the home crowd up. After that Arsenal destroyed them. Kevin Campbell got a couple, so did Paul Merson and Selley and Adams scored too. It was 6-0 to us after about eighty five minutes. It was unbelievable - but we still weren't finished. I thought our best player in the match was Eddie McGoldrick. Basically he was a disastrous signing but with about five minutes to go he burst forward after Merson put him through. Eddie scored a brilliant goal from thirty yards which hit the bar as it went in. We'd won 7-0 and Eddie was man of the match. I remember calling him a useless tosser the week after, mind.

On the way home in the coach, we found out that Man U had lost to Galatasaray in the European Cup and we were all singing *Always look on the Turk side of life*. It was an unbelievable night. But I won't be going back to Liege. I got home in the early hours and, after I'd had a kip, I blew my nose. The handkerchief was covered in jet black filth. God knows what I'd inhaled - maybe I should have taken the sample to a lab to be checked out!

Dave Noble - Arsenal fan from Canvey Island

Winning ten-nil on aggregate, we had cruised into the Quarter Finals to face Torino. Arie Haan, by the way, was immediately sacked by Liege; write off the Arsenal at your peril.

Having stormed through the opening European rounds, it gave the lads a chance to put right iffy domestic form. A 3-0 win at Carrow Road against the ultra smooth Norwich City also meant that we'd progressed into the Coca Cola Cup fifth round. Wright's breathtaking impudence in chipping Gunn from the edge of the area captured the headlines, and it meant we'd cruised past another technically superior passing team. Bolstered by the return from injury of Steve Bould and Tony Adams, the defence rediscovered its meanness. Adams was also about to rediscover the knack of hitting the back of the net for Arsenal. He'd recently gained notoriety, though, for taking the T.V. advert's advice to 'hit the hut' rather too literally. He and Ray Parlour, archetypal Essex boys that they were, had wreaked havoc in their local Pizza Hut in Hornchurch. Apparently bored with waiting for their garlic bread starters, they'd sprayed other diners with a fire extinguisher. As Graham Taylor said at the time - Gazza wasn't the only Englishman whose 'refuelling' technique between matches was suspect.

Kevin Campbell, once he'd shrugged off the flu-bug which hampered the team's progress, also returned in December and, for one last time, hit an excellent run of form up front. Smith and Wright combined to see off Chelsea's bunch of toilers and Sheffield Wednesday were beaten by an injury time Wright strike. The goals flowed over Christmas. Swindon were blown away on Boxing Day. Campbell's powerful running and sharp shooting shredded their amateurish offside tactics. Their manager, John Gorman, admitted in a press conference that he couldn't work out what his team was doing. But even after Kev's hat trick, he was upstaged by Wrighty. The gold toothed one's glorious chip from 35 yards followed a lovely parabola and crowned our 4-0 win. Two days later, Sheffield United were hammered 3-0. Kev poached a highly impressive double and Wright, inevitably, provided the denouement with his curling effort from outside the box. By the time Wimbledon had been sent off with an identical scoreline three days later, we'd scored ten goals in three days, hadn't conceded any, and were up to third in the league. Dixon, Winterburn, Adams and Bould were in awesome form and Campbell seemed to have rediscovered his confidence. On *Football Focus*, Jimmy Hill claimed that the Gunners would launch a New Year title challenge and he even began a 'Campbell for England' plea. Alas, the chinned one had spoken too soon.

Five winless games later, which included more draws against the likes of Oldham, and Arsenal's title challenge was well and truly dead. The midfield, with only Ray Parlour fully fit, spluttered dreadfully, but it was poor Kev who was firmly reinstalled as the crowd's boo-boy. His sudden plummet in form was baffling, though George had started to shift him out wide on the right again. Kev perfected the art of cocking up when clean through on goal, on a truly horrific FA Cup night at Highbury against Bolton in late January. We seemed to have done the hard part by drawing 2-2 up at Burnden Park but were roasted alive in the replay. Alan Smith scored an early goal, but somehow it was never going to be enough. Lee and McAteer ran the legs off our defenders all night and Dixon's and Winterburn's slips gifted them two easy goals. Bolton's boss of the time, Bruch Rioch, later told me : 'I'd never seen an Arsenal team look like that before. Squabbling between themselves and looking unfit; to be honest we tore them apart.'

As we tried to peg them back in normal time, Kev missed two gilt-edged chances. When the game went into extra time, the players had to endure seeing the highlights replayed on the big screen. Kev must have felt like he was on *Big Brother* and his shoulders visibly slumped when his horror moments were re-shown. Maybe he should have considered sending the tape to Beadle - at least he could have made a few quid out of it. Booed off at the end after Bolton won 3-1, Arsenal had now meekly surrendered their grip on both cups. Aston Villa had already beaten us in the Coca Cola Cup, after which even *Gunflash* castigated the players' efforts. These tame defeats said as much about the state of Graham's realm as any of the season's foreign conquests did. It was to be the Cup Winners cup or bust.

With the possible exception of Ian Wright roaring towards goal, Anders Limpar flying down the wing in an Arsenal shirt was the most thrilling sight at Highbury in the early '90s. By March '94, it was obvious that the relationship between him and George Graham had gone beyond the marriage guidance stage. We all knew it was just a matter of time before the final divorce settlement came through, but while Anders still wore the red and white shirt, there was always a lingering hope.

He appeared in Arsenal colours for the last time in two away games in early Spring. The team had hit another trough in form in the league and George brought back the super Swede after a three month absence. We took Ipswich apart 5-1 at Portman Road; Limpar's dashing runs directly set up two goals and his non stop effort made him man of the match, despite Wright's hat trick. For those of us privileged to be there, Limpar's last Arsenal game down at The Dell will live long in the memory. The proximity of the stands to the pitch at Southampton meant that every F-word and jarring tackle was audible. Being so close reveals just how fast top flight football really is, and, on that boiling Saturday afternoon, how turbo-charged Limpar was.

The game itself was memorable for Wright's epic hat trick. But Limpar's assists were just as stunning. For Wrighty's second goal, Anders turned Monkou the wrong way and, with telepathic anticipation, flicked the ball over his head towards Wright. He smashed in a volley with such venom that it threatened to tear through Beasant's net. Wright's hat trick came after Limpar's dash from his own half into the Saints' penalty area. Ken Monkou chopped Anders down once he'd threatened to blur into the distance. Wright tucked away the penalty - but those present realised who the architect of the victory was. Limpar never played for Arsenal again. Instead, he signed for Everton for £2m later that week and was immediately pitched into their grim relegation fight. He surely deserved better.

In his book, Graham paints a portrait of Limpar which is rather disturbing; a ball juggling wing wizard who began as 'my new match winner', who slowly lost the plot and the confidence of his team mates through an increasing lack of effort both on and off the pitch. In Amy Lawrence's book *Proud To Say That Name*, George does a hatchet job on Limpar again. He is portrayed as someone who lacked real confidence in his own ability and enjoyed the 'high-life- rather too much. In short, he was a figure who would have been more suited to playing for Arsenal ten years earlier - a Charlie Nicholas or Tony Woodcock type member of the 'song and dance brigade'.

After talking to several of his ex-team mates there are some grains of accuracy in Graham's version of events. But in truth, Limpar was a victim, the kind of player who was becoming *persona non grata* at Highbury in '94. Alan Smith commented that George was still adept at 'getting the best out of mediocre players'. He was not, however, able to get the best out of Arsenal's two greatest talents of the mid '90s - Merson and Limpar. Add that to his cold shouldering of Paul Davis and one could present a fairly watertight case that the real reason why Arsenal was floundering at times was down to George himself.

As I said in an earlier chapter, Limpar's insistence that he play for Sweden clearly rankled with Graham. By '93/94, George virtually declared open warfare on him, saying to Joe Lovejoy that 'Limpar doesn't work hard enough'. So Anders began to cut an increasingly lonely and unhappy figure. His appearances were rare but still often spectacular and memorable. One wonders how he would have fared under Arsène Wenger. Wenger would have surely dealt with him in a more supportive manner; encouraging him rather than castigating him in public and accepting that playing for Sweden would expand the player's horizons. Sadly, we'll never know. By 2000, Anders was winding down his career with Colorado Rapids in the North American Soccer league.

He talked to me for the first time about his final days at Highbury : 'By the time '93/94 arrived, I was fed up with the whole fucking situation. I decided to write a letter to Graham to ask if we could sit down and sort it out. I sent it and waited a couple of days and then he came to me, with the letter. He said : 'Anders, you don't need to send me a letter, you know you can come and talk to me at any time'. But everytime I did try to catch him after training he'd say 'oh I'm in a rush - I've got to go' or 'come and see me tomorrow'. And, as we know, tomorrow never comes. It was ridiculous, he treated me like a kid - he just wouldn't communicate properly with me at all.

In my final season, I started just nine games. Those guys who replaced me - Carter and McGoldrick - they were runners. They had good engines and all that to get up the wing, but that's all they were, runners not wingers. In my last two appearances for Arsenal we scored nine goals in two away games. I'm not being arrogant but I was excellent against Ipswich and Southampton. I thought I set up Ian Wright really well. The Arsenal fans sang my name during those games all the time and I think Graham hated that.

I went to him because in those two games, I really felt as if my form was coming back. I told him that I wanted to stay but I said to him 'It's up to you if you want me to stay'. He said 'No Anders, it's up to you.' The conversation went nowhere.

In the end, he told me that he'd got an offer from Everton which was too good to refuse. Then he walked out of his office and left me there with my agent. My agent couldn't believe how rude he'd been. Graham didn't say goodbye, shake my hand, or thank me. Nothing. That was it. The end of my Arsenal career. I've never been so heartbroken in my life. I just sat there thinking about how much I wanted to stay and all my great Arsenal memories. But it was finished.

Anders Limpar, speaking in 2000

When Limpar was allowed to drift away from Highbury, it revealed just how flawed and outmoded Graham's regime was becoming. We accepted Charlie Nicholas' departure because Paul Merson replaced him, Stewart Robson's because Steve Williams took his place and Lukic's sale because David Seaman was signed. But when Limpar was repeatedly dropped during his final season and finally left, he was replaced by Eddie McGoldrick. With the best will in the world, 'The Eagle' was unlikely to lob Scouse goalies from 45 yards or reduce defences to quivering jellies, was he? The tragic tale of Anders Limpar demonstrated that George was rapidly losing the plot.

We'd waited about four months to resume progress on the European trail. It gave our glamorous European counterparts time to enjoy their Christmas and New year break, and Arsenal the opportunity to get knackered on muddy pitches and dumped out of both domestic Cup competitions. Such is the joyful lot of English football. In the Quarter Final draw, Arsenal avoided the really big guns and drew Torino. Serie A clubs are hyped as being glamorous but, in truth, Torino were in a horrendous internal mess. Allegations of Mafia connections, bribery of referees, crippling debts and an unexpected relegation fight meant that when they ran onto the pitch in the Stadio Della Alpi, their fans had long deserted them. Only 34,000 turned up in a stadium which could hold treble that number. This certainly helped our cause as 5,000 travelling fans could actually make themselves heard, a novel experience in Latin footie grounds. They did manage to give us the traditional Italian welcome; the normal profusion of red and purple flares, burning Arsenal banners, whole swathes of fans jumping up and down... all offences which would probably result in a hanging in England.

Arsenal's line-up for the game was: Seaman, Dixon, Adams, Bould, Winterburn, Campbell, Jensen, Hillier, Adams, Merson, Smith. The press claimed it was a 4-5-1 formation but in truth it was a 9-0-1 line-up. The Gunners literally strangled the life out of Torino. Ian Wright was injured anyway and, apart from Tony Adams' header, they were barely troubled. David Hillier, in perhaps his best ever Arsenal game, clung to Venturin, their playmaker, like a limpet. This meant that Enzo Francescoli and a teenage Benito Carbone hardly saw the ball. The crowd howled at Arsenal's tactics and when the game ended 0-0, they set fire to their own flags and the Italian riot police closed in.

Torino indulged in their own blanket defending at Highbury two weeks later. With two defenders chained to Wrighty all night, the game seemed to be headed towards extra time. Only Paul Davis was likely to split open their defence and even he probably thought twice about pushing forward after the mother of all bollockings he'd received after the Liege game. When his floated free kick sailed over towards the penalty area, Tony Adams stooped to head the winner. We knew that a heavyweight semi-final clash was unavoidable even though Real Madrid and Ajax had tumbled by the wayside that evening. Two more fancied foes were out of the way, but svelte French giants Paris St Germain lay in wait in the semis.

Away trips to West European capitals are invariably joyous affairs for travelling footie fans. When you consider that we were drawn away in Paris with all its delights, you can understand why the away ticket allocation was immediately sold out. The huge swathes of red and white shirts on the ferries to Calais suggested that a few thousand also gambled on the chance of getting hold of tickets off touts. Fanzines from the time, and pub stories circa '94, vouched for the fact that Gooners took full advantage of the booze, superb grub, luscious Parisian women and other aesthetic pleasures on offer in the chique capital of Europe. Classy and stylish also were the dangers lurking within their side. They had a clean cut David Ginola, their anchor man Valdo and, of course, the sublimely talented George Weah. The rest of the team also had that innate French ability to caress the ball before rolling it away to a team mate.

Inside the Parc des Princes bear pit, the 46,000 strong Parisian mob screamed *'allez les bleus'*, and greeted the Arsenal players with as much affection as they had the aristocracy in the eighteenth century. With the *Marseillaise* ringing out, George stuck Steve Morrow on Valdo to snuff out his threat, and Bouldy man-marked George Weah. St Germain, adhering to their stereotype of highly strung histrionics, simply lost their cool. Valdo tried and failed to kick JJ, and Wrighty's marker punched him repeatedly in the back to put him off his game. Wright stole in to give us a priceless lead after just fifteen minutes and Jensen's blistering drive almost decapitated Lama. Ginola's late equaliser inevitably sent the Parisians ballistic but Arsenal's counter insurgency movement certainly made its point.

Two weeks later, and St Germain were greeted by a Highbury packed to the rafters, swaying and shouting to the tune of *'Georgie Graham and his red and white army'*. It may not have had *le gloire* of the Marseillaise, but it got Highbury rocking anyway. Arsenal's 'roughing up' of St Germain was more reminiscent of a mid '70s clash with Leeds than a European semi-final. Dixon and Ginola exchanged greetings as usual and this time, JJ was assigned to 'soften up' Valdo (in the Pesciesque sense of the word). Where else but Highbury could a silky Brazilian have been outplayed by a moustachioed Danish clogger? Arsenal's goal arrived quickly. Lee Dixon swung in a cross from which Campbell's flicked header clattered the post and flew in. The rest of the game saw Rai and Ginola maraud forward at every possible opportunity.

Tony Adams' monumental presence held them at bay but Ginola's open goal miss showed that the game was still on a knife edge, particularly bearing in mind that we had about seven players precariously balanced on a yellow card. It was Wrighty who went over the line - his 'striker's tackle' leading to his booking and suspension from the final. When the final whistle blew, Highbury exploded; against all the odds the team was through to its first European final for fourteen years. The real hero of the night was Kevin Campbell, but even then he was upstaged by Wright's emotional outburst. Some things never changed.

Inevitably, the rest of the league campaign was a feverish wait for the final in Copenhagen. League form, understandably, was patchy but there were some major highlights too. Ian Wright's diving header beat over-rated Cup finalists Chelsea and Paul Merson's delectable finish polished off Liverpool (read the second part of that sentence again, we didn't repeat the trick for the rest of the decade). He followed up with a superb chip over Neville Southall at Goodison Park in a 1-1 draw and Ian Wright silenced the Villa Park boo-boys with his clattering last minute winner. Inevitably, though, it was the 2-2 home draw with Manchester United which grabbed the headlines. Sharpe and Hughes scored their first half goals. Paul Merson's equalising volley flew past Schmeichel to grab a point and Wright seemed to have given us an astounding last minute winner after he'd bundled the ball into the net. The ref blew for a foul, thus we learnt that even farting near the red nosed Dane warranted a foul. Cantona's hilarious sending off (his second in three days) capped the evening. Tony Adams sportingly protested to the ref that the sending off was unjust; a noble gesture which I couldn't see being reciprocated at OT, could you?

That game demonstrated the urgent need to set up a workable membership card scheme at Highbury. During the season, black marketeers had been able to buy up wadges of tickets and flog them to punters at inflated prices. At the match against United, there were thousands of supposed United fans (with obligatory Home Counties accents), infesting the North Bank, having bought tickets from spivs outside. Several Arsenal fans who'd been to all previous home league games that season deserved to see this glamour match but were forced to miss out.

The match also spoke volumes for the merchandising revolution that was developing inside mid '90s Highbury. In the stand that night, I sat next to a chubby middle aged guy who was struggling with a bulging carrier bag. I peeked inside and it was stuffed with hundreds of pounds worth of 'official club products' e.g. replica shirts, mugs, and videos). It was, in effect, a David Dein wet dream. The guy unashamedly told me that he'd got his ticket from a bucket shop in London and that this was his one and only visit to Highbury for the year, though he was going to watch Chelsea V Spurs at the weekend. While he wasn't quite the real life version of the *Fast Show's*

Arsenal fan, he wasn't far off. The game was apparently a sell out, yet, apart from all the United fans in the North Bank, there was a huge number of these 'floating fans' and their numbers continued to grow each season. I know that other fans who watched Arsenal in the mid '70s and '80s feel aggrieved at the unwelcome presence of day trippers. It's a problem that all big clubs now endure, and further evidence that if you have the dosh you can gatecrash any party.

The problem with the influx of the more upwardly mobile Arsenal fan is that many of them seem devoid of passion. Content to sit chomping on their chips, whinging when people in front stand during goalmouth action, and keen to sit quietly watching the pre-match show on the big screen, one wonders why they're not at a County Cricket match. But then, the big screens must take some of the blame for diluting the atmosphere. Before they were around, the focus for spectators was purely the opposition and their fans. Now, with the D.J.'s incessant waffle, endless reruns of goals and highlights, and with Sonic 'the bloody hedgehog' and Gunner-bloody-saurus annoying us, fans' chanting is often drowned out when kick off approaches, anyway. Now and again though, the clock is turned back and the passion and verve from the crowd returns for big games. Copenhagen '94 for example was an occasion where you knew that the crowd's vocal support really did inspire the players.

The Cup Winners Cup Final was a battle which no-one really expected us to win. Our opponents, Parma, were a club which is the antithesis of everything Arsenal stand for. To put it bluntly, Parma are the Italian version of Blackburn Rovers. Propped up entirely by the wealth of a stinking rich success story from the free market, they'd invested heavily in glittering foreign talent and top class Italian players. By injecting 'new money' into the Italian game, they'd helped cause transfer inflation, just like Jack Walker did in the mid '90s. And in the process, they became the team everyone loved to hate in Italy. Maybe, then, the two clubs did have something in common.

On the football side, no-one could argue with the talent they had assembled. Admittedly, it's hard to think of Tomas Brolin as anything else than a tub of lard who ended up as a beached whale at Crystal Palace. But in '94 he was about five stone lighter, five yards quicker and he would be one of World Cup '94's stars. Faustino Asprilla and Gianfranco Zola were capable of lightening counter attacking and seemed set to tear Arsenal apart. Of course, the Gunners were decimated by injuries and suspensions. Wrighty was banned, JJ had virtually been sliced in half while playing for Denmark and David

Hillier and Martin Keown were also crocked. The Arsenal team that took the field, therefore, had a rough and ready persona to it. Press soundbites suggested that the Parma players sniggered at our journeyman team. Brolin allegedly said 'No Wright - no worries'. Their arrogance was misplaced.

Alan Smith describes events : 'We knew that George really wanted the Cup Winners' Cup. We'd won the cups in the previous year, but very quickly, it was clear the league was out of reach. He wanted to pit his wits against European clubs. As a result, he started to drop key players for league games and rested them for Europe. It was understandable, but it backfired in a way because it did create discontent amongst fans. The style of play at Highbury had completely changed. Gone were Rocky, Mickey, Marwood and Limpar. The flair wasn't there - but the determination was. That was crucial in the final.

Parma were silky smooth and Asprilla and Brolin in full flight was one scary sight. Skill-wise they were in a different league and, when Brolin hit the post early on, we had a really close shave. Who knows what could have happened if that had gone in? I felt I played one of my best ever games for the club. I was back as the leading striker and I had more room to move and operate, without Ian in the team. My goal was really out of nothing. It was a fantastic sight, seeing it hit the post and fly in.

After that, it was real 'backs to the wall stuff'. Paul Merson played very well and dropped back to defend. As well as the defence, Ian Selley and Steve Morrow played excellently, which showed the kind of team we were. Parma players were annoyed because they weren't allowed to play at all. When the whistle went, it was a superb feeling. Although my goal at Anfield in '89 came on an unbelievable night, scoring the winner in a final is totally different. It's something else really. Especially in a European final'.

Alan Smith, speaking in 2000

Dave Ritchie, an Arsenal fan from Clapham, tells of his recollections of the game thus. 'Copenhagen '94 was the best night of my Arsenal-supporting life. The whole trip was unbelievable from start to finish. There were about 25,000 Arsenal fans who went over to Copenhagen. *25,000 - that's about four times the size of a medieval army on the march. It's a* good city to visit anyway, all the squares and restaurants were jammed with red and white shirts. I remember we went to the Tivoli Gardens and all you could hear were Arsenal chants. We went to an old restaurant the night before the final and the plates were propped up on this old-looking Welsh dresser. Suddenly the *'Ian Wright, Wright, Wright'* chant started up and it was so loud and vibrant that some of the plates fell and smashed on the floor. And before you say anything - we paid for the damage!!

We spent the day of the final drinking Carlsberg, and it was a really great day. The Parma fans were there but we were happy to mix. There were no problems at all, which is how it should be. Inside the stadium, the noise was incredible. So much red and white too!! The Arsenal DJ had hijacked the p.a. facilities and kept playing Village People's *Go West*, which we'd now turned into *One-Nil To The Arsenal*. It was like a war chant - it was monstrous and awesome. I'd had a few beers - but it was!! I honestly think we'd almost won the game before it began - even without Wrighty.

Everyone knows that, on paper, Parma were the better side. Brolin, Asprilla; they were great players but, as George said, the travelling army virtually gave Arsenal a goal start. My memories of the game aren't that clear, actually. I had too much booze to remember the finer details. They're more vivid of the occasion. I do remember Alan Smith's winner, though. I've never celebrated a goal so hard in my life and the noise was so loud. I mean seriously loud. When the final whistle went, it almost split open my ear holes! We sang *'Georgie Graham's magic, he wears a magic hat, and when he saw the Cup Winners Cup, he said I'm having that'*. It was the best ever Arsenal event in my opinion. The feeling of going overseas with thousands of others is indescribable'

Dave Ritchie - Arsenal fan from Clapham

The stunning result was a triumph of organisation and willpower over flair and spontaneity. Patrick Barclay's headline in *The Observer* was: 'artistry ensnared in mean machine'. As the *'1-0 to the Arsenal'* mantra boomed out over the tannoy, we celebrated George's sixth trophy in seven years. He'd fulfilled the target he set himself at the start of the season and even gained some grudging respect for it. A block of fans unfurled the banner 'George knows' at the end of the game, and he'd judged his tactics perfectly once more for the big occasion. None of us though, could have predicted what would hit the fan within six months, not even the all seeing, all knowing, all conquering King George.

Alan Smith celebrates after winning the Cup Winners' Cup in '94

5

The Bitter End

The ludicrously propagandist '94/95 end-of-season Arsenal video is entitled *'What A Season'*. The review will never win any awards for its investigative reporting. However, if gongs were dished out under the category 'the ability to sweep things under the carpet', then this would be the most decorated documentary in the history of broadcasting. The season was a Babylon of sleaze, sackings and scandal, but this *Pravda*-like video pauses only briefly to mention that 'George Graham left the club under unfortunate circumstances in January'. No kidding.

Quite simply, those nine months were our very own *annus horribilis* and this chapter is not for the squeamish. Put in the hands of a master *film noir* producer, it could easily be turned into a cult classic movie. All the ingredients were there, after all. There was a tense and strained atmosphere, a vicious sting in the tail, and two classic anti-hero figures were publicly humiliated.

On the eve of the season, George Graham talked 'big' in the verbal sparring arena between the managers. He announced : 'I'm eyeing the title again', and that he wanted to become 'the first Arsenal manager to lift the European Cup'. Evidently he'd been busy writing a shopping list over the summer. The '94 World Cup had been a feast of fast, thrilling attacking football. Bergkamp, Brolin, Overmars, Baggio and Batistuta all displayed their stellar skills, and tabloids linked all five with a move to Highbury. Even the normally reserved George got in on the act, promising his players 'a World Cup signing that will blow your mind'.

These were fine words indeed, but the news that the club had signed Stefan Schwarz for £2m hardly threatened to destroy too many fans' cranial structures. He had the reputation for being a neat and accomplished left-footed midfielder, but he would grow rapidly pissed off with George's tactics during the season. The fact that he earned double the money other more established Arsenal pros were on, also made waves in the dressing room.

Chris Sutton's £5m transfer to Blackburn meant that the club again missed out on the number one British transfer target. George bid for the player, but Rovers leaked the news that they were paying him double the amount he'd have received at Highbury. Senior players were reportedly unhappy with this latest public humiliation in the transfer market, particularly when Ardilles' Spurs acquired Popescu, Dumitrescu and Klinsman over the Summer. For the first time since the early '80s, Spurs fans rightly believed that their club was in a better position than Arsenal to win trophies at the start of a season. It was a sobering thought, but, luckily, all three Spurs signings turned out to be expensive short term cosmetic padding for the lily-whites, despite Captain Mabbutt's belief that this would be 'Spurs' year'. Even in such turbulent times for Arsenal, the Totts would sack their manager and the Gunners would come closest to lifting silverware.

With none of the home nations qualifying for the World Cup, most Arsenal players had been resting over the Summer. Staggeringly, Eire's Eddie McGoldrick was the only member of the Gunners' squad to be involved in the World Cup (discounting Schwarz, who wasn't an Arsenal player until late June). The word 'involved' should be used loosely in Eddie's case because he didn't actually make it onto the pitch at any point, though T.V. cameras caught him passing water bags to thirsty Irish players during games. It was nice to see that Jack Charlton valued him as highly as we did.

Ian Wright had been keeping himself busy. He'd penned his book *Inside Wright - My World In Pictures*. In it, we saw him in a variety of guises; dressed as a builder, a 'gangsta', even as a footballer. The man gave us his insight and opinions on topical issues. He told us that he was 'really gutted' that Charles and Diana's marriage hadn't worked out, that trying on a new pair of shoes was 'a big thrill' and that George could get 'angry' when he had to. With cutting insights like that, no wonder LWT was so keen to turn him into a chat show host. Wright's growing penchant for self-publicity was starting to annoy sections of support, but his goals carried huge significance as the season wore on.

Wintry disaster seemed a world away after the first game of the season. We'd just hammered Manchester City 3-0, putting behind us the opening day calamities of the last two years. The Arsenal team was: Seaman, Dixon, Winterburn, Schwarz, Bould, Adams, Campbell, Wright,

Smith, Merson, Jensen. Graham persisted with playing Merson and Camp-bell wide in midfield, but elected to drop Paul Davis, whose Highbury days were numbered. Stefan Schwarz had an excellent first game, easily winning his midfield battle against ageing beast Steve McMahon. Schwarz's forte, as we'd seen against Napoli the week before, was a combi-nation of sharp tackling and crisp short passing, via his cultured left-foot. In other words, he was a super *de luxe* version of Hillier, Jensen and co. Ian Wright, Alan Smith and Kevin Campbell scored on a boiling day. The result was an excellent confidence booster for the latter two and the team in general. Amidst the optimism surrounding this result, it was easy to miss the danger signs hanging over Paul Merson. When a Premiership striker is left gasping for air after just ten minutes of the season's opening match, alarm bells ring. In his own words, the 'rock bottom' was about to be scraped. Arsenal's form would plummet just as spectacularly.

One month later, Arsenal had picked up just two points and two goals from five games. On our way into the murky depths of the relegation zone, we'd proved that we were unable to break down the division's best defences. With Bould's thigh injury and Dixon and Winterburn looking sluggish, the defence looked rocky too. Paul Davis later commented: 'The shape of the team was wrong. Stefan Schwarz was basically the only midfielder who could create anything - but he was also expected to cover the defence. He couldn't do it all. So the defence was often exposed and the strikers weren't seeing the ball enough'.

Admittedly, we were unlucky to lose to Leeds and Newcastle, but Liverpool hammered us 3-0, with acne ridden Robbie Fowler demonstrat-ing his obsession for belting goals past Seaman. Blackburn bored their way to a 0-0 draw at Highbury and Norwich did the same three days later. At this point, some season tickets were burned and poor Martin Keown was booed remorselessly after some 'shaky' early season displays. Most jarring-ly, *'Graham out'* cries were audible around Highbury. The joys of Copenhagen were quickly forgotten, and King George's divine right to rule was finally being questioned. The tabloids would soon help to ensure that the slow run up to his overthrow and public execution was the most grue-some of spectacles.

Tony Adams did his best to defend his colleagues. In the match pro-gramme, he asked fans to stop shouting 'shoot' at JJ every time he received the ball, claiming that the poor man's confidence was being destroyed. Rumours were, that in the Blackburn match, Jensen's shooting was so 'off-beam' that pilots descending into Heathrow airport believed they were under attack from Iraqi fighter planes which had strayed into North London airspace. Tone also requested that we 'pump up the volume' for home games. Most of us did our best, but the noise of shit hitting the fan soon blocked out all other sounds at Highbury.

Two things saved Graham from a pre-Christmas sacking; the K.O. punches handed out to featherweight cup opponents and Ian Wright's goals. We cruised past Cypriot beach bums Omonia Nicosia 6-1 on aggregate in the Cup Winners Cup. Wrighty tore them apart, home and away, but Graham said in the press that 'Omonia aren't a bad side'. What utter crap. Even a barely mobile Paul Merson sprinted past them in the away leg and punished them. Still, it was a nice break for the boys, and they came back with great tans, by all accounts. Wright and Adams, having between them seen off Hartlepool in the first round of the Coca-Cola Cup, then scored two towering headers at Upton park to destroy West Ham in a 2-0 league win. Our first victory in six seemed to have steadied the ship but a week later the perennially awful Crystal Palace came to Highbury and won 2-1. A *Gooner* contributor reckoned that not one pass from our midfielders reached its intended target for thirty first half minutes. Surely Ian Wright's hundredth Arsenal goal deserved a better backdrop than that.

The last angst-free Highbury match of the Graham era saw his team cruise past Chelsea. Bouldy was back to shore up the defence and Wrighty despatched two crackers with utmost venom. The celebrations which followed Kevin Campbell's overhead strike lasted long into the October evening. A week later the boys gained an impressive 3-1 win at Wimbledon. We'd hauled ourselves up into ninth position and the Kev and Wrighty partnership had sparked again. After Brondby were beaten in the second round of the Cup Winners Cup, optimism was once more the order of the day. Admittedly we'd almost blown it and should have conceded a last minute penalty, but Selley's and Wright's Highbury goals saw us through. George gushed public praise for Campbell's improved form, saying that 'Kevin will now get his confidence back'. He also reckoned that the 'team's bad performances are behind them'. Some bloody hope; Black November had arrived.

Have there ever been a more calamitous four weeks in Arsenal's history? Over these thirty days the name Arsenal FC sold more tabloids than any toe sucking, satsuma stuffing, love child spawning Tory MP of the time could ever do. It began innocently enough with a trip to Goodison Park. Stefan Schwarz dispatched a thirty yard rocket past Southall to give us the lead, but struggling Everton fought back for a draw. Off-field storm clouds gathered on the day we faced Southampton at the Dell. The tabloids got wind of the fact that Tony Adams was desperately unhappy with the situation at Highbury. Manchester United had apparently put in a whopping bid for him and he seemed set to zoom up to Old Trafford in May. Adams later explained that he felt totally flat at Highbury and the poor crowd for his testimonial (15,000 to see Arsenal take on Crystal Palace) had 'gutted' him. Like the rest of us, he was also frustrated with George's poor efforts in the transfer market.

The captain's talismanic presence at Highbury seemed to be one of the few bonds holding the club together and the thought of him defecting to United was a horrifying proposition. The rumours didn't help matters on the pitch. We lost 1-0 to the Saints on a surreal afternoon. Martin Keown wore the number 10 on his back, Eddie McGoldrick gave his worst ever performance in an Arsenal shirt (and that's saying something) and Jimmy Carter tripped over twice while he warmed up. For an even more bizarre backdrop, the away end waved 'Bank of Grobland' notes at Brucie, who was under investigation for match fixing allegations. This bank-note waving gesture soon became a case for wry reflection for all concerned. Maybe, for a while, George figured he'd been rumbled. He only had a week to wait.

Sandwiched between a woeful defeat at Leicester and a gutsy draw with Manchester United, the two cataclysmic stories broke. Bored with focusing on the Tory Euro rebels and John Major's inability to keep his troops together, the *Daily Mirror* turned its attentions to Paul Merson's personal life. 'I'm hooked on cocaine', ran the headline. Underneath was a shocking picture of an unshaven and gloomy looking Merse who'd obviously reached the end of the road.

This book is not the medium through which to analyse the reasons for Merson's downfall. For that, read the full harrowing account in his autobiography *Rock Bottom*. Suffice it to say that the lethal combination of booze and gambling combined to push a shy and insecure personality to the next 'gateway'; cocaine abuse. One of the finest talents of his generation faced ruin at the age of 26.

In reality, the revelations were stunning but somehow unsurprising. For several years, with Gazza away in Italy, Merson was the *enfant terrible* of the English game. Frequent headlines about pub brawls, his earlier confession about gambling difficulties, and public warnings from George already hinted that his off-field activities had gone beyond the stage of 'Merse having fun'. His antics, which, lets face it, many of us found amusing in the late

'80s and early '90s (especially his heckling of comedian Norman Collier at a club dinner), had ceased to be rib tickling. With George turning Highbury into a virtually flair free zone, we needed him on top form. Instead, he was often a passenger in the team. His weight ballooned and his 'let's all do the Merson routine' started to seem a bit sad. A sizeable minority of fans reckoned that the player should have been sold. *One Nil Down* eventually ran the headline 'Merson; should he stay or should he go?'

Inevitably, some tired ex-managers, whose own alleged vices hardly stood up against close inspection, screamed that Merson should be kicked out of football forever and be left to rot. Such ethics would have fitted in perfectly with the activities of the Nazi storm troopers in Hitler's Germany, when they rounded up anyone who didn't quite fit in with their master race ideology. It was pointed out that Merson was a lucky boy because Arsenal continued to pay his wages while he underwent three months of counselling and rehabilitation in the Priory Clinic. True - but then we know that footballers are cosseted beyond reasonable measure, as far beyond fans' financial understanding as the royal family. In a way, Merson had actually shown that having wadges of cash and too much time to kill could actually do more harm than good. All Gunners fans hoped that his rehab would be successful but some harboured real doubts over whether, in the long term, the years of inconsistency and abuse of his body actually merited him a spot in the Arsenal first team anymore.

Without Merson, though, Arsenal's form was excremental. One only had to look at the replacements in his number 10 shirt (Dickov, Keown, Carter) to know that even 'in drink', Merse was the superior option. Most of us, realising that we needed him, wished Merson all the best and hoped that he'd be back real, real soon. We could stomach the sight of Jimmy Carter no more.

The Graham scandal broke two days later. Playing it cool, the Sunday Mirror announced that 'a top Highbury official' received a large sum of money from the John Jensen deal in 1992. In truth, the story seemed irrelevant to most fans. Admittedly the thought that anyone should gain something from signing JJ was strange, but the term 'Highbury official' conjured up the image of an office boy in a grey suit.

Those early stories were shrouded in rumour and counter-rumour, and littered with buzzwords, like 'sweeteners', 'kick backs', 'unsolicited gifts' and, of course, 'bungs', which further clouded the issue. When the mist began to lift, all routes led, staggeringly, to King George. It was he, we were later told, who allegedly benefited from two 'kickbacks' from Norwegian agent Rune Hauge. The first was a payment of £140,500, allegedly his cut from the Lydersen deal, the second was £285,000, supposedly his take from the Jensen signing. We later found out that the board had known about the payments since August, and that George had apparently told them only *after* he realised that Hauge's tax returns were being investigated. For some, that was enough to prove George's culpability. The man himself begged to differ.

In Graham's book, he notes that the board told him in October that they no longer trusted him and discussions over his likely resignation were already in progress. The press sniped at him for the next couple of months, although they did tone down their use of the word 'bung'. They spent the Christmas period frantically clarifying with their legal people the difference between the 'b' word and the term 'unsolicited gift'. George and the club, in the meantime, maintained a position of stoic silence, which simply added fuel to the fire. Come February, when the Premier League enquiry was set up, and the press probed ever deeper into sleaze in football and politics, the term 'bung' would have as familiar a ring to it as did 'cash for questions'.

During this uneasy peace, Gunners fans realised that the Graham dynasty really was coming to the grimmest of ends. Whether the money was a bung or a gift, George, the white knight who'd ridden to our rescue in June '86; the immaculate, dapper boss under whom we'd won so many trophies, was now forever tainted. The Puritanical Scot who'd sounded so virtuous nine years earlier had supposedly pocketed large amounts of cash, shoved it in an offshore bank account and hadn't declared it to the taxman. An ex-player, who wished to remain anonymous, told me: 'I couldn't believe the stories. All those years when he'd been so tight over contracts, and then we find out he's been lining his own pockets. I could barely look him in the eye after that, to be honest'.

It was the perfect, irony-laden story for the ravenous tabloids who were convinced that football was awash with obscene amounts of cash and illicit payments. And, of course, George was boss of the Arsenal; everyone's favourite club to hate. He had always had an uneasy relationship with the press since his divorce from wife, Marie, and you can bet that half of them wet their pants when they learnt that he was at the centre of the scandal. Perhaps his business manager, John Hazell, was right when he admitted later that 'the press would never be happy until they had your head on a plate'. Still, the rapidly diminishing band of Graham worshippers reckoned that if results on the pitch could improve over Christmas and the New Year, the Scot may yet save his skin. They obviously didn't pray hard enough.

The last weeks of the Graham era were suitably dark and murky, played out on the Wintry evenings of December and January. Not only would George soon be gone, the clock was also ticking for several members of the '89 and '91 title winning sides. Illness and injuries combined to weaken the team still further at this point, meaning that Clown Prince Vince Bartram, Mark Flatts and Jimmy Carter were guaranteed games. With even the tea lady on standby, the following team scraped a draw at Forest; Bartram, Dixon, Winterburn, Schwarz, Bould, Keown, Hillier, Flatts, Campbell, Davis, Parlour. In his last ever Arsenal game, Paul Davis grabbed our late equaliser. Arsenal's player of the '80s deserved a more dignified exit than that.

Schwarz and Smith gave us a 2-1 win at Maine Road. Smudger's last Arsenal goal was masterfully swept in but knee problems meant that he, too, was almost finished. He recalls those macabre last days of the Graham era: 'I found it staggering when I learned what George had done. I'd always regarded him as the upholder of the badge. But George had simply been at Arsenal too long. The whole thing was so stale, there was absolutely *nothing* he could say which those players in the dressing room hadn't heard before'. Indeed Graham's defiant belief that 'something will turn up', was pure mindless Mr Micawber-type optimism.

Santa clearly decided to miss out Highbury on his sleigh ride that year. Arsenal's play was as anally retentive as any of Cliff's seasonal number ones and even the ghastly sight of Noel Edmonds in fuchsia and sage jumpers was preferable to witnessing the Highbury horror shows against Leeds, Villa and QPR. That we were supposed to draw any comfort from the fact that JJ scored his only Arsenal goal in the 1-3 defeat by Rangers spoke volumes for our desperate state. Admittedly, it was a superb curling effort, but if you stand in front of a dartboard and keep throwing, you'll eventually hit bullseye. The only problem is, you'll have maimed a few people in the process.

The injured and suspended players finally started to return in early January. Ian Wright's cracking effort and Kevin Campbell's last goal for the club beat fellow strugglers Ipswich and kept us bobbing above the relegation zone. Not even David Seaman's excellence could prevent Spurs beating the Gunners in one of the most ill- tempered North London derbies for years. Popescu's goal did for us but the normally ultra cool Stefan Schwarz's sending off, for a psychopathic lunge, told us more about the morale amongst the players than the result could.

Graham tried desperately to stem the tide flowing against him by splashing out over £3m on strikers Chris Kiwomya and John Hartson. The football world at large realised that Kiwomya was a panic buy. Even though he eventually entered the Highbury cult hall of fame, his signing from Ipswich failed to get juices flowing in North London. Burly Luton target-man, John Hartson, on the other hand, seemed to be an ideal long-term replacement for Smudger or Kevin Campbell, depending on who was axed first. Aside from the fact that he was the first Welshman in the team since Peter Nicholas (Oh gawd!!), he was, George informed us, one for the future.

Hartson made an immediate impact. He played excellently alongside Ian Wright in the draw with Everton and powered in the winner against Coventry at a muddy Highfield Road one week later. Johnny had the distinction of being the most expensive teenager in English football and, for a while, he seemed to represent excellent business. Seven days after Adams and Linighan had received their marching orders in a 1-3 stuffing by Sheffield Wednesday, King George took charge of Arsenal for the last time on Saturday, February 11th. *The Sun's* Brian Woolnough predicted that the boss would be sacked within a couple of days. He wasn't far wrong. At least George got to see the early benefits of Paul Merson's rehabilitation. In his first Highbury return game, Merse cracked home a superb half volley, which lifted our hearts at home to Leicester.

The fact that soon to be relegated City came back to scrape a draw, said much for the stark reality of our fortunes at the time. Graham commented afterwards that Merse's efforts justified his and the board's backing of their man, however difficult the circumstances. Maybe he was trying to make a none-too-subtle point to Hill-Wood, Dein and co. If so, the plea fell on deaf ears; King George was fired two days later.

A book was published on historical hypotheticals a couple of years ago. One of them asks: 'What if JFK hadn't been shot dead in '63? The author's opinion makes interesting reading. He postulates that the US would have been dragged into the Vietnam war, anyway; his alleged Mafia links would have been exposed and fragile health would have let him down. In other words, the 'Camelot image' would have been destroyed. Perhaps the author should have asked almost the reverse question about GG: 'What if George Graham had been 'taken from us' in 1991, or at a push, May '93?' The truth is that he would now be a Highbury icon. He would have been the Arsenal manager who, we reckoned, would have overseen the club's domination of the '90s and beyond. We'd flock to pay homage (Lenin style) to his marble bust, which would rest alongside Herbert Chapman's, and our new stadium would surely be named the 'George Graham Millennium Stadium'.

Instead, we've spent the last few years singing songs which question his mother's morals, rather than thanking him for the seven trophies he delivered during his eight years in charge. Graham's divorce from Arsenal was messy and acrimonious and there is a lot of anger on both sides. George may have dumped his Arsenal memorabilia in his attic during his spell as Spurs boss, and we've since gone on to enjoy glory without him, but the bad memories are slow to fade.

Although it was the FA hearing in March that banned him from football for a year, Graham had effectively been on trial since September 19th 1994, when he admitted to Peter Hill-Wood that he had pocketed the money. Essentially, the board and the subsequent FA enquiry asked four questions of him :

1. Did Graham 'engineer' the Lydersen and Jensen deals so that *he* could make a profit from them?

2. Did he only 'declare' Hauge's 'gifts' because he realised that the Norwegian was under investigation, so the news would leak anyway?

3. Did the £485,000, which George pocketed, rightfully belong to the club?

4. Was Graham aware that the money he received from Hauge was in connection (i.e. his 'cut') from the two transfers?

Between them, the board and the FA enquiry believed the answer was 'yes' to questions 3. and 4, meaning that not only had George acted against the best interests of the club, but he had also broken FA rules. Inevitably, there would always be a lingering suspicion that the answer to 2 was also 'yes', though this can never be proved. He was found not guilty over what would have been the most heinous crime of all; that of 'engineering' a bung, as stated in 1.

George has since hit back with some savage broadsides of his own, of course. He records his feelings about the whole affair in *The Glory and The Grief* and, most notably, at the time he appeared on Clive Anderson's *Talk Back* Show and stuck rigidly to his story. George has always insisted that the money was simply a 'thank you' present from Hauge for all the contacts, which he had opened up for him in England. In the process of writing this book, I have spoken to several 'Grahamites' who still claim that he was stabbed in the back. Let us, for impartiality sake, put forward the case for GG's defence, based on conversations with those fans.

'Managerial sackings at Arsenal over the last twenty years have been notoriously messy affairs, which often leave a bad taste in the mouth. Just look at the way the board handled Howe and Rioch's departures. There was certainly a hidden agenda behind those two exits. The way George Graham was treated was shocking, considering the fact that he was our most successful manager since Herbert Chapman.

There is no doubt that he had been foolish in accepting Hauge's money in the first place, which he admits. Stuffing wallets full of cash into a briefcase is, ahem, 'dodgy' and you'd have thought that someone as smart as George would have had the sense at least, to declare these gifts to the taxman. History shows that he eventually did this and the key thing is that George insists he never asked for the money. Such gifts are part and parcel of business life and there is no law in football, which states 'thou shalt not receive a gift'. The handovers also took place in the lounge bar of the Park Lane hotel. Now if George really knew he was receiving a 'bung', would he have collected it in such a public place?

In the city, it is a regular occurrence for expert brains to be picked (like George's was by Hauge) and rewarded with financial gifts. And, let's face it, if someone gave you a £425,000 gift, would you turn it down? It is interesting to wonder if those who repeatedly criticise him would have flatly refused the gift. Ultimately, the board panicked. They believed that by sacking him, Arsenal would escape further punishment from the FA. They chose to believe a combination of hysterical newspaper allegations, three I.K. Start officials (Lydersen's former club) who couldn't get their story straight, and a three man Premier Committee over their man who brought them seven trophies and countless millions of pounds in profits. David Dein's wealth is, in part, due to ownership of shares in Arsenal - the price of which were sent rocketing by Graham's success. Maybe the vice-Chairman and his associates should have remembered this before they acted so ruthlessly.

George had a valid argument when he pointed out that the Board had put up with the antics of Merson and Adams and forgiven them, while he was given no second chance. Then having made the agreement that he would leave his job at the end of the season and receive compensation, the board decided to sack him without him receiving a penny of this. All this came after the evidence given by the laughable FA enquiry, from which there emerged so many leaks and rumours that it was impossible for him to receive a fair hearing. George rightly blasted it as a 'kangaroo court'. Surely the case would have been thrown out long ago by a proper court of law. So if George's actions were a little shabby, the manner of his sacking was positively grotesque.

The Graham affair was all 'tip of the iceberg' stuff. The press' buzz word in the mid '90s was 'sleaze'. They were convinced that sleaze was everywhere - in politics, the city, football, wherever. John Major's disastrous 'back to basics' policy backfired and the press took delight in exposing men like Neil Hamilton and David Mellor as being less than honest. In the city, they'd investigated insider dealing and exposed Nick Leeson's activities in Barings Bank. With so much cash sloshing around in football with the Sky money, it was inevitable that they would start to investigate the football world, and George became the fall guy.

In the end, George was abandoned by the Arsenal board. He was made to pay for what, it has been rumoured, has gone on in football for years, all on the basis of public hysteria. Remember, this was the year that Venables and Clough were also under investigation. But then, it's not really surprising that the Arsenal man should be the one to be punished. That's been the story of the '90s. It's just that this time, the outcome was more tragic'.

While there are several relevant points in the case for the defence, it would have been impossible for George to have been given a mild 'slapped wrist' by the board. The FA had tied the Board's hands, anyway, and not to have taken appropriate action would have left Arsenal open, as was rumoured, to relegation and a series of huge fines. According to George, being a manager was always a case of setting an example to his players. The board obviously believed that his was a very poor one.

Financial irregularities aside, George's time at Arsenal was up. Those final tragic shots of him after our meek surrender to AC Milan in the Super Cup showed a gaunt, strained man who'd reached the end. Being dumped out of the FA Cup in the 3rd round by Millwall at Highbury was bitterly ironic. The club where George honed his managerial skills ended his Arsenal career - symbolically at least. The first division club won 2-0, and it could have been far more embarrassing. Events at Highbury had now turned full circle under Graham. He recorded in his book that he felt he'd 'lost' certain players, a view concurred with by several of that team. The side now required as much internal surgery as it had when he took over nine years earlier.

By the mid '90s, English football had changed, but GG was incapable of snapping out of his '89 and '91 mode of thinking. George's two title winning sides were stuffed with bargain price English players and homegrown lads. With the inflated state of the transfer market by '95, £600,000 signings from Stoke or Wimbledon were unlikely to win a team the title. One of the clear contradictions at the end of his reign was that he continually restated his wish to sign top foreign stars, but in public he was happy to say he 'mistrusted' them. How for instance, would he have man-managed Dennis Bergkamp? His behaviour towards Limpar and Ginola suggests that the relationship would have been stormy, and that Dennis' flying phobia would have resulted in only a brief Highbury stay.

In truth, we'd been meandering towards a gentle decline for a few years. As George had retreated further into his defensive shell, the team's play became more predictable. True wingers were dumped in favour of strong runners and creative midfielders were ditched for solid journeymen. Jensen had replaced Rocky, Hillier replaced Thomas and McGoldrick replaced the Super Swede. The youth academy production line had ground to a halt, and Adams, Merson and Parlour seemed more intent on pissing away their collective talents against a wall.

George Graham provided many of us with our best Arsenal memories; Anfield '89, Wembley '93 and Copenhagen '94. He gave us a defence whose longevity and reputation defied belief. He gave us Ian Wright, and he restored pride to our club. We're eternally grateful for that, but he believed that alone gave him the right to stay at the helm. Football management, though, is a ruthless and unforgiving business. George's protestations about 'what I did for that club' and the ungratefulness of certain directors smack of pure sentimentality to me - an emotion he's always professed to hate. Charlie Nicholas, David Rocastle and Anders Limpar would all testify to that. What went around finally came around, one might say. King George, why did it have to end that way?

When a regime collapses, there is, inevitably, a period of confusion directly afterwards. Statements on the future are vague, the masses don't know whether to look to an uncertain future or a glorious past and usually, some poor sod is thrown into the power vacuum. In Arsenal's case, it was Stewart Houston (aka cone man), who was appointed caretaker boss and, apparently, had designs on the job permanently. Houston did have some of Graham's qualities; he was Scottish, on the dour side and that's it really. For much of the time, Houston's pained expressions reminded us only of George's darkest days. Press speculation about a big-name successor (the usual suspects - Wilkins, Cruyff, Trevor Francis) told us that he would forever be a trusty lieutenant, rather than a general.

The pre-match atmosphere before the first match of the post-Graham era (Arsenal V Forest) was truly surreal. Arsenal fan, Matthew Allgood, recalls that in the Highbury Barn, pockets of fans huddled around in groups, to mutter conspirationally about GG's sacking, which occurred earlier that day. Due to printing deadlines, the programme had already gone to press earlier in the week, and George's notes began with: 'Rumours of my impending resignation have proved somewhat premature', which added to the eerie feel before the game.

Save for a few *'there's only one Georgie Graham'* chants in the first half, the crowd focused its attention solely on the need for an Arsenal home win. Star of the show was £2.3m winger Glenn Helder, who had been Graham's last buy. Looking uncannily like Lionel Ritchie, his dancing down the wing, his shuffles and drag-backs earmarked him as an Arsenal star of the future. Here, at last, we believed, was the natural successor to Anders Limpar. Helder's reputation was further enhanced by the fact that he'd recently replaced Marc Overmars in the Dutch national team. Within a few months, though, he was dubbed 'Graham's revenge' - and would struggle to keep even Eddie McGoldrick out of the side.

For now, though, Helder was superb in this injury and suspension ravaged Arsenal side. Chris Kiwomya's excellent off-the-ball running and cool finish gave us our first home win for four months. Three days later, Palace were destroyed. Kiwomya scored twice this time and Paul Merson grabbed another in a 3-0 win. It was a case of 'so far so good' under Houston. Andy Linighan's distribution from central defence immediately improved and our new found goal-scoring hero already had *'walking in Kiwomya wonderland'* chants booming out in his honour. So when you rock to the Bergkamp version - just remember that Chris was the trail-blazer. He never scored again for us, but his three goals that week ensured him a place in our cult hall of fame. It could be argued that his goals in February actually saved Arsenal from the grimmest fate of all.

The Gunners just about avoided relegation that season, but for a while, it seemed that the second tier of English football was about to claim its biggest victim since United fell in the '70s. Throughout March and early April, we won just once in eight ghastly games. We were slaughtered at Old Trafford, St James' Park and Ewood Park, and when Robbie Fowler cracked in Liverpool's last minute winner at Highbury, our arses were dangling perilously close to the snapping crocodiles below. The principal problem was with the defence. Lee Dixon and Nigel Winterburn seemed to be fulfilling George's prophecy that they needed to be replaced. Dixon, in particular, appeared to have regressed to his ropey form of '92. The transfer talk had clearly unsettled Tony Adams and his worsening injuries and fragile frame of mind unsettled Keown, Linighan and Bould, none of whom was fully fit, either, at that stage.

That the season's two crunch matches were against the combine harvester drivers from Norwich and Ipswich spoke volumes for our situation.

In the end, our fellow strugglers were blown away. Helder's masterful wing display set up John Hartson for a brilliant double against the Canaries, which virtually consigned them to Division one after their 5-1 defeat. Ian Wright's spectacular hat trick obliterated Ipswich 4-0, and Paul Merson's excellence in both games led to admiring gasps from the press. Arsenal travelled to Aston Villa on Easter Monday, knowing that victory would secure our Premiership position. Five thousand travelling Gooners rose to Wright's brilliant combination of pace and deadly finishing, and John Hartson's power and positional sense. Both scored twice in a 4-0 win. The team had a very close shave, finishing just six points clear of the relegation zone, and the need for major restructuring was obvious to everyone.

In the midst of managerial chaos and relegation strife, the Gunners still produced three astonishing performances in the later stages of the Cup Winners Cup. Arsenal appeared to have messed it up in the first leg of the Quarter Final at home to Auxerre. The Wright/Kiwomya partnership mis-fired and the French team squeezed us back into our own half. Only Wrighty's penalty grabbed a draw. It didn't help that it had been pissing sleet all day, and half our team seemed to spend their time sliding around in the slush rather than actually creating chances.

Written off by the critics, Arsenal were expected to be submerged under a wave of classy Gallic counter attacking in France. Auxerre threw every-thing at the Arsenal defence. Future Spurs disaster Moussa Saib rattled Seaman's crossbar from 35 yards, and Spunky brilliantly defied their strik-ers on three occasions. It was desperate stuff. Bould and Adams, united once more, blocked and repelled each attack and Martin Keown, who'd begun to get the boo boys off his case, kept their influential captain, Martins, quiet.

Inevitably, Ian Wright came to the rescue. In the second half, two French defenders collided and Wrighty curled in an unstoppable shot from the edge of the area. The score remained at 1-0 to the Arsenal and in the next day's press, the *Daily Mirror* waxed lyrical about the team's 'guts and glory'. Perhaps the best aspects of Grahamism weren't dead after all.

Cup Winners Cup Semi-Final; Arsenal V Sampdoria, April'95. Both legs of the tie were cardiac arrest-inducing, bollock-busting occasions. These games were as intense and thrilling as football can be - all helped by the fact that we'd pulled out such a plum Italian glamour team in the draw. Inevitably, the games evoked happy memories of the Juve games some fif-teen years earlier. These two matches proved to be equally as raw and blood-boiling. The first leg, at Highbury, was played in the best atmosphere we'd had for years. Sampdoria were star studded, with Mancini, Lombardo, Gullit and Platt their main men. Even when the latter two were ruled out through suspension, the dangerous Jugovic was drafted in. On the night, swathes of London based Italians swarmed into Highbury to crank up the atmosphere by a few more octanes. The consensus was that Arsenal would play it cool and entwine the Samp players in Schwarz and Hillier's web. It didn't quite turn out that way.

The Italians put Arsenal under intense pressure for twenty minutes. Seaman's excellence denied Jugovic and Lombardo, but their fans sensed blood. Without warning, the game swung dramatically. Lee Dixon's thirty-yard firecracker singed Zenga's fingertips, and two minutes later Tony Adams' goal was struck off for a supposed push on their goalie. Zenga's doe-eyed look of innocence, flashed back on the Jumbotron, incensed the crowd. We only had a minute to wait for justice. Ray Parlour cut in from the right and fed Hillier, whose cracking drive was parried by Zenga. Steve Bould crunched in the rebound, and Highbury went ballistic. Ninety seconds later, Bould's flicked header looped over Zenga and dropped into the net. The scorer's slack jawed expression suggested he was trying to feed Wrighty - but who cared? A Steve Bould double? Put it this way - it seemed to us a miracle of biblical proportions.

Two goals up at half time, and the game seemed to be over. But Jugovic pulled a goal back and, once again, Highbury was treated to some desperate helter-skelter stuff. GG would have despaired. Paul Merson's magnificently weighted pass let Wrighty hook us back into a two-goal lead, at which point the North Bank roof nearly exploded. Yet Samp hit back again. Jugovic's late goal gave us a slender 3-2 advantage going into the return match. In the *Daily Express*, Steve Curry described it as a clash between 'latin mastery and Anglo-Saxon muscle'. As we streamed out from Highbury that night, drenched in sweat, and with ear drums stinging from the deafening chanting, it was clear that Arsenal's fans and players would need to strain every sinew in the return leg, and more besides.

There have been a handful of games in this club's recent history which, as they unfolded, you realised must go down as 'Arsenal classics'. The Sampdoria V Arsenal match in Genoa is now rightly up there with the '79 FA Cup Final and Anfield '89. The match in Genoa rocked and reeled with the two sides tormenting and testing each other for over two hours.

Alex Marks, an Arsenal fan from Swiss Cottage, describes events: 'If I had to choose one game from the '90s for pure excitement, it would be the away match in Genoa. It was my first foreign trip with Arsenal since the Juventus match in 1980. The atmosphere was so intense because the tie was balanced on a knife-edge. Sampdoria had strengthened their team. Mancini returned and man-marked Wrighty, Vierchewod came back into central defence.

We didn't look comfortable at the start of the game. The home crowd was really going for it, with the smoke bombs and the fires, and on the pitch their boys really went for us. Mancini put them ahead and they slaughtered us in that first half. The trouble, though, with Italian crowds is that they get impatient really quickly and, when Samp couldn't score again, they turned on their own players. In the second half, Mancini let Wrighty go at a corner and he scored. He'd now scored in every tie in the competition. We just went mad and now we were back in control of the tie. To be honest, I thought that was it. We'd 'locked up the back door' so many times under George, that I guess we took it for granted that we'd do it here. I suppose we got cocky. Kiwomya replaced Wrighty, and Keown, Hillier and Schwarz dropped really deep. I couldn't believe it when Belluci scored twice for them in about two minutes. I just thought 'Oh shit, how the bloody hell are we going to pull this back without Wrighty on the field?' We were 3-1 down on the night and most of us figured that the game was up.

Schwarz's free kick was just staggering, wasn't it? I never actually liked him much. He always seemed to be a moaner, but when he levelled it on aggregate, I'd have married the man, if I could. It was all level at 5-5 on aggregate, which sounds like a make believe scoreline. I suppose all it needed was Pele to get the winner like in *Escape To Victory!* Their fans were absolutely gutted, they thought they'd got it when Belluci was swinging his shirt around his head but now they knew that we'd never lie down and die.

When it went to penalties, we were cacking ourselves. Our seats were quite close to ground level and I realised just how physically big David Seaman is. More importantly, he had this kind of arrogance and aloofness, which must really intimidate the opposition. In the shootout, he was immense. You could see that their players were getting more nervous the closer they got to the penalty area. I think we all aged about ten years during the shoot out.

McGoldrick's penalty was, as you'd expect, bollocks. But I could have cried when Merson missed his. Dixon and Hartson scored theirs and Tony Adams' shot was what you'd expect from him - head down, blasted in. Pure courage. When Seaman saved his second penalty from Jugovic, he just threw the ball away. Like saying 'don't even try it'. On that final one, when Lombardo had to score to keep them alive, hardly anyone could watch. Not our fans, not theirs.

I'll always remember Seaman's brilliant save and Wrighty leading the players' charge to pile in on top of him. Fantastic stuff - we were in the final! I've been to two games in Italy since, against Lazio and Fiorentina, and we've never lost there. Travelling to Italy must bring out the fight and the spirit in us, mustn't it?'

Alex Marks - Arsenal fan from Swiss Cottage

The pictures of a beaming David Seaman wandering around the pitch, draped in a Union Jack, were some of the most memorable of all '90s Arsenal images. Having beaten the tournament favourites, we breathed a collective sigh of relief that 'average' Spanish opponents Real Zaragosa awaited in the final, rather than Chelsea. Zaragosa only had one player we'd heard of; Nayim. So we relaxed and prepared to become the only team in history to retain the Cup Winners Cup. This most trying of seasons was destined to have a happy ending after all. The pessimists who pointed out that, in 1980, we'd beaten Italian giants in the semis and fallen to Spanish side Valencia in the final were laughed out of court. After all, lightning doesn't strike twice, does it?

The final was played on a beautiful Summer's evening in Paris. The team looked ready to finish the season in style - Merse's new 'suede-head' and his glowing demeanour showed the benefits of his rehabilitation. Seaman looked serene after the semi-final heroics and Wrighty was surely set to break another record. The game was tense. Esnaider hooked them into the lead in the 70th minute with a lightning shot on the turn. But John Hartson, confident and mature beyond his years, snatched an equaliser. There was pure bedlam on a balmy Parisian evening. The game meandered through the remainder of the second half and into extra time. Paul Merson had a golden chance, but missed. Hillier and Schwarz tightened up on Nayim and Tony Adams stuck rigidly to Esnaider. This was still, in reality, Graham's Arsenal. Indeed, the fact that Schwarz and Hillier, dogged terriers both, were vying to be Arsenal's man of the match, suggested that GG was pulling the strings from afar. The *'Seaman, Seaman'* chants began as another penalty shootout seemed inevitable. Then of course, the *'We'll win, 'cos we're Arsenal'* mantra boomed out.

The Spaniards, aware that they would be unlikely to beat Seaman in spot kicks, launched one last attack. Andy Linighan weakly headed away one of their punts. Latching onto it was Nayim, who had been dawdling just over the half way line. He spotted that Seaman had strayed off his line and unleashed a speculative lob. Seaman desperately backtracked and tried to claw away the monster punt. If he'd been about a foot further back he'd have managed it but the shot scraped against his fingertips and dropped into the net. The Spanish fans immediately launched into their own terrace fiesta and the final whistle went about twenty seconds later.

It was the worst possible ending to a horrible season; an ex-Spurs player had scored the winner against us in the last minute of a Cup Final. Although he'd departed three months earlier, this was truly the *fin de regime* of the Graham era. For Arsenal to have won the final, playing in such a blanket-defending, midfield-harrying, 'hoof it up' style, would have meant that we'd have clung onto the myth that George's way was still the right way. And, as we'd seen over the last three league campaigns, it wasn't anymore. The sight of David Seaman, tangled up disconsolately in the netting, was replete with ironies. Our Semi-final hero was, according to the press, now the villain. And yet, without Seaman's excellence, we wouldn't even have made it to extra time. It was the perfect paradox in a season where heroes had fallen so readily.

This truly was the bitterest of ends - more importantly it was the chance for a new beginning. Manchester United and Newcastle were showing that the way forward was to put the emphasis on bold attacking and creative midfield play. As David Miller pointed out in *The Times*, 'Arsenal must prepare to broaden their horizons'. It was time for a total overhaul at Highbury, and some legends slipped quietly away. Paul Davis was freed to join Brentford and Kevin Campbell joined Nottingham Forest for £2m. Kev's Arsenal career, having begun so brightly, ended in scarcely a whimper. Whatever the reasons for his decline; playing out of position, being in awe of Ian Wright, it was a stark warning to all teenage starlets. I wonder if John Hartson took note? Alan Smith's knee injury forced him to retire. It was a desperately sad end to his career. Still, with two golden boot awards and a place in our scorer's hall of fame, he had excelled himself. Thanks Smudger. And finally, Jimbo Carter 'jet setted' off to Portsmouth, where being crap is considered a virtue.

The Gunners were on the verge of entering a glorious new era, but, for the next few weeks, we had to put up with smart-arsed Tottenham fans taunting us with *'Nayim from the half way line'* chants. Christ, the past nine months had been so bad that three months of Formula One and County Cricket seemed positively enticing, for once.

King George departs - February 1995

Seaman's heroics defy Sampdoria in a penalty shoot-out

6

Who's The Boss?

The previous season was unquestionably Arsenal's worst of recent times and, over the summer, it was tempting for Gunners fans to involve themselves in other sports, kidding themselves that they really gave a toss about Tim Henman's Wimbledon challenge. But supporting football teams often requires a leap of faith and soon, the *'Nayim from the halfway line'* chants lost their sting. The close season turned out to be even more knicker-wettingly exciting than the 'Charlie Nicholas Summer' of '83.

The rumours began virtually seconds after Nayim's lob landed in the back of David Seaman's net; Arsenal were tracking Dennis Bergkamp. Few believed that he'd actually sign, though. After all, hadn't the club made bids for Keane and Sutton in the last few years, only for the players' personal terms to wreck the move? It seemed to be just another fiendish press trick. Arsenal's tight wad attitude to transfers had already reached music hall joke status, after all. The club's recent limit was £2 m for Stefan Schwarz, who had decided to clear off to Italy after only a year at Highbury, sick of GG's and Houston's tactics.

So when Dennis was unveiled for the first time on June 20th, resplendent in his red Arsenal shirt, we virtually combusted with excitement. The tabloids were clearly caught unawares - the best headline *The Sun* could muster was 'HELLO KAMPERS - Den for Hi-de-Highbury'. The Dutchman was unquestionably a star. Although he'd endured a torrid two year stay at Inter Milan, with the *paparazzi* invading his much valued privacy, the memory of his goals for Holland against England showed that he was simply on a different skill level from most of his contemporaries. For Arsenal fans, his signature suggested that the Gunners really were about to ditch the functional veneer of George's later teams.

Tall and blond, Dennis' chiselled looks would have granted him instant access to the Aryan Super Race. A journalist wrote at the time 'he looks different, he looks cool, he looks like a super-hero'. More importantly, the aura surrounding him was quite unlike anything we'd seen at Highbury before. Dennis was a thoroughbred from the Ajax stable which had spawned the likes of Cruyff and Van Basten. On Gary Lineker's BBC1 documentary, *Dreaming of Ajax*, shown in the mid '90s, viewers saw at first hand the type of training a young Dennis would have gone through. Far removed from the 'hoof it up field, break his legs' school of thought, which is evident in the minds of many English coaches, young Dutch footballers are encouraged to play in all positions on the pitch. They are instructed to use both feet (so no Nigel Van Winterburns make it through) and treat the ball as if it were a 'best buddy'. The philosophy may not have exactly been pure 'total football' but all Gunners fans fervently hoped that the Dutchman's arrival would hasten the club's symbiosis into a more stylish outfit. His bold statement that 'I aim to become the best player in England', was enough to make the gonads tingle.

When he was joined at Highbury two weeks later by David Platt, England's goal hungry midfield captain, collective hysteria from Gunners fans reached a pitch only previously heard in New York's Shea Stadium when The Beatles were in town. Rumoured to have bought a plot of land in Cheshire, the smart money was on Dave going to Old Trafford, which made his capture seem all the more triumphant. Having started out at Crewe, Platty's subsequent career saw him play for Villa, Bari, Juventus and Sampdoria, which made him the most expensive player of his time in cumulative transfers. After his arrival in London N5, he'd cost clubs a grand total of £22m. Crucially, he'd been virtually the only success of Turnip Head Taylor's disastrous England tenure, scoring 27 goals on his numerous ventures into the penalty box. In our newly found beatific state, we were convinced that Platty was the evangelist destined to breathe new life into a moribund midfield.

Arsenal had yanked out a big boy wedge of over £12 m to pay for the two players. Having shattered its much valued wage structure, the board realised that in order to compete with the likes of Newcastle and Blackburn, the 'readies' had to be splashed, and *be seen* to be splashed in the capitalist haven that is the Premiership. Our embittered ex-boss muttered about what he could have done if he'd had that kind of cash at his disposal. George had a point, but the legacy from his sacking was that David Dein now took a lead role in all transfer negotiations. Interestingly, Dein has always insisted that the money was there for George to spend. The board has always been happy to hint that GG simply wasn't willing to buy big in his final years at Highbury.

Either way, it was very clear that the nature of the manager's job at Arsenal had changed. With Dein in command of transfer negotiations, the dictatorial powers enjoyed by George would no longer be granted to his successor. In short, the new boss would be in charge of 'team affairs' but there was a grey area when it came to signing new players. Whoever took over would 'nominate' signings, while Dein completed the negotiations. Immediately, there were all the signs of a classic '90s conflict of interest between the footballing and financial aspects of the game. As we would soon discover, this uneasy dichotomy had far reaching consequences for the new manager.

Bruce Rioch was appointed Arsenal boss on June 8th 1995. His name had been touted around since George's sacking - although Bobby Robson and, ominously for Bruce, one Arsène Wenger were rumoured to be the club's favoured choices. Still, for a club anxious to rid itself of its 'sleaze' tag, Rioch had the perfect image. Immaculately turned out, Scottish and with a reputation for tough discipline and neo-Puritanical views, he sounded rather like GG circa 1986. It was well known that he preferred young players to be settled with a family, rather than out socialising regularly. Platt and Bergkamp were ideal Rioch players, arriving with 'squeaky clean' labels stamped on their foreheads.

The new boss immediately witnessed another chapter being written in the book of boozy Arsenal stories when Ray Parlour was involved in the 'prawn-cracker-gate' affair in late June. Parlour, Tony Adams and Chris Kiwomya had been on an all-night bender in Hong Kong during the club's close season tour. At dawn, Parlour tried to grab a cabby's attention by lobbing a bag of prawn crackers into the bonnet of the taxi. Taking exception to this, and after being punched on the nose by Parlour, Lai Pak Yan chased our Charlie Dimmock look-alike around the car with a wooden club, before Ray was finally arrested and fined by Arsenal and a Hong Kong Court. 'Witnesses' Kiwomya and Adams were apparently too pissed to remember anything.

It was, in a *Loaded* type way, highly amusing and Ray was immediately elevated to the magazine's 'platinum rogues' gallery, but the 'prawn-cracker-gate' affair was enough to show Rioch that Arsenal's problems were deep rooted and not just confined to on-pitch events. The club's reputation for being stuffed with a bunch of piss-heads was not entirely without foundation.

Clearly one of Rioch's tasks was to fumigate the stink of booze from Highbury, just as Graham needed to do in '86. Rioch's managerial background was not dissimilar to George's. He'd learnt how to manage on a shoestring at Torquay, Millwall and Middlesbrough, but he'd really made his name with first division Bolton, who'd recently been promoted to the Premiership. Gunners fans had certainly been impressed with his side's energy and passing game when they knocked us out of the FA Cup in 1994.

Smartarses claim that Rioch was never 'big enough' for the job. Despite having won the title with Derby in the '70s, he'd never played for Arsenal or served his managerial apprenticeship at Highbury - the first since Billy Wright not to have done so. This is a case of being wise after the event, as most had originally supported the club's 'new broom' philosophy. More worrying at the time were the rumours about Rioch's confrontational nature. At Torquay he'd allegedly broken a player's jaw in a training ground bust up and his 'in yer face' bollockings metered out to under-par players were legion. In short, he had a decent reputation for getting the best out of journeymen and young stars. How would he cope with seasoned pros who'd already won the lot?

Rioch began his tenure in a brisk and positive manner, trotting out in the *Evening Standard* all the statements expected from a new Arsenal boss. He spoke of 'tradition', 'the huge challenge' and, of course, the fact that 'Arsenal are the biggest club in the country'. Grateful fans also believed that Rioch had persuaded Dein to bring Platt and Bergkamp to the club. But did he? Conspiracy theories now suggest that the deals were a *fait accompli* before he'd even arrived, though Rioch denies this. The scenario was given a further twist by a rare Wenger *faux pas* in the late '90s, when he hinted to a journalist that he may have had some input into Bergkamp's signing. As with all good mysteries, his slip could be a red herring, but it's a compelling thought that if Wenger was already the *de facto* manager by June '95, then in effect Rioch was immediately relegated to the role of a caretaker.

Ominously for Bruce, Tony Adams compared the atmosphere in the Arsenal dressing room after Graham's dismissal to that of a rowdy classroom lacking discipline. Again, if the Wenger conspiracy theory is correct, Bruce must forever be seen as a hapless supply teacher, at the mercy of the class until a more respected figure arrived. Certainly, player power had increased during Houston's inter-regnum. Although 'cone man' believed that 'prawn-cracker-gate' had done for his chances of becoming Arsenal boss on a full time basis, it seemed that the damage had been done before then and the board never fancied him as George's long term successor.

Despite his growing 'personal problems', Tony Adams' influence had grown after GG's sacking and, in *Addicted*, Adams admits that he felt resentment at Rioch taking over '*my*' club'. Ian Wright's on-field petulance was also growing exponentially. Dropped by Houston at Blackburn in February, Wrighty dropped his shorts to reveal his backside to the cameras as he prepared to come on as sub. The man himself denied that it was a none-too-subtle 'kiss that' gesture to Houston, but such an act would not have occurred at GG's Arsenal.

Maybe Bruce would have done well to have read up on Vince Lombardi's advice to managers. Rioch's predecessor believed Lombardi to be a kind of 'guru' for up and coming football bosses, and the American's belief that ego and player power were the twin cancers most likely to destroy a manager was something with which Bruce soon became familiar. In short, Rioch's aim was; make Arsenal a more attractive side to watch, guide the team into a top five spot at least, allow Platt and Bergkamp to settle in, continue to strengthen the squad, and gain the respect of players and fans. Even the labours of Hercules seemed simple in comparison.

Far from being the usual tepid affairs, pre-season friendlies at places like Southend and St Albans suddenly seemed appealing. St Albans hadn't seen an invasion like it since the days of the Romans, as 4,000 Gooners descended on Hertfordshire to see the new boys in action. Bergkamp's mesmerising chip over their keeper told us that a soccer God was in our midst. Platt's torrent of goals convinced us that he was the link between midfield and attack, which we'd craved for so long. It was a smug assumption that showed just how intoxicated we were that Summer.

Before mindless optimism gave way to realism, Arsenal's Premiership season got underway amidst unbelievable hype. The first game with Middlesbrough could have sold out four times over, such was the expectation surrounding the two international superstars. The board, making their first sensible decision in years, made sure that only 20,000 season tickets were sold. They could have cashed in on the upsurge in expectation and sold about 30,000 but that would have created a Newcastle 'lock-out' type scenario where it was impossible for non-season ticket holders to gain a seat.

Recently spruced up by their sugar-daddy Chairman, newly promoted Middlesbrough arrived, ready to spoil the party. With Highbury in ferment on a glorious afternoon, Platt and Bergkamp ran into the arena, to be greeted by the Arsenal masses. The line up for the game was: Seaman, Dixon, Winterburn, Keown, Bould, Adams, Platt, Wright, Merson, Bergkamp,

Parlour. It would remain Bruce's favoured formation, save for Helder replacing Parlour on occasions. Bergkamp didn't score, although his tackling and vision again suggested that he was on a higher plane. Ex-Spur Nick Barmby gave Middlesbrough the lead before Ian Wright's thunderous header secured a slightly anti-climatic 1-1 draw. At Goodison Park three days later, Rioch's Arsenal won for the first time. Merson and Bergkamp threaded through inch-perfect passes for Wright and Platt to score the killer goals in a 2-0 victory.

Dave's trademark dash and finish from the centre of the park was a carbon copy of his England strikes, as were his finger-wagging celebrations, but the goal couldn't disguise his general lack of effectiveness in the early season encounters. 'He's not yet readjusted from Serie A', reckoned most journos, but discerning fans realised the issue was more complex than that. By the time Coventry squeezed us to death in a Highfield Road 0-0 draw, and Forest snaffled a point at Highbury, despite Platt's superb volley, the Gunners had already played four knackering games in ten days.

The team was unbeaten and the fans had seen some benefits from Bruce's more enterprising tactics. But, in truth, arses had not yet been set on fire in Rioch's Brave New World. Amidst the din of the pre-season media circus, he'd stated his aim to implement a passing game at Highbury. Outlining his plans to me in 1999, he said: 'You could break down my aims into two distinct areas. Firstly, I wanted goals to be scored from all over the pitch, rather than concentrating on one player to get them. Secondly, I wanted the ball played out skilfully from defence and knocked around in midfield - with less reliance on balls over the top. It would be difficult because the players had to get used to it. I hoped that, as disciplined pros, they would just get on with the job'. His plans were likely to push several noses (and one in particular) out of joint and, if fully implemented, would result in a large turnover of players. The new boss was linked strongly with his Bolton protégé Jason McAteer who, it was hoped, would inject extra pace in midfield and out wide. Indeed, Rioch's main problem remained in midfield.

For all his boy-scout earnestness, Platt was certainly not the solution to the dearth of creativity in that area. Aside from his goals, the situation actually seemed to have worsened since the previous season. Davis and Schwarz had departed and, in those pre-Wenger days, Ray Parlour remained ineffective in many games, seemingly more interested in pizza toppings and booze. Rioch's early midfields were a hotchpotch of journeymen and attackers/midfielders playing out of position. The typical midfield was: Platt,

Keown and Merson. Hillier or Jensen would fill in if injury dictated, though at least Bruce marked Jensen's cards by giving his shirt number to Platt.

Not only was Rioch frustrated in his attempts to fully develop the passing game, it meant that Platt was already made a scapegoat. An early season edition of *One Nil Down* informed him that it was 'time to deliver'. This was perhaps a tad unfair, but if Platty truly was the 'best of British', then no wonder Wenger plundered French hypermarkets for his midfield produce. The limitations within Platt's all round-game were alarming; an inability to pass or tackle effectively and a frightening tendency to drift out of games. In that respect, he was no different from the rest of the midfield - but this was *David Platt*, England's saviour on so many occasions.

In hindsight, he was the right signing at the wrong time. Platt had always flourished in teams with a lone striker, or where the strikers weren't of the highest quality. His trademark 'late gallops' meant that he was at his best playing in the 'hole' between attack and midfield. The problem was that Bergkamp also functioned best in a slightly deeper role. In those early games, with Paul Merson pushing up from midfield, the hole was too crowded. It was an issue which Rioch never fully addressed. Some reckoned he'd have been better off playing Wright and John Hartson up front, and simply dropping either Dennis or Platty - leaving one player in the hole. Another school of thought suggested that Inter Milan's Paul Ince, a more defensive midfielder, would have been a preferable acquisition to Platt. Arsenal would be strongly linked with Wrighty's best mate, but Bruce probably realised that he was having enough trouble dealing with one monumental ego, and didn't need two 'guv'nors' on the same patch. As for the issue of Hartson - Bruce never fancied him much as a player anyway. Platt temporarily resolved the problem by sustaining an early season knee injury. Little did we know that his two month absence would enable Rioch to stumble upon a more dynamic formation.

After two consecutive draws, the lads squeaked a 1-0 win at bottom of the table Manchester City. It was a dreadful game, enlivened by Eddie McGoldrick's hilarious display as a sub. Showing his usual poise in his final game for the club, it prompted Jimmy Armfield to comment on Radio Five Live that 'you have to laugh otherwise you'd cry'. Eddie had recently told a *Times* journalist that he 'wouldn't cross the road to spit on an Arsenal fan', such was the mutual respect between us. I bet he'd have missed, even if he'd tried, though. Not even Wrighty's last minute winner at Maine Road, complete with his high kicking celebrations after Bergkamp's cross, could disguise the fact that the Dutchman hadn't yet scored after five games. The memories of a Charlie Nicholas type goal drought flooded back, and Bergkamp seemed set to be axed from the team.

Matters came to a head when he didn't score against Hartlepool in the first leg of the Worthington Cup third round. Dennis set up a couple of goals for Tony Adams, just like he had for Wright at Maine Road, but that cut no ice with the tabloids. *The Mirror* labelled him a 'Hartlefool' and added 'Bergy can't even score against 10 men'. Fanzines also fretted about his lack of goals and *One Nil Down*, bemoaning the number of high balls which flew over his head, advocated a 'no flying zone' around him. Dennis obviously took this too literally!!

After ninety minutes of a thrilling 4-2 victory against Southampton, he answered his critics in the most imperious way. Rioch decided to reintroduce Glenn Helder to the team in order to get more width. Shorn of his Lionel Richie locks, Helder played a blinder. Suddenly, Rioch's 'passing plans' began to take shape. Early in the first half, Helder tore down the left, crossed, and Bergkamp cracked in a right foot volley. Highbury rose to his majesty, and the Dutchman's confidence visibly surged after this rush. The game seesawed with Bergkamp as the pivot. Adams and Wright nudged us ahead of the Saints before Dennis delivered the most exhilarating *coup de grace*. Cutting inside Monkou, he unleashed a mortar shell from thirty yards, which cannoned in off the post. The scorer thanked the gods and punched the air in delight. Saluting him, the North Bank realised that a Highbury legend was born.

The team hit peak form in mid autumn. Lee Dixon and Nigel Winterburn, having virtually been consigned to the knackers' yard by George, started to rediscover their best form. The sight of the pair bombing up and down the wing once again proved that George had made another grave error of judgement at the end of his reign. Players appeared to grow more comfortable with the new tactics and results and games, at times, were sensational. After Sheffield Wednesday's Chris Waddle pulverised Arsenal for thirty minutes, Dennis' curling free kick pulled us back into the game. His sumptuous backheel fed Winterburn for the equaliser and, later on, Rioch threw on subs Dickov and Hartson, with the game delicately poised at 2-2. Both scored excellent goals to give us a 4-2 win and put us third in the league behind Newcastle and Manchester United.

The loathsome Mancs cruised into Highbury in early October. Oozing arrogance, Cantona, Giggs and Cole darted menacingly around the Arsenal penalty areas. Naturally, the Arsenal reject missed a hatful of chances before

Bergkamp stole in behind Irwin and slipped the ball past Schmeichel. In a stupendous rearguard action, George's classic 'back five' formation stood firm. *The Sun's* Martin Samuel compared Steve Bould's display with a Ronald Koeman performance and Nigel Winterburn's last ditch tackles foiled Scholes twice. United inevitably lapsed into sulk mode and only their red nosed Danish goalie kept the scoreline down to 1-0. It was a miracle that he found the time to make his spectacular saves from Wright and Hartson, as he spent most of the second half calling Steve Bruce 'a lazy, blind fucker', much to the Clock End's amusement.

Arguably, the best performance of all was the 3-0 demolition of Leeds at Elland Road. Paul Merson walloped in the opener past a stranded Lukic and then proceeded to lead Carlton Palmer a merry dance for the remainder of the game. The Gunners' other goals were both of the highest quality. Bergkamp's instinct and sorcery enabled him to flick home Bould's header, and Ian Wright's masterful chip simply took the breath away. Equally as encouraging, too, was the up-beat manner of defeats at Bolton and Spurs; bizarre but true. All travelling away fans knew that both results were a travesty of justice. The everlasting vision of Bergkamp's goal at White Hart Lane still stirs the soul, coming as it did after a breathtaking move which snaked across the pitch. It put into perspective Alan Sugar's decrying our signing of Bergkamp as 'cosmetic padding'. Embittered after Klinsmann scarpered back to Germany, Sugar reckoned signing 'Carlos kickaballs' was destroying the game. For all Tottenham's pretensions to being London's glamour club, the real foreign talent now headed to Highbury. Only the Gunners were capable of keeping the Catherine Zeta Jones type players. They would forever be lumbered with the Anne Widdecombes. Any flirtations they had with big names would inevitably leave them broken hearted. Spurs fought back to win, but such was our first half domination that only the most dim witted of their fans actually believed their side deserved victory.

At Bolton, the Gunners had nine clear attempts on goal. Wrighty and Winterburn scraped the post and Helder was denied twice at point blank range. Yet John McGinlay's solitary goal was enough to win the game for them. Before anyone gets the impression that ill fortune was wrecking progress on the pitch, though, it's as well to remember that Mark Bosnich put two chances on a plate for Wright and Merson in the 2-0 win over Aston Villa, which kept the Gunners in third place.

If Rioch was looking for good omens, then he must also have been delighted with the team's progress in the Coca-Cola Cup. George won it in his first season at Highbury and, judging by the early round romps, Bruce seemed set for a repeat. Bergkamp and Wright battered Hartlepool at Highbury. In a truly awesome display, Bergkamp's stunning close control and quick reactions brought him two goals, and Ian Wright's clinical hat trick gave us a 9-0 aggregate win. The 'fire and the ice', as they were becoming known, would destroy better teams than Hartlepool over the next two years with their combination of burning energy and cool thinking. John Hartson, who'd not yet made a full appearance in Rioch's side, crashed in an excellent goal at home to Sheffield Wednesday in the next round, a match enlightened by Merson's brilliant second half ball juggling, which showed the extent of his rehabilitation. Two weeks later, ninety minutes of exhibition football in the pissing rain crushed Barnsley 3-0. Keown and Bould pounced for two sharply taken goals, before Dennis' rifling 25 yarder put Arsenal into the Quarter Finals.

Despite some early teething problems Rioch seemed to be creating the 'feel-good' atmosphere he'd wanted by early November. Publicly, senior pros praised the new boss, none more so than David Platt, who said that Bruce 'deeply impressed me as a person with his vision of how the game should be played'. A journalist likened Bergkamp's influence to 'watching Shakespeare, where before there had been *Carry On* films'. Trouble was looming, though - and Bruce's first major problem arose when Dennis was injured.

His hamstring strain couldn't have come at a worse time. Not only did his six-match absence show how over-reliant the team was becoming on his aura and ability to open up space for others, it also knocked the team out of its rhythm. In *The Independent*, Glen Moore described the Bergkamp-less Gunners as an 'orchestra without a conductor', and Arsenal were about to revert, temporarily, to a more primeval state. Taking the Dutchman's place was John Hartson, who hardly fitted in with Rioch's vision of the model pro. 'A player who spent too long suspended or on the treatment table', he later said. Hartson's situation demonstrated exactly how far perceptions of Arsenal had moved on over the last few months. Previously, he'd looked an excellent signing, but now, compared with the stream-lined Bergkamp, he looked cumbersome - a throwback to an 'old fashioned' target man. Admittedly, he did chip in with some useful New Year strikes but Dennis' arrival had clearly knocked the Welshman's confidence. In truth, Hartson didn't really look any better than a journeyman for the rest of his Highbury career, during which his waistline and collection of red and yellow cards grew exponentially.

Equally as concerning for Bruce were the long-term injuries sustained by Steve Bould and Tony Adams that Winter. Looking rusty and unhappy, Bould had been sent off at home to Chelsea and Adams away at Southampton. Bould was diagnosed with a career-threatening thigh injury which ruled him out for the rest of the season and, crucially, Adams sustained a long-term knee problem. After the captain's monumental performance against Manchester United, Rioch had said of him: 'When you come to a club you rely on the captain to get your message through - Tony keeps the dressing room together'. Adams' leadership qualities were crucial for team collectiveness and, interestingly, he expresses feelings of guilt in *Addicted* because he was 'not there for Bruce from Christmas onwards'. With Adams absent from the team and the dressing room, we would all feel the fall-out, none more so than Rioch himself. Indeed, four consecutive draws in November, notable only for Platt's return to the team and excellent equaliser at Villa Park, and Lee Dixon's last gasp point saver against Chelsea, gave the first hints of gathering storm clouds in Bruce's Brave New World.

The Highbury grapevine was starting to quiver about Bruce. Many fans remained unsure about the new manager and *'Brucie Rioch and his red and white army'* didn't sound as convincing as the 'Georgie Graham' version. Some claimed Rioch's dour public style had all the appeal of a '70s insurance salesman. A letter in *The Gooner* went further, stating that Rioch was actually a Scottish version of John Major. The key issue remained his refusal to sign a contract. This inevitably left him open to suspicion from supporters, who questioned his loyalty and commitment to the club. Rioch later suggested there was much more to this than meets the eye, but he was having some difficulties in the man management department. There had been the public flash of temper from Ian Wright when he was subbed against Manchester United (he'd refused to shake Rioch's hand), and a 'mole' spread rumours that Bruce had gone 'ape-shit' at Wright after a couple of games. Already, Rioch was becoming isolated from the directors and was virtually resident out at London Colney.

One consolation for him was Paul Merson's majestic destruction of QPR on Boxing Day. His first, a cracking volley and his second, a slithering dribble past their goalie, added to Wright's opener and gave us a 3-0 win. Merse presented us with a delicious Christmas gift, but Arsenal's overall progress was more fraught than being stuck with the in-laws for two weeks. Robbie Fowler, with his by now bog standard hat-trick, destroyed us at Anfield and not even a fit-again Bergkamp could stop us being shat on 3-1 by

Wimbledon. Robbie Earle gave Martin Keown a torrid afternoon and new boy Adrian Clarke, who'd looked good on Boxing Day, was taught a painful lesson by Vinnie Jones. Poor Adrian, his confidence knocked, would only surface twice more in the first team before he was flogged to Wycombe.

The excrement really hit the fan after a highly embarrassing FA Cup third round exit against Sheffield United. As raw and unlikeable as Wimbledon, they fought like dervishes at Highbury before winning 1-0 in the replay. Such a spineless performance, reminiscent of the Millwall debacle a year before, led Bruce to lambaste the team publicly in the press afterwards. He even spoke curtly in the normally ultra bland manager's notes, saying 'The skipper played with the determination he always shows. I wish everyone had followed his example'. A year later, it emerged that he and Ian Wright had had a heated *tête-à-tête* in the dressing room at half time. No doubt the board quickened their knife sharpening in the background when they heard of this altercation.

With faint title hopes destroyed, Bruce's route to salvation appeared to lie in the Coca Cola Cup. His predecessor found the competition to be a way out of various holes and so attentions now turned to the Quarter Final. The thought of a mouth-watering tie with Keegan's league leaders, Newcastle, was enough to draw a screaming 38,000 crowd to Highbury. Dripping with expensive ornaments, like Asprilla and Ferdinand, they were brilliant but crucially, highly-strung. The tie turned out to be one of the most memorable matches of the '90s. Inspired by Ginola, the Geordies came with the intention of dazzling our grizzled old defence with their skills. Lee Dixon, John Jensen and Nigel Winterburn had other ideas. Dixon, in particular, adopted Peter Storey's persona for the evening and subjected the Frenchman to several, rumbustuous challenges. Within five minutes, Ginola was booted into touch by Dixon and ended up on the lap of a startled Junior Gunner in the front row of the West Stand. Early in the second half, he was back in the dressing room, sent packing by the referee after elbowing Dixon in the chops.

It was one of those Highbury evenings where Ian Wright was simply inspired. His energy and searing pace set the stadium alight. Admittedly, Sir-nicek should have kept his first half volley out, but Wrighty's classic flying header late on from Helder's cross was as close to symmetrical perfection as you can get, especially if you were seated in the North Bank directly behind the goal. The post stopped him from grabbing a hat trick and Bergkamp deserved a third. Arsenal had secured a magnificent 2-0 win in a savage atmosphere and, to complete the entertainment, there was a hugely amusing bust up between Rioch and *Brookside* Scally Terry McDermott on the touchline. Underwhelmed by his lack of charisma on T.V. interviews, some were convinced that, maybe, Bruce had the stomach for a fight after all.

Having tiptoed through the minefield into the Coca Cola Cup semi-final, the team slowly pulled itself out of the Winter rut to put together a decent run in the league. Losing just three more times before the end of the season, from January onwards, travelling fans witnessed some excellent performances. Dennis Bergkamp, now fully fit once more, plundered a cerebral winner at Forest and John Hartson, replacing the suspended Ian Wright, savaged West Ham all afternoon at Upton Park. He also grabbed the winner just to prove his point to Bruce. One of the reasons for these victories was that Rioch's bold new 3-5-2 formation helped the team overcome the absence of Bould and Adams. Martin Keown was finally moved back into central defence alongside Andy Linighan and Scott Marshall, while the two full backs were free to masquerade as 'wing halfs'. It was only a temporary measure - but the tactics continued to reap dividends. John Hartson's double against Manchester City, including a spectacular dipping forty yard volley, put us two goals ahead but the delicious finale was provided by Lee Dixon. Receiving Bergkamp's superlative pass, he latched onto the ball and drove it low past Immel to give us a 3-1 win. A week later at Selhurst Park, Nigel Winterburn's cracker sent us on the way and even David Platt silenced his boo boys with a goal in a resounding 3-0 away win.

For a display of top attacking footie though, the Riverside Stadium in Middlesbrough was the only place to be. Juninho, 'Boro's supremely talented Brazilian midget, gave us the run around in the first half and threatened to run riot, but Merson and Platt nudged Arsenal ahead before Glenn Helder cracked in his first (and last) Gunners' goal to give us a thrilling 3-2 victory. Despite his occasional flashes of brilliance, though, Helder was clearly not the long-term solution to the team's lack of width. His masterful early displays - given extra spice by the 'Helder shuffle', duped us into believing that Graham's last signing was Limpar's worthy successor. But Premiership defenders discovered - in Seaman's words, that he was a 'one trick pony', which his often woeful application and crossing proved. Still, as we'd seen with Kiwomya and Carter, every dog has its day. It didn't stop Helder becoming the latest victim of Highbury's boo boys though, particularly now that the previously maligned Keown's excellent performances were starting to attract rave reviews from fans and press alike.

Martin Keown's second spell at Highbury, which began in early '93, appeared to be headed for disaster. Asked to play in a variety of positions by successive managers, one of Highbury's own sons seemed in danger of being told to bugger off for a second time. Famously, back in '86 Keown, who'd emerged during the dark days of the Howe and Cartwright regime, had unwisely asked George Graham for an extra £50 a week; no clues needed as to what George told him he could do. This time though, angry fans seemed set to drive Martin away, rather than a wrathful manager. Under Rioch, Keown was originally forced to perform in midfield. At first, he looked totally unsuited to the role. He moved like a crab, and frequently shuffled sideways to little effect. Most damningly, he was prone to panicking and stumbling over the ball. Occasionally, as a last resort, he'd hoof the ball forward. High kicking like a can-can dancer, he'd shout to the strikers 'get on the end of that', as the orb ended up in the stand. Booing Martin in the mid '90s was as monotonous a Highbury event as the DJ playing *Eighteen Til I Die* before games. The Keown renaissance began when, still in his midfield role, he saw fit to begin nutmeging his midfield opponents, one of them a very pissed off Roy Keane. Keown's control began to improve and his pacy runs started to trouble the opposition.

Still, it took a decent run in central defence to fully restore fans' confidence in him. The Keown of old returned and his sharp, combative approach blunted several team's attacks in the New Year. Rioch later admitted: 'Martin wasn't a midfielder, and I remember that fans had a real go at him at times. But, in the long-term, I think it improved his all round game. It helped his distribution and it helped his awareness across the pitch. At the time, it was a case of 'needs must', I'm afraid'. Football fans don't always mind being proved wrong and it was a pleasure to see Keown's confidence surge in the New Year. Appointed captain for the first time at Forest, his excellent form later helped him win the Supporters 'Player of the Year' award. Of course under Wenger, Keown would become even more vital to Arsenal's cause. By then his scuttling style caught the eye for the right reasons - as did his red boots.

But, in early '96, the highest compliment you could pay him was that he did an excellent job replacing Adams and Bould. Finally he was even granted his own chant. *'Boom, boom, boom, let me hear you say Keown-own-own'*, sang the away end at Upton Park, to the tune of a dance classic of the day. By now, most of us belatedly realised, that despite his six year stint at Villa and Everton, he really was an Arsenal man to the core. He also spoke positively about Rioch's influence at Arsenal, but not even the acting captain's support could save his boss from approaching disaster.

Conspiracy theories aside, the events of late February and early March finally did for Rioch, some five months before he finally departed. Two goals up at home against Aston Villa in the first leg of the Coca-Cola Cup Semi-final, Bruce's team seemed to be cruising towards Wembley. Bergkamp's two Highbury goals, the first a raking thirty yarder, the second a delicious finish, elevated him to footballing valhalla. Then, inexplicably, the lead was lost. Dwight Yorke and Savo Milosevic punished some lousy defending to make it 2-2, and but for David Seaman's excellent stop from Dwight Yorke, Villa could have won the match. The Midlanders had the best defensive record in the country and, in the second leg, they squeezed us so hard the pips squeaked. Man of the match Paul Merson's raids down the wing came to nothing, particularly as Gareth Southgate marked Bergkamp so tightly, you'd have thought they were fused at the hip. After a few near things, Nigel Winterburn's crunching left footer hit the post and flew behind. The game ended 0-0 and the Gunners were out on away goals. Rioch cursed his luck - after all, the team hadn't actually lost a game. If Winterburn's shot had been a couple of inches to the left, we'd have been at Wembley to face an impotent Leeds United, where Bruce would surely have emulated GG by lifting the trophy in his first season. Upon such small distances hinge managerial careers.

Ten days later Ian Wright handed in a transfer request. In *The People* he cited the fact that 'the boss has different ideas from me on how the game should be played'. Years later in *The Sun*, though, he went public and said that 'Rioch labelled me as a Charlie big potatoes'. Ostensibly Wright was unhappy with Rioch's new passing style. He admitted in *Inside Wright* that he was used to thriving on service which was 'direct and over the top'. Wright realised that there was no place for such directness in the new system. And no doubt, the fact that Graham's 'pet' was now treated as just another player also knocked his confidence. Another damaging exposé against Rioch came when John Hartson went public and claimed that the boss 'treated me like a dog'. (Well, if you *will* urinate against trees after a few beers, what do you expect?) Both Wright and Hartson hinted that Rioch wasn't a good listener, despite Rioch's early pledge that 'I'm not one for a give 'em hell approach'. The fall out from Wright's transfer request was felt immediately. An anonymous director, delivering what was effectively the *coup de grace* on Bruce's authority, allegedly said to Wright 'you are going nowhere'.

Unwisely, Bruce had allowed a damaging personality clash to fester with the club's star player. Most fans seemed to agree with the Highbury director, though more circumspect writers on *One Nil Down* suggested that Wright's time at the club should come to an end. They suggested that his insatiable hunger for the ball had sapped Hartson and Helder's confidence (though he didn't 'bully' Bergkamp did he?) and that, in order to fully revamp the side, Wright would have to be sacrificed. But as Tony Willis warned in his editorial column, Bruce was the man who was unlikely to survive these public bust-ups. Willis commented that: 'it is a tough character who alienates his senior players and the *de facto* chairman and still comes out on top'.

But as Arsenal cruised towards the pre-season target of a UEFA Cup place, Ian Wright poached two goals in our 2-1 win over Leeds, and a week later, he helped destroy Newcastle's title ambitions. Scott Marshall's only ever Arsenal goal gave us the lead; the young Scot's excellent end of season form in central defence already led some to dub him as Tony Adams' long-term replacement. Wrighty's cheeky chip over Sirnicek resulted in a 2-0 win over the Geordies.

With Spurs, Blackburn and Everton breathing down our necks, Arsenal went into the last game of the season aware that only a win over Bolton would guarantee a UEFA Cup spot. In truth, three straight draws in the league and a defeat at Hillsborough, where Helder was booed off the park by travelling Gunners to a chorus of 'you're not fit to wear the shirt', meant that we'd almost blown it but, heh, who wants an easy life anyway? The Bolton match spoke volumes for the state of Rioch's Arsenal. Ian Wright, only semi fit after a hamstring injury, sported a bloody silly peroxide blond haircut, stomped around ineffectually for an hour, and went off in a huff when Rioch subbed him, refusing to shake the manager's hand.

In the meantime, long since relegated Bolton went 1-0 up and clung onto their until the 86th minute. It was akin to being constipated; we repeatedly threatened to crap on Bolton but some painful blockage meant that we were left howling in frustration. Aptly, Dennis Bergkamp was the key to salvation. After eighty six minutes, he controlled a ball in the area, layed it back and David Platt thumped in the equaliser. The guy in the Clock End who'd gained notoriety throughout the season for shouting 'earn your money, Platt' was temporarily silenced. Dave had come good, in the nick of time. We'd forgive him everything if his goal got us into Europe, but Spurs were doing well up at Newcastle and could still pip us to the place.

With two minutes left, Bolton were finally killed off. Platt, with fire in his belly at last, threaded through the ball to Dennis Bergkamp. The Bergmeister controlled the pass in an instant and rolled the ball forward. In a flash, he'd delivered the most scorching of thirty-yard winners. Highbury was virtually incinerated in a burning frenzy of celebration. Dennis had indeed delivered and all that pre-season hype was not misplaced. Arsenal were back in Europe.

At the final whistle, Rioch and Ian Wright walked around the pitch, applauding the crowd, with their arms around each other's shoulders. It was a bizarre embrace on Wrighty's part, particularly in light of what had happened 45 minutes earlier. It was probably as genuine and heartfelt as Tony Blair sending Ken Livingstone a 'Good luck in your new job' card after he'd won the Mayor of London election. At a basic level, Rioch had fulfilled our expectations. He'd begun to rebuild the shambles that George had left and, for the most part, improved the aesthetic quality of the team. Doubts remained, though, especially because he was still refusing to sign a contract. Wright later said to a pressman: 'Here I stay. I've patched up my differences with Bruce'. But that image of the two men embracing remained a strange vision for watching fans. The obligatory *'Ian Wright, Wright, Wright'* chant boomed out, interspersed with blasts of *'Brucie Rioch and his red and white army'* ringing around the stadium. In hindsight, maybe, *'This Town Ain't Big Enough For Both Of Us'* would have been a more suitable chant.

The Bergmeister arrives

7

Wenger's Arsenal

It is a shame that Nick Hornby's *Fever Pitch*, the angst-ridden account of an Arsenal fan's life, was concluded in 1992. Just consider the bizarre material Hornby could have used if he'd included the events of season '96/97, and its preceding close season.

While the rest of the country basked in Euro '96 mania, sang Skinner and Baddiel's *Three Lions* to its heart's content, and pissed blokes everywhere copied Gazza's dentist's chair antics, Arsenal fans were becoming more animated about the club's embarrassing failure to sign any of the *glitterati* on show in the Championships. Tony Adams, who'd earned rave reviews as England Captain, along with penalty stopper *non pareil* David Seaman, embarked on a three week bender, where he finally crossed the line between heavy drinking and alcoholism. What is more, we were mightily annoyed with the timing of Bruce Rioch's sudden sacking (two weeks before the new season began, and a matter of days after he'd finally signed his contract) and the subsequent lack of information from directors on what really happened.

Of course, just as Arsenal once again became a national laughing stock, along with John Major, a miracle happened; new manager Arsène Wenger introduced a revolutionary continental playing style to Highbury. In some ways the season's upheavals were not surprising. After all, cruising comfortably down the easy route has never been our *forte*. We'd rather scramble up treacherous tracks with red danger signs all along the route. Such is the Faustian lot of a Gunners' fan.

After Rioch's dismissal, the choruses of 'we told you so', from the anti-Bruce faction were deafening. They reiterated the fact that he'd come and gone an outsider, never effectively able to come to terms with the aura and expectation surrounding a mighty club like the Arsenal. An oft used phrase at the time was that 'while Bruce had left Bolton, the Wanderers had not left Rioch'. It was reported that he held up his former protégés, like Alan Stubbs, as examples of professionalism to the likes of Lee Dixon, who had won the lot. Tellingly, Ian Wright later said of Rioch: 'There he was, a manager who'd never been in the top flight, put in charge of a dressing room full of internationals'. Some of Wright's team mates seemed to agree that Rioch was more suited to working at a smaller club. And just like that other 'outsider' Billy Wright, who'd been sacked almost exactly thirty years before by Arsenal during the '66 World Cup, Bruce was dismissed at a time when optimism surrounding English football had never been higher.

His detractors also highlight the stories about his man-management techniques, which became more exaggerated with the passing of time. A bawler and a shouter, he was said to be fond of throwing cups and plastic bottles around the dressing room. On one occasion at Blackburn, Rioch booted over a whole water dispenser and flooded his player's feet. But it was the problem of communication which continually dogged him. 'Eyeballing' his players, screaming and virtually spitting in their faces was one of Bruce's habits. As David Seaman pointed out in *Safe Hands*, managers simply can't treat highly paid pros like that anymore. Such an outmoded approach created an image that he was out of his depth at Highbury. An exasperated Rioch once claimed that he 'felt like Marje Proops' when dealing with the myriad of personal problems in the Highbury dressing room. But that was the reality of the situation at the club in '95, and counselling skills were a prerequisite if he was to be successful. Players' personal demons needed to be exorcised, egos needed massaging and fragile confidence had to be boosted. Bruce wasn't always successful in meeting these challenges, although Merson and Adams still speak highly of him.

He was sacked on August 12th, a couple of weeks after finally signing his contract. His delay over putting pen to paper annoyed many fans and led the board, as was mentioned at the AGM, to 'question his motives'. In *One Nil Down*, Tony Willis had been predicting for months that he would only last a season at Highbury. Indeed, Rioch's impending death warrant seemed to be about the worst kept secret in London. William Hill had noticed a sudden flurry of bets on his imminent departure. Realising there had been a serious leak (I wonder where that started) and that several punters had access to important information, they closed the book.

At the time, it seemed that the failure to add to the squad cost him his job. Bruce had drawn up the most mouth-watering list of potential summer signings, 'nominating' somewhere in the region of thirty players. These included the de Boer twins, Lee Bowyer, Tim Sherwood, Gary McAllister,

Edgar Davids, Alan Shearer, George Weah and, er, John Lukic. Only Johnny arrived on a free transfer from Leeds. It was nice to see him back and everything, but it was like going shopping to Harrods Food Hall and coming back with a tin of baked beans. The rest were lost in the murky 'Bermuda triangle' area between David Dein and the manager. This came at a time when Arsenal were roasted in all but one of their pre-season friendlies, losing even to the mighty Rushden & Diamonds. Ironically, though, it was David Dein who was jeered by fans after a defeat in Florence, not Bruce. Such insults were not forgotten by Dein; hell hath no fury like a vice-Chairman booed, apparently. Peter Hill-Wood later commented that 'Bruce gave us a list of players but you cannot sign world-class players if their clubs won't sell. In a way, it was an impossible task that he set us'. Pete conveniently forgot that Shearer, Bowyer, McAllister and Zidane did all move on that summer. At the September AGM, it was alleged that Dein had asked Rioch several times about whether he wanted to sign Davids - but Bruce apparently dallied for too long and the chance was gone. Allegedly, this had happened before and according to one of Dein's cronies, the vice-chairman was 'fed up with being made to look a c**t around Europe'. Although the lack of transfer activity speeded up Rioch's departure, the die had long been cast.

In reality, Bruce never stood a chance as Arsenal boss. Even if Wenger wasn't yet destined for Highbury in '95, Rioch lacked the vital ingredient needed by any Highbury manager in the '90s - advanced political skills. As Joe Lovejoy wrote in *The Independent*, 'the skulduggery which brought Graham down meant that Rioch took over a job with very different parameters to that of any of his English counterparts'. To paraphrase Tommy Doc: 'Henry Kissinger wouldn't have lasted 24 hours at Arsenal', such was the intrigue behind the scenes after the Graham affair. The Scot was an experienced manager but, as a stubborn disciplinarian who believed in rigid ethics, he was always going to clash with smooth businessman David Dein - one of the football world's foremost politicians. Rioch's annoyance that Dein was meddling too much in team affairs is nothing new. Terry Neill and George Graham have said exactly the same thing in their autobiographies.

Rioch's undiplomatic approach meant that his relationship with Ian Wright was a fraught one - 'Ian probably felt disappointed that I'd shouted at him. Looking back, both of us are probably disappointed', he later told me. As our top scorer, Wright had powerful allies within the club and his 'let's suck up to David Dein' article after Rioch's departure, was seriously vomit inducing. In it, Wright confirmed that the decision to sack Rioch was the correct one. And would anyone else but Wrighty have got away with such petulant behaviour towards the end of the previous season? His dash onto the pitch after the Bolton match (in which he hadn't even played the last 45 minutes), stole Bergkamp's rightful thunder. Wright has carried out several hatchet jobs on his ex-manager - notably in Amy Lawrence's *Proud To Say That Name* and his revised version of *Mr Wright*. He also let it be known that he nicknamed Rioch 'Dagenham', because he was only a couple of stops short of Barking.

Since his sacking, Rioch has kept his counsel over his one-year reign at Highbury. He agreed to discuss with me the events surrounding his dismissal: 'I don't agree when people say that I wasn't up to the challenge of managing Arsenal. I don't think that it's necessary to have played for them to realise the stature of the club. I'd won the title with Derby in the '70s and had played for Everton and Villa, so I was used to pressure with big clubs. And, with Bolton, I was used to handling Cup matches against the likes of Everton, Liverpool and, of course, Arsenal.

There's been a lot said about my refusal to sign a contract. The facts are these; I joined the club in June '95 and verbally agreed terms with the board. On October 28th - that's four months later, I was presented with a draft copy. Four months is a long time to wait and already I was thinking - 'This isn't quite right.'. I was then given an amended copy in January. Another three months gone. Then I was told things like 'the Chairman's in Scotland' and 'he can't sign it yet'. This kind of stalling made me feel uneasy. I think it would make anyone feel uneasy. So the situation dragged on. I couldn't win at Arsenal. Quite simply, I discovered they'd always wanted Wenger, even before I became manager. David Dein had been talking to him and they were good friends. Even Peter Hill-Wood admitted that they'd spoken to him while I was still manager (Hill-Wood later admitted this at the AGM in August '96). The problem was that he was under contract in Japan, so Arsenal had to wait for another year. But for me, it was always just a matter of time'.

Bruce Rioch, speaking in 1999

Arguably, Bruce was the right man in the wrong decade. If he'd been appointed boss ten years earlier, his brand of discipline and emphasis on the passing game would have reaped dividends. But, ten years later, top flight footie had changed beyond recognition. Certainly, he did not possess a wealth of foreign contacts (an essential '90s attribute for a top Premiership boss), or speak a host of foreign languages. Fittingly, for someone whose managerial reign still remains such a mystery, Rioch has not produced an exposé autobiography. On the official Arsenal video - The Wonder Years, Alan Davies described him as 'a man who many people have forgot (sic) was ever in charge', meaning that the club is happy to pretend he never existed. He lacked the flair and subtlety to have taken Arsenal to Wenger-type heights, but his achievements were considerable.

He began to implement the passing game, which ultimately made Arsène Wenger's job easier, and he was able to give constructive advice to Paul Merson and Tony Adams when they needed it. Neither of these accomplishments are mean achievements. Even his belief that Arsenal would not realistically challenge for another title with Wright in the side ('a fantastic goal-scorer - but it's a team game') was one shared by other players. But here's the rub; within a few weeks, we'd virtually forgotten about Bruce anyway, and once his goals began to flow again, most forgave Ian Wright for his show-boating at the end of the previous season. Footie fans reckon that bosses and directors are cold hearted - we can be the most amoral and unsentimental of all when the club's welfare is at stake.

Johan Cruyff, Bobby Robson and Arsène Wenger were Arsenal's principal managerial targets that Summer. There was even a vocal 'we want George' lobby amongst more lunatic Arsenal fans. Presumably, this group also sympathised with the 'bring back Maggie' faction in the Tory Party. In the farcical 'interregnum', the redoubtable Stewart Houston was again appointed caretaker manager. Poor Coneman - forever the Prince Regent, never the King. Cruyff's reputation for being 'difficult', together with a heart condition, eventually ruled him out. The club, in yet another p.r. balls-up, refused to confirm that hot favourite Wenger was taking over in October, even when two French midfielders, Remi Garde and Patrick Vieira, arrived just after Rioch departed. How dim did the board think we were? Only someone of Gazza like intelligence could have failed to spot the obvious French connection.

A midst the chaos, the Premiership campaign began on August 17th. The players unveiled our new home kit - the coolest design of the '90s, but for a while, it seemed like that was the only thing which would go according to plan. A combination of knee injuries and the 'drying out' process kept Tony Adams on the sidelines. Platt was already out for a month and Ian Wright's troublesome hamstring injury sidelined him too. Vieira and Garde didn't appear either. Patrick had a knee injury and Garde had apparently ricked his back on the aeroplane travelling to England. It hardly inspired confidence, but it was eventually a pleasure to be proved wrong about £3.5m signing Vieira. Garde, on the other hand, would make even Darren Anderton look super fit.

Still, one only had to look at opponents West Ham to feel rather better about things. Their two big foreign Summer signings had already vanished. Paulo Futre stormed off in a taxi because he wasn't given his favourite number 9 shirt by Harry Redknapp, and Marco Boogers proved he was a modern day Lord Lucan by doing a runner and hiding in a caravan. The game was a cruise and eased our nerves, despite the fact that Ray Parlour and Steve Morrow were the Gunners' only available midfielders. Dennis Bergkamp was head and shoulders above the rest, and he cracked home a penalty. John Hartson, playing as Bergkamp's striking partner, thumped in our second to give us a routine 2-0 win. We then travelled up to our version of Room 101 - Anfield, to suffer an inevitable 2-0 defeat to Liverpool, despite some decent build-up play.

Newly promoted Leicester were beaten 2-0 at Filbert Street, despite Emile Heskey testing Seaman on several occasions. Dave received a rapturous round of applause from the fans after each brilliant save. After his Euro '96 heroics, Seaman had proved even more popular than Cliff when he appeared in the Royal Box at the Wimbledon Championships - though luckily he didn't try to sing *Congratulations*. Dennis Bergkamp scored another penalty after Steve Walsh's rugby tackle, and late substitute Wrighty sealed it with a tap-in after Winterburn had harried Kasey Keller into a mistake. For now, Houston decided to persist with the three at the back policy employed by Rioch. The system didn't always function too well early in the season. Of Keown, Linighan and Bould, only Martin had the pace to cope with the nippy forwards we faced. All three were given some terrible roastings at the end of September, not helped by the fact that a rusty John Lukic was brought in to replace the crocked David Seaman.

Defensive frailties made for some stunning matches, though. After all, what option had we but to attack? The red-hot clash with Chelsea's foreign legion was arguably the best of the season. Vialli and Le Boeuf put them 2-0 up, helped by Johnny's slippery fingers and Bouldy's early season clumsiness. Paul Merson's stinging shot just before half time began the fightback, and Martin Keown's goal levelled the scores. With cries of *'Coneman, bring him on'* ringing out, Stewart Houston finally deemed it appropriate to introduce Wrighty, who lobbed us into an incredible 3-2 lead with five minutes left. Cue white heat at Highbury. Two minutes into injury time, that Dickensian street urchin Dennis Wise pick-pocketed Chelsea a point, after Lukic again remained glued to his line. It had been a six-goal thriller but despite all their ridiculous pretensions to being London's top club, the Kings Road tarts wouldn't beat us for the rest of the decade. Two goals down at Villa to sulky Serb Milosevic's double, the boys launched another epic comeback. Paul Merson's excellent header gave us hope and, in the ninety first minute, with 35,000 Brummies shrieking for the final whistle, Andy Linighan's delicate header snaffled us another point. Merson's excellence was such that, in *The Independent*, Ken Jones led the calls for him to be restored to the England team.

Coneman resigned two days after this draw, fully aware that he'd never become Gunners' boss, and he accepted the managerial post at QPR. His reign at Loftus Road was unsuccessful, but he mysteriously appointed Rioch as his number two and did us all a few favours by buying several of our unwanted reserves. Nice one Stewart. Houston's departure came at a time when the board was still prevaricating over the likelihood of Wenger's arrival. In the meantime, youth team boss Pat Rice was appointed caretaker manager II. Rice was, in effect, our fourth boss in eighteen months. With a record like that, anyone would think that we were actually trying to outdo Manchester City.

September's AGM promised to be about as enjoyable an experience for the board as the recent Tory Party conference had been for John Major and his cronies. When Friar, Hill-Wood, Dein and Fiszman filed into the room, they approached the platform with all the joy of prisoners going to the electric chair. They were well aware that angry shareholders had some fairly direct questions to ask about the leadership of the club, and what really was happening regarding the manager's position.

The 'gang of four' stuck rigidly to the party line. Hill-Wood said little about the Rioch affair, other than giving a slight variation of the banal claptrap which appeared in the club programme. He did admit, however, to talking to Wenger before Rioch got the sack, and that 'communication' problems had done for Bruce. Other than that, Nigel Hawthorne's character in *Yes, Minister*, Sir Humphrey Appleby, would have been delighted at how little the officials actually said at the meeting.

The biggest mystery of all, though, continued to surround major shareholder Daniel Fiszman. Officially, he controlled 33% of the club's shares, but it was announced that he and Dein had 'shared interests' in 7,176 shares. In effect, Fiszman now owned 45% of the club's shares. Peter Hill-Wood on the other hand, owned only 0.86%, but he was still the mouthpiece for the club. Fiszman, we were told, had 'interests' in the diamond trade and, with all the focus on other clubs' sugar daddies at the time, fans wanted to know if he was about to pump some of his fortune into the club *a la* Jack Walker. Judging from the club's inactivity in the transfer market, a fresh injection of cash was urgently required. Fiszman demurred from saying anything at the meeting and opted not to comment on the nature of his arrangement with Dein. By doing that, it simply led fans to question his motives for joining the board and to wonder what the future direction of the club really was. At a time when effective communication between the board and fans was paramount, the meeting inevitably threw up more questions than answers - most of which have remained unanswered to this day.

Despite the never ending waffle, the board finally confirmed that Wenger would be joining in late September. In the meantime, he had to forward his directives to Pat Rice from Japan, where his contract at Grampus Eight had another few weeks to run. He addressed the crowd in 'big brother' style on the Jumbotron screen before the Sheffield Wednesday match. It was hardly an 'up and at 'em' Churchillian-type speech, more an indecipherable Marlon Brando drawl. The acoustics were so poor that about the only thing we could understand was 'let's win tonight'.

For forty-five minutes, table topping Wednesday played Arsenal off the park and went 1-0 up. Five minutes into the second half, big brother Arsène, watching via the internet, told Rice to send on the terminator. Patrick Vieira, all six foot three of him, replaced Ray Parlour. Immediately, we saw that a prototype of the new-age midfielder had indeed been sent back from the 21st century. Vieira's awesome physical presence and short, accurate passing, induced terror into Wednesday's previously well organised ranks. He simply controlled the centre of the park in a manner not seen for years at Highbury. His display led Mike Collins to comment in *One Nil Down*: 'The muscular strength of Mickey Thomas was there, as was the speedy box-to-box athleticism and the subtle vision and touch of Paul Davis'. The Frenchman's impact that night was instant. David Platt scored a cracker to pull us level, before Wrighty's tornado-like hat trick gave us a 4-1 win. His third goal was his 150th for the club, making him our second ever-highest scorer. Wrighty inevitably milked the applause, but even he was aware that Vieira's league debut was the most impressive we'd seen since Wright himself had destroyed Southampton five years earlier.

Two more wins kept us right on the tail of leaders Liverpool. Up at Middlesbrough, John Hartson replaced Dennis Bergkamp and chipped us gloriously into the lead. Wrighty took advantage of Boro's terrible defending to put us 2-0 up. Already, their new striker Ravanelli was in desperate need of attention from men in white coats. Throwing his arms around theatrically after he crashed shots against our post was hilarious, as was Juninho's annoyance with travelling Gooners for shouting at him *'get your midget off the pitch'*. Pat Rice's successful caretaker role ended with a farcical 2-0 win over Sunderland. Paul Stewart - that ex-Tottenham donkey of the highest order, got himself sent off for two ridiculous handballs and, when Kevin Scott clattered into the fit-again Tony Adams, they were down to nine men. All nine stayed behind the ball until Parlour and Hartson killed them off with two late strikes. Despite all the trials and tribulations at the start of the season, Arsenal's early form was promising. The incoming manager must have been impressed.

Arsène Wenger finally arrived in London on Friday, September 27th. When David Dein got his man, he knew he was employing the archetypal modern manager. Like all new bosses at big clubs, he was asked to do hundreds of interviews in the first few days. For those of us brought up on George's classic: 'The quality players just aren't available this year', Wenger's use of buzz words like 'internationalism', 'warm-downs', and 'globalisation' was a refreshing change. A journalist actually suggested that Tony Blair and Wenger should have a 'trendy speak' competition. Who would have prevailed? Surely Wenger's use of 'transnational movement' would have out manoeuvred Blair's 'stakeholder economy', and Arsène's 'supple muscles' would have bent Tony's 'sympathetic ear'.

But the employment of such lingo hadn't forged the Frenchman's excellent reputation. Wenger's managerial skills were honed in the French league and Japan's J- league. As Monaco's boss, he'd shunned the principality's beaches and casinos, to turn a team, watched by only 5,000 in most matches, into title winners. No mean feat, when you consider that Tapie, Marseilles' President, was allegedly bunging money at teams to induce them to lie down and die at that time. At Grampus Eight in Japan, Wenger turned a ragbag outfit, floundering at the bottom of the league, into runners up within twelve months. He had a burgeoning reputation for combining a fearsome intellect - economics graduate and speaker of five languages (including fluent Japanese - which is a real bastard to learn), with a steely determination and, when appropriate, ruthlessness.

That Wenger's excellent references came courtesy of Glenn Hoddle and George Weah helped him even more. Glenda had spent a couple of years in France with Wenger at Monaco where his game was entirely suited to the more languid style of the French league. He spoke gushingly of Wenger's willingness to work with players individually after training, and focus on the positive aspects of their game. Crucially, Hoddle spoke of Arsène possessing 'an English mind, but also a German mind, which is very disciplined'. Wenger was born in Alsace - a French region based very close to the German border. Students of history will know that this region was once pinched by Germany, so he grew up in a dual-nationality culture. With the Premiership becoming more cosmopolitan by the week, his skills at international negotiation would prove crucial.

When George Weah had arrived at Monaco for £100,000, the shy Liberian was overawed by the demands of European football. Within months, he'd become one of the most sought-after players in France. 'Wenger has the ability to turn a player into anything he wants to be', Weah later added. When the African finally won his 'World Player of the Year' award he dedicated it to Wenger. Within a few weeks, we'd all see at first hand the incredible benefits of the Frenchman's positive input.

His arrival was a classic example of how Premiership football clubs were mutating as the millennium roared towards us. British managers had long claimed that 'boozing sessions help the team to bond'. Wenger disagreed - saying that 'one beer after a game is ok. Any more is a problem'. Players' diets were also about to change. British footballers were notorious for nominating their favourite meal to be steak and chips. The classic pre-match snack, of course, was scrambled eggs. Both of these culinary delights were now strictly off limits at Highbury. Players were encouraged to stick to white meats and pasta in their normal diet, and pre-match meals would include celery dips, steamed broccoli and boiled fish. Wenger's reasoning was that these foods contained vitamins which would be needed during games. Enough talk of nutrition, though, this is not *Nigella Bites*, after all. In short, lardy, boozy Arsenal footballers were passe. John Hartson's Highbury career, therefore, was almost over.

The reception greeting Wenger when he became boss was distinctly lukewarm. In *Addicted*, Tony Adams' thoughts probably mirrored many of the players' opinions. Adams recalls thinking: 'What does this Frenchman know about football? He wears glasses and looks more like a schoolteacher. He's not going to be as good as George'. It was rumoured that most players wanted Cruyff, and Wenger's reputation for being scholarly, a loner and a workaholic saddled him with a label for being 'different'. It didn't take long for libellous gossip about him to spread. The whispering campaign reached such a crescendo that, on November 8th, it was rumoured that he was about to resign. Anyone who reckoned that he didn't have the stomach for the job changed their mind after he reduced a bunch of brain-dead press hacks to gibbering wrecks on the steps outside Highbury. 'What are you accusing me of?' Wenger asked them. Realising that to speak up would be libellous, the reporters backed off, jostled by a few Gunners fans. And then, of course, it emerged that Wenger had a long-term girlfriend in France and was an expectant Dad anyway. I hope those journalists sleep easy in their beds at night.

Yet he still had much to prove to the doubters. On a whistle-stop tour to Germany in September, he'd overseen Arsenal's defeat against Borussia Moenchengladbach in Cologne, and Tony Adams wasn't over-impressed with Wenger's decision to change the shape of the side at half time in the second leg. The Gunners lost 4-6 on aggregate. Some also reckoned that, having worked only in the French and Japanese backwaters, he wouldn't cope in the pressure cooker Premiership atmosphere. They under-rated his steely determination. Within a couple of weeks, he was speaking in reverential tones about 'the unbelievable team spirit' within the Arsenal side, and with some tasty looking encounters coming up against old foes, he'd get a crash course on how passionate, physical and frighteningly quick English football really is. *The Sun* boomed 'No more Arsing around' when he was appointed. Gunners fans fervently hoped that the managerial chaos was over and that, under Wenger, Arsenal's fortunes would surge once more. This time, we weren't to be disappointed.

The Frenchman's first league match as Arsenal boss was at Ewood Park against Blackburn. The team gave little indication of the foreign revolution that was to come: Seaman, Dixon, Winterburn, Bould, Adams, Keown, Platt, Vieira, Merson, Hartson, Wright. What an archetypal English afternoon that was. The weather was blustery, and the bollock-crunching tackles flying in from both sides made the crowd wince. God knows what Arsène made of the sensational aerial battle between John Hartson and Rovers' *Braveheart* extra Colin Hendry. Inevitably, the new boss' arrival galvanised a few players into action. David Platt actually tackled back to assist the defence for once and, in his last decent game for the club, Hartson dovetailed perfectly with Ian Wright - who was inspired. The Welshman's towering header set up Wright for the first, which he dispatched with utmost coolness, and Vieira's lightning burst and glorious through ball set up the gold toothed star for his second. The final score was 2-0. Bogey team Blackburn had been destroyed on Wenger's 'debut', and a club that was a laughing stock two months before lay in second place.

When George Graham's new Leeds side visited Highbury a couple of weeks later, you could be forgiven for thinking that a messiah was returning. He received a rapturous reception - far removed from the hate that filled the air during his tenure as Tottenham boss. Strange, isn't it, how in fans' eyes managing Spurs is a greater crime than allegedly pocketing hundreds of thousands of pounds? The Graham era at Highbury was now beginning to seem a distant memory. His Leeds side was stuffed full of huge central defenders, tough midfielders and powder puff strikers. In short, it was a team even more aesthetically repellent than the Arsenal side at the end of his reign. With Dennis Bergkamp returning from injury and orchestrating our attacks, Leeds' thugs were blown away. Dixon scored after forty four seconds, Bergkamp scored another, five minutes later, and Wrighty completed the rout. King George - once a winner with us, was now just another pauper boss at the bottom of the league, forced to look on as we surged to the top of the Premiership. How the mighty were fallen.

Fifteen thousand Gooners descended on Selhurst Park in early October to witness a game with Wimbledon, which Wenger described as 'not football'. Vinnie Jones, presumably already rehearsing for *Lock Stock And Two Smoking Barrels*, laid out Wrighty with a haymaker on his jaw, and then clashed heads with Adams and Bouldy. The upshot was that both central defenders, complete with split skulls, resembled Basil Fawlty in *The Germans* episode. In between the carnage, it was a gripping match. Vieira, relishing his battle with Jones, ran at full tilt for fifty yards, and set up Wrighty for the opener and Merson's sharp left footer put us 2-1 up. Marcus Gayle punched the ball into the net, giving them an undeserved draw and knocking us off top spot, but we'd be back.

The boys gave an excellent account of themselves at Old Trafford, going down 1-0 after Winterburn's own goal. Keown, Bould and Adams were monumental in repelling Cantona and Solksjaer's attacks, but Wright and Schmeichel were on the way to forming a similar kind of relationship to Winterburn and McClair. Wrighty continued to remain annoyingly unable to get the better of the red-nosed Dane in league games. Ole' big gob made two outrageous stops from him and proceeded, apparently, to give Wright a gob full of racist abuse. Naturally, the FA decided to do nothing. 'It's very difficult to prove exactly what was said by viewing TV evidence', said an FA official. Tossers!! Still, with games against Spurs and Newcastle coming up, there was no time to sit and sulk.

'The most intense atmosphere I'd seen at Highbury since Paris St Gemain '94', was how *Gooner* editor Mike Francis described the match with Tottenham in November. Leytonstone *Gooner* Colin Arthur describes events: 'The Arsenal-Spurs match was the game where I realised that Wenger's revolution really was having an affect. It was his first North London derby, and he must have wondered what it was all about. It was pissing down with rain so hard - I sat in the front of the North Bank and got drenched. It was pretty ugly stuff at first. Patrick Vieira had a running battle with Neilsen and Wrighty, and Calderwood did nothing but argue all afternoon. The game seemed to be heading for a draw. Ian Wright scored a penalty but the Spurs cheats got an equaliser when they should have thrown the ball back to us.

Under George, I'm sure we'd have shut up shop. But Georgie had gone and, with five minutes to go, the fans around me started shouting *'Arsène Wenger and his red and white army'*. It spread through the whole stadium and even the East Stand looked like they were joining in. Tony Adams decided to roam forward and the sight of him volleying in with a minute to go was indescribable. Then Dennis finished them off. It was probably his best ever goal for us. Wrighty knocked in a brilliant cross. Bergkamp controlled the ball and curled it in to make it 3-1. And then he slid on his knees in the mud, screaming to the skies. Wasn't it Alan Sugar who said Dennis wouldn't be interested in the mud and the rain? You should have heard the din from the Arsenal fans going into the tube station afterwards. *'We beat the scum 3-1'*, everybody sang. Now Wenger really had arrived.

Colin Arthur, Arsenal Fan from Leytonstone

These staggering scenes were matched a week later up at St James Park. Newcastle's Alan Shearer was at his most belligerent, and proceeded to cheat and dive all afternoon. But the Geordies couldn't destroy the Arsenal. Lee Dixon's spectacular flying header put us on the right road, before Shearer decided to hurl himself to the ground again after a brush with Tony Adams. Tone received his marching orders and the Geordies poured into the gap. Shearer equalised, naturally. And just how were we supposed to love 'good ole' Al when he played for England? Wave after wave of Toon attacks rained down on Seaman - before Ian Wright silenced those bloody annoying *'Blaydon Races'* chants with a sensational late winner. After crushing the Saints 3-1 at Highbury three days later, with Merson majestic and late sub Paul Shaw grabbing his first Arsenal goal, we were roaring clear at the top.

Wenger's belief that 'we can win something' was founded on the team's excellent league form between early September and November, on Vieira's impact and the intense team spirit. We were about to hit choppy seas, though. It was nothing disastrous - just a lull after the initial euphoria. At home to Derby, Tony Adams' superb flying header and Vieira's sensational last minute 30 yarder salvaged a deserved point, after Sturridge's strike seemed to have won it for them. But then a psyched-up Nottingham Forest contrived to defeat the Gunners on the day Stuart Pearce took over as their boss. Haaland's goals hauled Forest off the bottom of the league, and then struggling Sheffield Wednesday held us to a goalless draw at Hillsborough.

Boxing Day visitors Aston Villa also grabbed a point in a 2-2 draw, even after Merson and Wright had scored excellent goals. Injury-hit Middlesbrough proved to be Arsenal's only Christmas victims. They were beaten 2-0 in Arctic conditions after Wright and Bergkamp led sciatica-ridden Bryan Robson a merry dance in his last ever competitive game. The visitors' misery was compounded when Ravanelli missed a last minute penalty - cue the inevitable tears and tantrums. Actually, it was a wonder that Boro turned up at all - they'd not bothered to do so a week before and their two point deduction meant they would be relegated at season's end. That win put us back up to third in the table and left the team, seemingly, in a strong position to challenge the Mancs and the Geordies in the New Year.

A journalist casually enquired of Paul Merson in late December whether or not he would be making any New Year's resolutions. 'I've already given everything up' came the reply. When he told the same hack that 'I expect to finish my career at Arsenal', few fans doubted that would happen. Gone were the lurid *Loaded* and *FHM* exposes; in their place came improved performances and daily attendances at Alcoholics and Gamblers Anonymous meetings. By Christmas, he was already touted as a contender for the PFA player of the year award, such were the quality of his displays.

Of all Arsenal's players, Merson in particular appeared to relish Wenger's philosophy of working on a one to one basis with players. For a man so used to therapy sessions, Merse gained much from 'the incredible belief that Arsène has given me'. The Frenchman worked on his strengths; namely powerful running, sweeping passes and spectacular finishing. In form as he was, he proved to be a cornerstone of the stylish team his manager was sculpting. His catalogue of goals was impressive - not least his excellent finishes against Borussia Moenchengladbach, and the pile driver at home to Southampton. Merson looked at his most effective in a deep-lying position, ably moving forward to support Wright and Bergkamp. Skill-wise, only the Dutchman could match him; witness Villa's and Sheffield Wednesday's defence and midfield backing off in fear every time he received the ball in the Highbury matches.

But, as Merson has always said, recovering alcoholics live a day-to-day existence, aware that problems and demons lurk around every corner. Yet again, he'd fooled us into believing that he could maintain these standards for the whole season. He couldn't, of course. A New Year hamstring injury ruled him out of several games. Not only did that knock the tempo out of the team, it also jolted Merson out of his stride. By the time he returned, Bergkamp's excellent form in Merson's old position, together with a new arrival, meant that, suddenly, one of Highbury's own faced an even more uncertain future.

Wenger's revolution had, for the most part, been glorious. Without chopping and changing the side, the lads were now 'expressing' themselves. Wrighty's T-shirt unveiled at the Spurs game told us 'I love the lads', and Patrick's first ever Arsenal goal against Derby was greeted with an orgy of celebration from his team mates. Arsène was also proving to be a master of psychology, regarding the Wright issue. The Frenchman said of Wright: 'If he can do one thing well, let's concentrate on that. At his age, why work on the negatives?' There's a masterly equivocation if ever there was one. Wenger had boosted his striker's confidence (a far cry from Bruce's approach) while, at the same time, truthfully admitting Wrighty was entering the twilight of his career.

As well as Paul Merson's excellent displays, Tony Adams' performances demonstrated the full extent of the 'Wenger effect'. When Adams had admitted in August that he was an alcoholic, it came as little surprise to those party to the Highbury grapevine. All year, 'spies' claimed that he'd been seen around London and Essex in various states of drunkenness, sometimes with crutches 'n all. *One Nil Down* reported early in '96 that Adams was sent home on New Years Day - 'totally unfit' to play football. Read *Addicted* for a raw and unvarnished insight into the drinking culture in English football. As to why Adams crossed the line into alcoholism, suffice it to say that, as a teenager, he wanted to be a 'good' drinker in order to impress Rix, Sansom and the other jack-the-lads in the Highbury dressing room. During his career, heavy drinking sessions acted as a 'crutch' to help avoid dealing with intense feelings - the sort which emerge when thousands of people bray at you for example. But during the weeks following Euro '96, Adams realised that booze was now his greatest enemy. Like the Merson affair, the question which Arsenal's manager had to address was, did Tony still justify his place in the team?

The answer was a resounding 'yes', and the captain's performances for the rest of the season showed that Wenger was lifting some of the shackles with which Graham tied him down. Doubtless George would have been horrified with Adams' sojourns into the opposition penalty box, and it would take time for Gooners to get used to it as well. Adams clearly relished his new freedom and Wenger realised the importance of keeping his captain 'on side'. Michael Hart wrote in the *Evening Standard*: 'the hard core resilience of this team springs from defensive players. In terms of attitude, they've set the tone of the side for nearly a decade'. A dressing room without this 'resilience', which was embodied within Adams, could be a treacherous place as Arsène's predecessor discovered. In the early stages of Wenger's revolution, it was befitting that the captain should be leading from the front.

The new found freedom of expression also had its down side, and several players were becoming stroppy when the going got tough. Dennis was already getting touchy when mere mortals dared to lay a finger on him, and Patrick Vieira's savaging of Teddy Sherringham in the North London derby didn't go down too well at the FA, though it was fine by us. Patrick was banned for a couple of games, which seriously disturbed the balance of the team over Christmas. We already knew about the atomic power of Wrighty's gob, of course. One linesman was hardly enamoured to be described as a 'muppet' - much less David Pleat, who Wright labelled 'a pervert' after the Sheffield Wednesday match. His sending off at Forest was harsh, but then opponents were discovering that the best way of stopping some of our players was to kick them and pull their shirts.

Such is the eternal fate of the talented footballer. Still, that didn't really excuse John Hartson's appalling disciplinary record, did it? Studs up overexcitement from Vieira was one thing, but Johnny's ridiculous string of obscenities at the ref, and subsequent red card in the last minute against Middlesbrough, was something else. Wenger always refused to criticise his players in public - which in a way is admirable, but within a couple of years, this *laissez-faire* attitude may have cost the team games and trophies.

After Liverpool crushed the Gunners at Anfield in the Coca-Cola Cup, Wenger dropped heavy hints that reinforcements were needed. Wright's brace of penalties couldn't disguise the fact that the boys looked fatigued at times and the squad lacked cover in key areas. In order for the boss to get the streamlined appearance he wanted, numerous warts and growths needed to be removed. In the spirit of Blair's New Labour, he'd so far tried to please everybody. But now, with scalpel in hand, he began to demonstrate his more ruthless side and cut away the masses of dead wood lingering in the reserves. Wenger farmed out Glenn Helder on loan to Benfica for the rest of the season. The Dutchman never appeared in an Arsenal shirt again, though strangely he remained on official team photos for the next two years. So did Chris Kiwomya, who hopped over the Channel to join Le Havre for the next eighteen months.

Offloaded almost immediately for a cumulative profit of £1.5m were Eddie McGoldrick, David Hillier and Paul Dickov. The feisty Dickov was sold to Manchester City and Eddie joined him there for £300,000. He'd been swanning around in the reserves doing nothing for a year, other than sniping at us in the press. 'At least I've got a big house' was one of his stranger jibes at Arsenal fans. It was no surprise that with Eddie bumbling around, the Maine Road club was crashing through the leagues at alarming speed.

David Hillier was sold to Portsmouth, and with Jimmy Carter on the wing for the South Coast club, these must have been golden times for Pompey. Having begun brightly enough back in '91, his ridiculous brushes with the law had long since turned him into a laughing stock. Found with traces of cannabis in his blood, he'd protested 'I thought it was a cigarette'. A few months later, he was caught stealing two holdalls from an airport departure lounge. If Dave had looked up, he would have seen a CCTV camera recording his every move. Not exactly a criminal mastermind was he? Arsène gave his scalpel a rest for a while, but in the New Year, bigger names would be on the move.

If disciplinary problems had begun to undermine the title challenge, the FA Cup 3rd round is often an opportunity for hope to spring eternal in the New Year. Opponents Sunderland had put up a good display at Highbury to grab a draw, but the replay up at Ice Station Roker Park was memorable. On a Wednesday night, just four days after Tony Adams' own goal condemned us to a 1-0 defeat in the league there, the Mackems stormed forward in the last Cup match to be held at their old stadium. Two minutes into the second half, Dennis Bergkamp, who'd been loitering on the edge of the box, dragged the ball back past a bewildered Sunderland defence, and from 25 yards, lofted an elegant shot high into Sunderland's net. Dennis and team-mates celebrated with hands over their mouths - no piece of commenting could do that goal justice after all. Commentating on Sky T.V., Andy Gray told his colleague to 'shut up - you can't describe that'. Youth team graduate Steve Hughes' flying header - his first in an Arsenal shirt, wrapped up the tie.

By the time George's Leeds visited us in round four, Manchester United and Liverpool had already crashed out of the competition, leaving us as red-hot favourites. We were well and truly 'Georged', though. Tangled up in a maze of central defenders and clogging midfielders, Rod Wallace's early goal was enough to knock us out. It was a horrible experience, truly grotesque. We began to understand just how Parma must have felt in '94 when the likes of Morrow and Hillier tripped up their silky attackers in craftily spun webs.

Two successive Highbury league matches in February, with Manchester United and Wimbledon, took on the guise of 'must win' occasions. We'd steadied the ship with an excellent 3-1 win over Everton. Paul Merson scored his last ever Arsenal goal and Dennis' majesty and Vieira's raw power produced two more goals. It wasn't lost on several observers that Wrighty's listless New Year form was becoming a worry. Subbed at half-time against Everton, the team looked much more balanced without him. Still, that would be forgotten if he could destroy the Mancs. No such luck. Cole and Solksjaer virtually killed the game after half an hour. Not even Dennis' late reply, or Wrighty's attempt to break Schmeichel's leg, could save us. The clash between the two was reaching Ali V Frazier proportions, although at least Smokin' Joe demolished Ali on one memorable occasion, didn't he? All Wrighty got for his pains was a bollocking from the FA and another blank day against United. The grim reaper figure of Vinnie Jones killed us off on the following Sunday. On a day when an injury crisis meant we had a back three of Garde, Morrow and Marshall, treble-chasing Wimbledon volleyed and bulldozed their way to victory.

Title pretensions virtually destroyed, Wenger continued to sculpt and shape the Arsenal model of the future. Eighteen year old Nicolas Anelka arrived from Paris St Germain for an 'undisclosed fee', with a reputation for being one of the hottest striking talents in Europe. A shy, introverted teenager, he managed to communicate to journalists that he was 'moving not for the money, but for a place in the team', and that 'Arsenal are a club of greater stature than St Germain'. He'd spin virtually the same line two years later, only this time we wouldn't be so flattered. Anelka was seen as a future replacement for Wrighty, and in the latter part of the season, he'd have a few chances to show what he was made of.

In order for Wenger to get down to some serious summer cash splashing, he needed to recoup money. To that end, John Hartson's £4 m sale to West Ham in March represented excellent business, and was greeted with general hilarity by the football world at large. His fee would rise to £5 m if West Ham won the European Cup, and presumably £10 m if Harry Redknapp ever became US president. Hartson had begun brightly enough in '94/95 but by the late '90s he simply wasn't what was required. The view that 'he was never really an Arsenal player' is a little harsh, though his subsequent career doesn't really suggest that he could have spearheaded a title challenge at Highbury. Sadly, he's more famed for failing medicals and getting into fights than actually scoring goals these days. Andy Linighan, our FA Cup Final hero of '93, was sold for £1 m to Crystal Palace. His place in the hall of fame was secured, and he'd eventually won over the boo boys to become an excellent deputy when called upon. Cheers, Andy.

With FIFA's insistence on turning European competitions into cash laden, rich men's playgrounds, a Premiership runners-up spot would give us a crack at the Champions (sic) League. With crunch games to come at Highbury against Liverpool and Newcastle, this target was still in reach, and optimists clung to the faint hope that the title could be secured. The Gunners' form in March was excellent. Bergkamp and Wright ran amok at Goodison and scored our goals in a 2-0 win. They were helped by Stephen Hughes' excellent form on the left-hand side of midfield. That scoreline was repeated a week later at home to the doomed Nottingham Forest; the Bergmeister's double was a fitting reward for his majestic form. A third straight win came at the Dell on the 15th. Steve Hughes again played excellently - he scored, as did Paul Shaw, who grabbed a second in another 2-0 victory.

Liverpool's Spice Boys visited Highbury on an infamous evening in late March. The Southern press hyped it as a final chance to haul ourselves back into the title race, but United were already several furlongs clear. Before the game, Wenger insisted that we'd revert to 4-4-2 during the close season, but for now left the team untouched. In the meantime, Dixon and Winterburn weren't roving wingers, they were full backs who didn't quite have the pace of old. Dixon sometimes looked the part, marauding forward and dispatching curling crosses into the box, but Nige seemed to hit a block once he crossed the half way line. The ghost of George, perhaps? His annoying habit of doing this disrupted several attacks against Liverpool. Everyone knows what happened that night. Seaman's blunder gave Stan Collymore a simple tap in and Robbie Fowler's actions have gone down in folklore as an example of how refs were turning into robots. Fowler protested to the ref that Seaman *didn't* haul him down in the area but Ashby gave the penalty anyway. The Scouse striker was so embarrassed that he deliberately fluffed his spot kick but Jason McAteer followed up and scored. Even Wrighty's late goal couldn't stop them pinching the points again - they'd more than got their revenge for '89.

With the season nearing its climax, we crushed Chelsea 3-0 at Stamford Bridge. A furious Ruud Gullit claimed afterwards that 'Arsenal waltzed through the game like a team playing an exhibition game'. The match gave Anelka his first chance in the side as a late sub. We were impressed with his speed and touch and, no doubt, he noted the quality of Wright's smash and grab goal and Dennis' imperious finish to give us a 2-0 lead. David Platt finished them off with his first Arsenal goal since September.

Platty was about to launch a late season bid to avoid winning the 'player which fans would most like to see replaced' award. His supporters (that's the tiny minority who didn't sit in the North Bank and the Clock End and shout 'Fuck off Platt, you useless bastard'), believed that his no nonsense, no frills calmness had allowed Vieira to settle in smoothly. There's some mileage in that view but, for £5m, Platt should have been shining like a beacon. He'd change some minds in the following season, but for now he was about as popular as the Millennium Dome; overpriced and overhyped, most wanted rid of him after a year. Yet he scored the first in a 2-0 win at home to Leicester, and then put us into the lead at home to Blackburn. Rovers, hovering above the relegation trap door, decided to kick and scrape through the game. At 4.47 precisely, Chris Sutton's forcing of a corner after we'd booted the ball out of play to help one of their injured players, seriously endangered his life. Vieira and Dixon told him what low life scum he was, but Flitcroft scored from the corner which meant Rovers stayed up. How gratifying it was to see Blackburn and Sutton get their rewards two years later when they were finally relegated.

Arsenal qualified comfortably for the UEFA Cup, but finally blew the chance to participate in the Champions League after Newcastle's late winner at Highbury. The team finished third in Wenger's first season - quite an achievement considering the mire in which we found ourselves back in August. The new style of play was indeed revolutionary, clearly demonstrated in the final game of the season at Derby. Rams' fans were giving the last rites to the Baseball Ground, but Bergkamp's *objet d'art* chip, Wright's double and Anelka's speed destroyed them. This couldn't disguise the fact that crucial home defeats against the Mancs, Scousers and Geordies had cost us dear. We totally agreed with Wenger's bemoaning of the lack of width in the team and bite in midfield. Tony Willis tersely pointed out in *One Nil Down* that '.. next year, Arsène, nearly won't be good enough'. The reality was that we were still slightly short of being *bona fide* title contenders. But it was nothing that the addition, say, of a speedy Dutch winger and a pony-tailed French midfielder couldn't rectify.

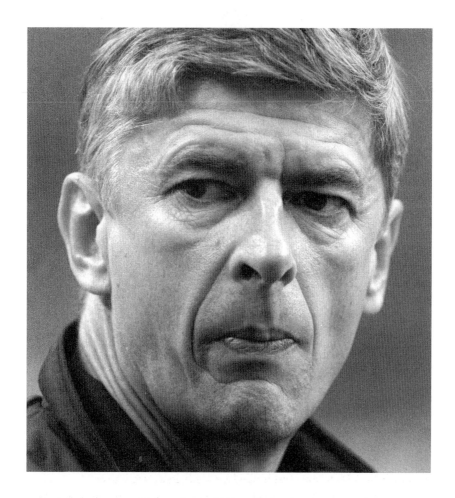

A new era dawns at Highbury with Arsène Wenger

8

At The Double

ootball has never been as hip as it was in the Summer of '97. *Loaded* magazine had recently dubbed it 'the new rock 'n' roll' and the merchandising revolution, especially replica shirt sales, reached its height. Our home shirt (70% of which had the letters W-R-I-G-H-T stamped on the back), and the classic early '70s top were both sold out. In trendy Islington cafes, where footie talk would have been an anathema ten years before, debates on the meaning of terms like 'Cool Britannia' and 'girl power' were interspersed with discussions on Arsenal's numerous Summer signings.

The Premiership football package, now presented with Mandelsonian type slickness, took on a truly cosmopolitan image. It was all perfectly in tune with the post-Bosman era and freedom of movement under EU law. Arsène Wenger had taken on board the P.M.'s wish that we should indulge in a spot of 'global interfacing'. His contacts abroad meant that the new arrivals hailed from a variety of European countries. Emmanuel Petit, Gilles Grimandi and Chris Wreh all played in France, Marc Overmars in Holland, Alberto Mendez in Germany, Luis Boa Morte in Portugal, Alex Manninger in Austria and Matthew Upson plied his trade in exotic Luton.

Overmars and Petit were given the full red carpet treatment when they disembarked from the aeroplane. They were rightfully stamped with the label 'first class'. Overmars, who'd overcome the doubts about his fitness after cruciate damage, had won the European Cup with Ajax and seemed to be the speedy winger we'd craved since Anders Limpar's departure. Petit was known only to followers of the French game. He came with excellent references as a tough tackling, impressive distributor of the ball who could play in midfield or defence. The others, in truth, were unknown rookies who were marked with the label 'for the future'. Wenger reasoned that United and Liverpool had the country's best young players, while the Gunners had superior power in the 25-30 department. Many of these signings were a bid to redress the balance.

With Arsène continuing to show that he was a good European, home grown Paul Merson was sold to Middlesbrough. A vocal school of thought expressed its displeasure at the Merse's departure. It reasoned that this was the thin end of the wedge, and that floods of foreign imports would soon have damaging long term effects on the development of English players. This was not xenophobic ranting - we'd all seen the disastrous effects which Boogers and co. had on West Ham in the previous season. And, of course, the Merse was a London boy - after his departure only Woolwich-born Wrighty actually hailed from the capital but, in the brutal world of accounts and finances, Merse's sale *did* make sense.

Receiving £5m for an inconsistent 30 year old represented excellent business. We admired him for his courage to battle against his addictions, and we'll always remember the young colt from '89 and '91 who helped spearhead the title challenge. With rose tinted specs, it is easy to forget that he could be anonymous in games for weeks at a time. In the previous season, for instance, he hadn't *actually* scored since February. But occasional flashbacks and newspaper reports prove that he did often disappear in games. It's somehow apt that he was stuck on having scored ninety nine goals for Arsenal. A player of his skill should have guaranteed himself a spot in Arsenal's goal scoring hall of fame, rather than occasionally coming up with the goods. Whatever the final judgement is on his career, the reception he receives at Highbury when he returns proves one thing; he'll always be a Gooner at heart.

With the new foreign signings, and Wenger's revolution starting to pay dividends on the pitch, Arsenal, amazingly, were becoming trendy. The screening of Nick Hornby's *Fever Pitch* further elevated the club in the nation's consciousness. The fact that Colin Firth was chosen to be the Arsenal fan in the film certainly helped, and our merchandising department must have loved him. The actor, who'd sprung to fame in *Pride And Prejudice*, modelled the '71 'Double' top for virtually the whole film - handy as the Christmas shopping season approached. The movie also promoted footie as an aesthetic and cultural experience, rather than simply twenty two men kicking a ball and/or each other for ninety minutes.

Such pretentious shite inevitably had some weird side effects. On trains, Sloane Rangers, spotting the red and white shirt, wanted to know whether or not we too talked about D.H. Lawrence and Keats, as well as the offside trap. Luvvie leeches like Melvyn Bragg professed their undying love for the club in the press, and Laurence Marks had already begun to pen his diary *'A Fan For All Seasons'*. Due to the changing perceptions of football, our players were also becoming hot commercial property.

Wrighty was touted as a future chat show host, which just shows how much football had changed in the '90s. Hard to imagine Smudger fronting his own talk show, isn't it? We'd already seen Wrighty in Nike ads and he was snapped up by Mercury for one of their One-2-One commercials. In it, our star striker professed his 'total respect' for Martin Luther King's non-violent approach in the '60s to civil rights issues. It was all slightly ironic, bearing in mind that Wrighty was taking anger management sessions in a bid to curb his hot temper. Of course, we were already used to seeing David Platt in McDonalds ads. Maybe Arsène should have put out his own ad to fellow managers telling them about 'The McPlatty - yours for £3.50. To take away, PLEASE'. Only kidding Dave. Even he managed to redeem himself in the '97/98 season.

After a mercifully sleaze 'n' scandal free summer, we couldn't wait for the big kick-off. The stadium looked magnificent - all freshly painted and gleaming in the summer sun. Liam Brady was back in his new role as head of youth development. The club had also modernised its image. It was the first to cruise down the information superhighway and set up its own official website. Catering inside the stadium was set to become even better. You could now buy Nachos covered in chilli sauce at half time if you wished. Ultimately though, we didn't really give a toss about many of these things. It had been more than three years since we'd won a trophy. The delicious smell of Mexican grub wafting through the North Bank was all very well but, in reality, the inhabitants of Highbury's global village wanted to get high on the odour of silverware polish come May.

From the outset Wenger decided to pursue his idea of a 4-4-2 formation throughout the season. His plans immediately hit a snag because pre-season injuries robbed us of key men. Martin Keown's horrific shoulder injury, sustained in Le Tournoi, would keep him out of action until November, and by now we were used to Tony Adams not joining the fray until later in the season. With Lee Dixon also out, Remi Garde filled in at right back alongside Bould and Grimandi in central defence. The line up for the opening game against George's revamped Leeds had a slightly raw look to it: Seaman, Winterburn, Vieira, Bould, Wright, Bergkamp, Overmars, Parlour, Petit, Grimandi, Garde.

In boiling temperatures, the Gunners struggled to overcome their muscular midfield and shackle new boy Jimmy Floyd Hasselbank. Ian Wright crunched in the first goal of the season, his shot screaming past Martyn from the tightest of angles. Petit, who'd taken Platt's role in midfield, seemed a little overawed in the Summer heat. Overmars also faded in the second half - like the team. Hasselbaink grabbed their equaliser and, in truth, the Gunners only just hung on for a draw.

Coventry's Sky Blues visited Highbury on a steaming evening three days later. Dennis gave the first indication that he was about to challenge for the mantle of our greatest ever talent. His monumental display included a supreme trap and volley, all in one movement, which scraped the bar, and his dipping volley was brilliantly pushed away by Ogrizovic. Scott Marshall had an excellent game in central defence, quite easily repelling Dublin's aerial threat. When his early header rattled the post, Vieira cracked in a shot which Oggy palmed out; Wrighty thumped in the rebound. When his old Palace buddy Richard Shaw cocked up a simple second half backpass, he slid in a second. It had been a 2-0 cruise on a balmy evening. Ian Wright now stood poised on the brink of Gunners' immortality. He needed just two more goals to break Cliff Bastin's record. With a game at Southampton approaching, it seemed his moment had arrived.

Away match tickets were at a premium in that glorious August of '97. Everyone wanted to be present when Wright made history, but getting a seat at the Dell was difficult at the best of times. Undeterred, Arsenal fans snapped up tickets from touts by the bucketful, and large numbers were present in the Southampton home end. Hampshire police don't much care for Londoners, though. Anyone who didn't boo the Gunners relentlessly was chucked out of the ground, it seemed. They missed an awesome display from Dennis Bergkamp. Wright turned provider for our first goal - his delicious through ball allowed Overmars to cut inside the area at speed and smash an unstoppable shot past Beasant for our first. The Saints drew level, though, and threatened to take the lead, before Dennis got moving.

Thirty minutes into the second half, he got the ball on the halfway line, danced and dazzled his way past Dodd and Benali, and bore down on goal. The following day's tabloids freeze-framed the Saints' defenders faces. They were open mouthed in bewilderment and awe - rather like the famous shot from the '30s of Alex James carving up Manchester City's defence. Bergkamp paused and curled in a stupendous shot. We didn't so much celebrate as genuflect. Here, indeed, was a talent every bit as great as James or Brady. When, five minutes later, Benali tried to stop Dennis scoring his second, by virtually ripping the shirt from his back, he was shoved imperiously out of the way.

Bergkamp strode on and rifled in a thunderbolt which screamed past Beasant. David Lacey wrote in *The Guardian* that: 'In Italy he (Dennis) might have stumbled across a Benali selling souvenirs, but not in Serie A'. Bergkamp would discover during the season that the Premiership is littered with Benali clones who'll employ any means possible to stop their opponents. But after this 3-1 result, fans were left asking themselves how the Dutchman could possibly improve on that display. It would take him only four days to do so.

Every sport has fans who claim that when they witnessed a certain game, race or fight, they knew they'd seen greatness. Examples: US author Norman Mailer drools about Ali's seemingly impossible comeback against George Foreman in 'The Rumble In The Jungle', and athletics fans will remember forever the gold-shoed Michael Johnson winning two gold medals in the Atlanta Olympics. To complete the triumvirate, Arsenal fans who were at Filbert Street on August 27th 1997, will forever recall Dennis Bergkamp's awesome performance. Yet again we turned up expecting Wright to break Bastin's record. That didn't happen, but the Ice Man's display was more than adequate compensation.

Leicester stuck two of their lumbering giants - Walsh and Elliott, on Wrighty all evening to take him out of the equation. This left the Bergmeister free to wreak havoc. His divine hat-trick defied footballing reality. His first goal was curled high into the roof of Keller's net from thirty yards. The scorer was modest about the strike; telling *Goal* magazine 'It's just technique. You should be able to do it with your bare feet'. His second goal was a beautifully timed lob over the stranded goalie, courtesy of Vieira's pass.

Despite his heroics, Arsenal were still level after 92 minutes. Gilles Grimandi ('just a French Gus Caesar', according to one *Gooner* contributor), was in his early season fuckwit mode, which meant that Bould was exposed to Heskey's raw power time and again. He and Matt Elliott had cashed in on the Frenchman's hesitation to make it 2-2. Two minutes into injury time, Platty chipped forward an excellent ball to the roving Dennis who juggled the ball, teased Elliott and clipped his shot into the net. Pure bedlam in their poor excuse for an away stand; but then the sods popped in a 96th minute equaliser. It had been a classic match and even Alan Hansen drooled over the Dutch master's play. He wasn't so impressed with our suicidal defending, though.

After the aberrations at Filbert Street, the defence took on a more familiar look. Lee Dixon returned to replace Garde, but Tone and Martin still weren't ready to face Spurs. In the most obscenely one-sided North London derby we'd seen for years, Overmars, Bould, Bergkamp and an increasingly stressed-out Wrighty all tested the tensile strength of Tottenham's stanchion, but we ended up drawing 0-0. Sol Campbell and David Ginola apart, Spurs showed just what a ragged, half arsed outfit they'd become; Overmars v Sinton, Wright v Armstrong, Vieira v Sedgeley, proved that the battle for North London supremacy was a case of heavyweights v featherweights. And, just think, Alan Sugar reckoned that Bergkamp was just 'cosmetic surgery'. So what did that make Ginola then? You almost felt pity for the incoming Christian Gross, a dead ringer for a *Doctor No* type Bond baddie, but not a top grade footie boss.

Fast forward two weeks; Diana and Dodi had been killed in Paris and, in an emotion charged World Cup qualifier, Wrighty broke his scoring drought to hit two against Moldova. To say that he was 'doing it for Diana', which the tabloids claimed, may be stretching the truth but, with Wrighty, you never know. Naturally, the London press hype reached hysterical levels regarding Bastin's record. The forthcoming Highbury match against Bolton gave him another chance to smash it and, this time, he didn't disappoint.

Arsenal fan Matthew Allgood recalls events: 'Avenell Road, 5 p.m., 13.09.97: Ian Wright is performing his version of the *"Full Monty"*, removing all his kit and throwing it out of the dressing room window, down to the delirious throng of Gooners below. Someone, somewhere, has a pair of his underpants for a trophy, although the Nike 179 - JUST DONE IT T-shirt was torn up. A hilarious end to a record breaking day, which saw Wright equal, then break Cliff Bastin's record of 178 goals for the club. Bolton had briefly threatened to spoil the party, having led on the quarter hour mark with Alan Thompson's diving header. However, with Bergkamp in imperious form, their lead was never likely to last for very long, and his slipped ball through to Wright helped tie the game up and enable him to meet Bastin's total. The shirt came off prematurely, to reveal a white vest inscribed "179 JUST DONE IT". It was removed, five minutes later, this time for real, when a two yard tap in confirmed him as Arsenal's greatest ever goal scorer. He admitted afterwards that it was the easiest goal he'd ever scored.

He didn't just break the record, though - he smashed it by getting a hat trick. It was an unforgettable moment. There's an old saying which says 'side before self every time'. I think that's right, 99% of the time - but in every way Wright was an exception wasn't he? He was a one off. I think any milestone like that is worthy of recognition - there's got to be some room for *individual* achievement in football. And don't forget that Wright got a hat trick that day in a 4-1 win, so it was crucial for the team. Amidst everyone going mental in *The Sun*, I'll always remember David Seaman running half the length of the pitch to celebrate with him, and Lee Dixon joined him, too. The team obviously couldn't have been more delighted for him. What a player, he showed the enthusiasm of a ten year old and the ability of a star. With that combination, no wonder we empathised with him.

Matthew Allgood, Arsenal fan from Cuffley

Record bustin' Wrighty inevitably walked into another controversy when *The Express'* pedant Mike Langley claimed that he'd broken no record at all, because Cliff Bastin's goals were racked up in the league and FA Cup only, with no help from European or league Cups. In a sense, he was right, but anyone who's ever actually watched '30s footie footage knows it was an infinitely more pedestrian game, back then. Comparing strikers from different eras is a pointless exercise, anyway, given changing fitness levels. For most of us, Wrighty was the greatest goal monster in Arsenal's history.

Wenger maintained that he subbed Wright in the Bolton game to allow him a standing ovation. That was very nice of him, but the significance of Anelka's late introduction wasn't lost on certain sections of the crowd. Neither was Wenger's masterly equivocal statement: 'It will be a hard decision to tell him (Wright) he's no longer part of my team'. For all the pomp and glory surrounding the gold toothed hero's achievement, his Arsenal career had already reached its zenith and was about to go into rapid decline. Save for his excellent display for England in Rome, the tornado had burnt itself out. We'd soon discover that an in-form Nicolas Anelka was the key to title chasing success, not 36 year old Wrighty.

By late Summer, most contemporary writers admitted that Arsenal had been remodelled; in other words, several of our players were considered cool. The phenomenon first came to light just after Wright broke Bastin's record. *Marie Claire* ran a poll asking its readers to name their sexiest Premiership footballer. Criteria included looks, haircut and 'aura'. Staggeringly, three Gunners made it into the top ten; Overmars, Petit and Bergkamp. This was a bewildering state of affairs for those of us who'd grown up with the likes of Willie Young and Kevin Richardson in the team. The only Arsenal players in living memory who'd raised a hint of *frisson* among the girls were the two Charlies; George and Nicholas. Good looking and elegantly coiffured players were traditionally custodians of the non-trophy winning zone that was White Hart Lane. The doughty Arsenal had no time for such fripperies.

The change had been coming for a while, though. After Euro '96, David Seaman immediately became a 'rent-a-personality', and Wrighty added to his repertoire by signing a deal to publicise 'Chicken Tonight'. Equally as revealing were the soundbites released by some of our players. Manu Petit revealed that in his spare time, he liked to 'expand my mind - I find shopping a very liberating experience'. What a change that was from the likes of Paul Dickov, who'd confessed that his favourite passtime was watching Chubby Brown videos - especially *The Helmet Rides Again*. More stylish and cerebral footie demanded more glamorous players.

Another London side undergoing a makeover was Chelsea. Ken Bates' empire building and modernising of Stamford Bridge continued apace, but that couldn't disguise the club's knuckle-scraping past. Maybe the Chelsea supremo needed to remember the old adage: 'form is temporary, class is permanent'. The disgustingly ostentatious Chelsea Village, and a single title won back in the '50s, is no substitute for genuine tradition, like the stylish marble halls and Chapman's legacy from the '30s.

Facing Arsenal at Stamford Bridge, the Blues approached the match in the manner you'd expect from a club lacking true class. Mouthing off in the press beforehand about the fact that they were now London's premier club, simply highlighted their tacky *nouveau-riche* veneer. True aristocrats don't need to indulge in such bragging. When the match kicked off, Dennis Wise foolishly picked on Vieira and Le Boeuf decided to square up to Petit.

Two lovely strikes from Dennis Bergkamp cancelled out Poyet's and Zola's goals for the Blues. With the game finely balanced at 2-2, Chelsea became more spiteful by the minute. Le Boeuf was rightly red carded after one petulant reaction too many. From that moment on, they retreated like cowardly bandits in a *Magnificent Seven* movie. With Chelsea camped inside their own area, Arsenal pressed for a late winner. When Nigel Winterburn received the ball from thirty five yards out, with three minutes to go, their defence relaxed. After all, he hadn't scored for eighteen months. Two seconds later, travelling Gooners almost combusted with delight when his screaming shot swerved past de Goey to give us a 3-2 win. Even Arsène temporarily lost his cool and hugged Nige, who was running around like a demented chicken.

Goal sprees continued apace throughout September. West Ham were resoundingly whooped amidst a tornado of first half brilliance. Bergkamp teased in the opening goal and Marc Overmars pelted forward, fed by Dennis' slide rule passes, to score an excellent double. Overmars wasn't yet playing at full tilt but at least he'd showed his blistering potential. Winning 4-0 at half time, the boys eased up after the interval. Gunners fans amused themselves by chanting: *'You've got Iain Dowie and we've got Dennis Bergkamp'*. Equally as pleasurable was the hammering dished out to hapless whipping boys Barnsley. Roasted 5-0 in *The Sun*, the Premiership newcomers simply couldn't cope with Ray Parlour's excellent display on the right side of midfield, or Patrick Vieira's distribution. Platt and Parlour scored their first goals of the season and an out-of-sorts Wrighty scored his last ever Highbury goal. Inevitably, it was Bergkamp who stole the show with a wondrous double. The second goal, expertly curled past their goalie, led Matt Dickinson to claim in *The Times*: 'Wenger learning to count on the perfect 10'.

A journalist remarked in September '97 that Dennis Bergkamp seemed capable of 'virtually anything'. All except flying, of course. Dennis' bad aviational experience in 1994 with the Dutch World Cup squad meant that he'd refused to fly to Greece to join the Arsenal team for the UEFA cup tie with PAOK Salonika. The side looked lost without him, and was lucky to lose only 1-0. Though Bergkamp scored in the Highbury return, PAOK pinched a late goal to win the tie. It was disappointing but, tactically, the Greeks looked superior. It was to be a familiar failing of Wenger's early European ventures.

Dennis' aerophobia showed how reliant we remained on his mercurial talent. As a player, he fits in perfectly with the conventionally held view that Dutch footballers are neurotic geniuses. 'Aloof', 'intensely private', 'deep thinking', and 'highly strung', are four adjectives one often affixes to Cruyff and his ilk; Dennis is no exception. He is notorious for refusing interview requests and, on the rare occasions when he accepts, he insists on discussing tactics only. So Dennis' soundbites are as precious and unique as many of his goals. In late '97, *Goal* magazine was granted an interview with him. This was during the period when virtually every Bergkamp strike seemed to be a contender for Goal of the Month and Alan Hansen minutely analysed his every move on *Match Of The Day*. In the *Goal* interview, Bergkamp reiterated the fact that, to him, playing football was not only enjoyable, it was also a form of science. To reach the highest level required the most rigorous practice and dedication.

His soundbites in David Winner's excellent book *Brilliant Orange* are most revealing of all. In Holland, Bergkamp is regarded as an artist, according to the owner of the Rijksmuseum - a man more used to discussing

Rembrandt. Aesthetics clearly mean a great deal to Dennis, who confesses that poaching 'ugly goals' is not his forte, and that he 'lacked the killer instinct to poach them in the first place'. Such brittleness is considered by many to be a symptom of arrogance, a trait which the author believes cost Holland three World Cups. Indeed, Bergkamp's nickname in Holland is 'Denise', such is his unwillingness to 'get stuck in' at times. It is befitting that a perfectionist like Bergkamp should have reserved his best form for the beautiful afternoons of August and September. It was a period where he believed: 'I am getting close to the highest I can get'. Such perfect conditions almost demanded great goals and outrageous skills. It was no surprise, therefore, that as the leaves on the trees turned red and orange, Bergkamp's fortunes - and Arsenal's form, hit choppy seas.

An uncomfortable trip to Selhurst Park heralded the end of a beautiful Summer and the beginning of a spate of injuries and disruption (a two month descent to disaster - so the press reckoned). Crystal Palace's Herman Hreidarson, the Eagles' Icelandic defender, earned his corn by following Dennis around the park all afternoon. His employment of 'novel' defending techniques, meant that Bergkamp probably needed to have Hreidarson's boot surgically removed from his rear end after the match. It was a scrappy 0-0 game, and Arsenal's form was certainly not helped by Overmars' absence. The referee missed a blatant shove on Wright in the Palace area and later booked Dennis for over-protesting after a foul. That booking, Bergkamp's fifth of the season, meant he'd miss three games. The Dutchman's magic spell was broken and, in truth, his form wouldn't hit such staggering heights again.

A week later, Villa's Ricardo Scimeca man-marked Dennis and, with Ian Wright's form plummeting, another 0-0 draw ensued. Premiership defenders cottoned on fast to the fact that if the Dutchman was hustled out of the game, the Gunners seemed unable to construct other routes to goal. Manu Petit's sending off was another major blow; after an uncertain start, he had begun to look the part in midfield. His punishment for touching referee Paul Durkin was a four match ban, which meant that he and Dennis would miss crucial clashes against the Scousers and Mancs.

Inevitably, the Gunners crashed to defeat at Derby a week later. Sturridge and Wanchope made the defence, and Nigel Winterburn in particular, look fools, as they rampaged to a 3-0 victory. Big Ron's new Sheffield Wednesday side then cruised to a 2-0 win at Hillsborough. In the midst of this grim run, the boys produced one vintage Highbury display which defied the form book and, at season's end, carried huge significance. The visit of Manchester United in early November provoked an afternoon of fear and loathing in North London. United had surged ahead in the title race and the match was an unceasing frenzy of attacking football and superb goals. Nicolas Anelka, who'd looked out of sorts at Derby on his full debut, chose the perfect moment to open his goal account for the Arse. Controlling the ball on the edge of the box, he drilled a twenty five yard shot past Schmeichel.

When French counterpart Patrick Vieira's physics-defying effort swerved in ten minutes later, the ground was in uproar. Not that Pat remained cheerful for too long. After scoring, he slid to his knees, tearing ligaments in the process. With Vieira hobbling out of the action, United fought back. Ex Spur Sherringham's double pulled them level by half time, and his insistence on kissing his shirt in front of the North Bank made the atmosphere even more spiteful.

The second half contained just one moment of significance. David Platt's header from a corner bisected perfectly Gary Neville's bonse and the crossbar. 3-2 to the Arsenal; the North Bank boiled over with excitement and Platty tore away with joy. Urging his team mates to chase him, they obligingly piled on top of him in celebration. For once, Platty's wonderland was indeed a beautiful place.

A gritty 1-0 win up at Newcastle appeared to confirm an upturn in fortunes. Ian Wright's barren run ended with him nodding the winner. But the vest under his shirt, inscribed 'At last', spoke more for his lack of confidence and wretched luck in front of goal. The win against the Geordies turned out to be nothing but a temporary respite. McManaman's wonder goal for Liverpool inflicted upon us our first home defeat for nine months, but the season's nadir arrived a fortnight later against Blackburn.

Destroyed 3-1 at home by a rampant Rovers side, several player's form scraped the barrel - especially Wrighty's who, after a fractious display, was heckled at the final whistle. Police were later called after he remonstrated with fans in Avenell Road, from the dressing room window. Just two months earlier, the scenes were very different after he'd broken the record. Naturally, the whole incident was overblown, but here was clear proof that his love affair with the fans was in danger of turning sour. His first team career was practically over.

Shamefully, even Tony Adams was booed by some brain dead elements in the crowd. It was a grim moment, but it highlighted the fact that back, ankle, and knee injuries were threatening to end his career. The news that he would take a month's sabbatical in the South of France to regain fitness hardly improved fans' moods.

Press exposés focused on the defence's age and fragility, and internal wrangles within the club. Peter Robinson in *The Observer* reckoned: 'The great Arsenal back four, the buttress on which success was built, may at last be dismantled'. Others talked of a 'continental rift', 'Anglo-French friction', and a 'creaking *entente cordiale*'. *The Mirror's* Mike Walters went even further, suggesting that 'Gallic subtlety is in danger of marginalising English grit'. The root of the Gunners problem - injuries and suspensions aside - was that even when the team had performed well in the Summer, the new signings hadn't effectively gelled within the team. At various times, Bergkamp, Wright, Overmars and Vieira showed individual genius but, as Bob Wilson said: 'the true Arsenal qualities have to come out.... it's not enough just to pass the ball around'.

In *Addicted*, Adams admitted that, during the pre-Christmas period, he didn't feel as if the defence was receiving adequate cover from Petit and Vieira. Under George Graham, when Adams had won all his medals, the defence was brilliantly shielded by the likes of Rocky and Mickey. Leaks suggested that the English players believed Petit and Vieira were indisciplined - 'forty-five minuters', is how a couple of senior pros described them. After the Rovers match, the players had a forthright team meeting where Bould, Adams and co. weighed in with observations on how they felt the French duo needed to operate within the team. They clearly listened well to the suggestions; in the New Year they would become the most effective midfield partnership in the country, creatively and defensively. The Blackburn match and its aftermath was the turning point of our season.

With big clubs, history has a habit of repeating itself. Back in 1970, after Arsenal lost 5-0 at Stoke, the players held a ruthlessly honest team meeting, where tactics were rethought and attitudes were re-examined. The class of 1970 were immediately written off as title challengers. The trophy was more or less awarded to the most high profile team of the day - Leeds. So it was in late '97 - the bookies declared Manchester United to be virtually unbackable. The '70-71 team, of course, went on a long unbeaten run after the Stoke debacle and ultimately completed the Double.

When, ten days after the Blackburn game, a far Eastern betting syndicate arranged for the lights to go out at half time during our game at Wimbledon, Arsenal's season was, literally and metaphorically, plunged into darkness. The match, which we seemed set to lose anyway, was abandoned, and injuries, loss of form and suspensions meant we were now thirteen points behind the leaders. The fact that we now had a match in hand was small consolation. Title hopes were in ruins and Arsenal, according to conventional wisdom, were a shambles. No one could have foreseen that four months further down the most joyous of roads, Wenger's Arsenal would remain undefeated in twenty six consecutive league and FA Cup games. From chaos, there emerged glory; it's the Arsenal way of doing things.

One of the myths surrounding the '97/98 season is that the team's form in August and September, and from mid February onward, was the key to success. That is partly true, but Arsenal's unbeaten displays through late December and January mustn't be ignored. This spell allowed the team to consolidate league form, tiptoe through tricky cup ties and, subtly, alter tactics. The matches were not pretty but they allowed younger players to gel within the team, suspended or injured players to return, and Wrighty to be phased out for good. It was a transitional few weeks when, in Eric Morecambe's words, the team started to play 'all the right notes, but not necessarily in the right order'.

Ugly scraps with Leicester, Spurs and Coventry yielded five points from three games. It represented an upturn in form, and the defence - marshalled by Keown and Bould, started to regain its shape. The players certainly relished the physical side of these encounters. Steve Bould won his tussle with Spurs' panic buy Jurgen Klinsmann (cosmetic pudding, Mr Sugar?) and Vieira spent his afternoon at Highfield Road trying to kick any Sky Blue player that moved. Patrick then lived up to his reputation for being increasingly 'difficult' when he argued the toss over his blatant handball. Momentarily transformed into Michael Jordan, he virtually slam-dunked the ball away before the referee sent him packing. With the boys still lying back in sixth place, cup competitions took on a special significance.

The January ties represented Ian Wright's swansong in an Arsenal shirt. Up at Port Vale in the FA Cup 3rd round replay, he damaged a hamstring. Fortunately David Seaman helped us scrape through the penalty shootout. Wrighty did return briefly for the Coca Cola Cup Quarter Final against West Ham, when he skipped across Upton Park to rifle in the winner. But as his aborted move to Benfica suggested, his time was up. His late season return represented pure nostalgia rather than a significant contribution. It was time for the younger guns to boom in our attack.

Wenger's switch to a 4-3-3 formation also began to pay dividends. He rotated any two from Vieira, Petit, Platt and Hughes (depending on who was fit or suspended), to play alongside the hugely improved Ray Parlour in midfield. Marc Overmars was pushed further forward to join the attack. It was an inspired decision; witness the Dutchman slamming two excellent goals past George's Leeds team in a 2-1 win at Highbury, despite the inevitable white shirted wall of defenders blocking his path. The first leg of the Coca Cola Cup Semi-Final against Chelsea was the perfect example of his ability to flit menacingly between midfield and the opposition penalty area. His partnership on the left with Stephen Hughes worked brilliantly; Overmars netted the first, and cut the ball back for Hughes to clatter in a second. *'Hughesie for England'*, screamed the tabloids, such was their excitement at finding an English midfielder who actually knew where his left peg was.

The Kings Road tarts deserved to be tonked, but old enemy Mark Hughes' late away goal gave them hope for the return match. As it turned out, the second leg disaster was the only crucial aberration Wenger's Arsenal made during the New Year period. Crushed 3-1 on the night by the Blues, Chelsea deservedly cruised to the Coca Cola Cup final. As ever, though, their lordly London neighbours would soon have rather more important matters on their minds. In reality, the more glamorous FA Cup provided the first real sign of things to come. By late January, Tony Adams was ready to return to defensive duties. Fit and rejuvenated, he'd be virtually ever present for the rest of the season. For the fourth round clash with Middlesbrough, Arsène was able, virtually, to pick his first choice line up for the run in (save for a couple of defensive alterations): Manninger, Dixon, Adams, Bould, Winterburn, Vieira, Parlour, Petit, Bergkamp, Anelka, Overmars. This quicksilver line up tore first division Boro' apart. Overmars and Parlour killed the tie within twenty minutes. Such was the Gunners' dominance, Michael Henderson wrote in *The Times* that 'on another day, they could have declared at half time'. Even Paul Merson's reply for the Teesiders was fairly pleasurable, and Gunners fans streamed away confident that at least a decent FA Cup run was in the offing. And a lot more besides, as it turned out.

At season's end, Arsène Wenger compared Steve Bould with Franz Beckenbauer. 'I call Steve the Kaiser', he said. Arsène was half joking, but it showed just how crucial Bould was to the team, and how much his play improved throughout the season. During Tony Adams' absence, he was appointed acting captain, and did an excellent job alongside the more pacy Martin Keown. Both Wenger and ex-boss George Graham agreed that he was, arguably, the most under-rated player in the Premiership. This is due to the fact that he seemed the archetypal blue-collar Graham type player. Bought for a bargain £390,000 from Stoke, he'd been loaned out to Torquay during his early career. He was certainly a graduate of the 'hard knocks' football academy. It was the kind of upbringing which Graham believed gave a player the hunger to succeed when he finally arrived at Highbury; the kind of hunger which Lee Dixon and Nigel Winterburn also had.

Bouldy's appearance led 'experts' to neatly pigeon-hole him into the 'English clogger' category. Towering, balding, hard as nails, and prone to welly the ball upfield, he was often seen as the meanest component of Graham's mean machine. Just to emphasise the essential 'Englishness' of Bould, George Graham wrote in *The Glory and The Grief* that he was the 'sort of man's man you want alongside you in the trenches'. Yet Bould was plagued by a troublesome thigh injury during much of his Highbury career, which meant he often missed chunks of the season. Consequently, he was overshadowed by the likes of Keown, O'Leary and, of course, Tony Adams.

It's ironic that even when Bould displayed the best form of his life in late December and January '98, the press bombarded us with daily bulletins on Adams' progress. Paul Davis once said to me: 'Tony always got the credit for the clean sheets - but, so many times, Steve saved us at the last minute'. So it was in early '98. Reassuring though it was to know that Tone's stay on the *Cote d'Azur* was reaping dividends, back in freezing Blighty, Bould was busy repelling the likes of Heskey and Klinsmann at a crucial juncture of the season.

Another beneficiary of the Wenger effect, Bould believed that Wenger extended his career 'probably by another three years'. The Frenchman worked on his defensive strengths but also encouraged him to bring the ball forward and develop his passing skills. But Steve's canny tricks at set pieces had always drawn admiring glances from the likes of Alan Hansen. From corners, he'd mastered the art of shoving his marker in the back, enabling him to flick the ball onto an onrushing Arsenal player. His occasional goals also suggested there was more to his game than defending. Bould's first goal against Sampdoria in '95, as commentator Martin Tyler put it, was finished like a 'craftsman'. Despite that Bould will rightly be remembered for play-ing his part perfectly in the Gunners' famous back four for a decade, which helped Arsenal win so many trophies in the '90s. And that is no mean achievement, is it?

With the team safely through to the FA Cup fifth round, performances began to shift into a higher gear. Manchester United, meanwhile, slipped up in two consecutive games against Leicester and Southampton, and gallant Barnsley dumped them out of the FA Cup. Though Fergie was not yet shitting bricks, he was beginning to skulk around with an even more miserable expression on his sour face than usual. The Gunners also had three games in hand but this would count for nothing unless they could put together a most improbable string of victories. The fact that we faced five life threatening London derbies during February made the task more daunting, though the disrupted fixture list meant we had three Highbury league games in a row. This break gave the team a chance to embark on a crucial little run of victories.

Another spate of injuries and suspensions led Arsène to bemoan the number of games played in Britain, but it gave him the chance to introduce more youngsters into the team. These were players who had previously looked unconvincing but would all have crucial contributions to make by the end of the season. Late on in the home game against Southampton, Platty joined rookies Nic Anelka and Chris Wreh up front. It was an unorthodox Wenger strategy but Platt had one of his most effective games yet. Anelka looked inspired - coolly slotting in a well constructed third goal and adding to excellent finishes by Adams and Bergkamp.

The Highbury clash with Chelsea was billed as London's battle royale. Apart from ourselves, the Blues were the only side with a hope of catching the Mancs. Stamford Bridge's self proclaimed 'entertainers' arrived with a six man defence (such ambition), but Steve Hughes proved to be the game's x-factor. Two storming goals, which left de Goey grasping air not only gave Arsenal three crucial points - it also destroyed Chelsea's season. Adept as they were at raising their game for Cup matches, they were no match for thoroughbreds. A few days later, Ruud Gullit was sent packing. The Gunners were now becoming London's true exponents of 'sexy football'. Chelsea were capable of producing the foreplay, but only Arsenal could provide the fulminatory climax.

Wenger's selection problems reached their zenith in mid February. Vieira, Petit, Overmars et al were absent when Crystal Palace visited Highbury. This gave Vernazza, Boa Morte and Gilles Grimandi a chance to press their first team claims. In truth, Palace were such an awful side that Arsène could have fielded a Tea Ladies XI and still been confident of winning. But the Eagles, with beached whale Tomas Brolin wobbling about all over the pitch, somehow kept the score to 0-0 before Grimandi's cross-cum shot flew into the net. This, at last, got the boo-boys off his back. Wenger had said of Grimandi's 'teething' problems that 'if the crowd at his former club, Monaco, got on his back, he could always go and talk to them'. In hindsight, his goal takes on massive significance. An injury-hit team under-performed against crap opposition, but still win 1-0. 'Tis the stuff of Champions. Palace also had the temerity to scratch out a draw at Highbury in the FA Cup fifth round, before Anelka and Bergkamp destroyed them in the Selhurst Park replay.

A gritty 0-0 draw in the league followed at Upton park; Keown's head was sliced open after one aerial duel too many, Boa Morte missed a last minute sitter, and Alex Manninger pulled off two stupendous saves from Hartson and Berkovic to scab a point. But of all the clashes in London, the match at Wimbledon was truly the beginning of the gallop to glory. On the eve of the match, Wenger said of Arsenal's title hopes: 'I honestly believe we can do it. But then perhaps I'm a little bit crazy'. Wimbledon - if ever there was a team to throw spanners into works, and fart in the face of con-vention - it was the Crazy Gang. Blood splattered memories of the previous season's game at Selhurst Park were still fresh and, at Highbury, they'd always proved to be a major pain in the arse. On the night, Vinnie Jones was his usual thuggish self and Jason Euell did his best to puncture Manninger's bubble. Up front, however, Bergkamp appeared, finally, to instill good habits into Chris Wreh.

Reputably signed on the premise that he was George Weah's cousin, his wretched early performances suggested that his presence on the field could only be explained by this fact. In his rare appearances, he'd seemed adept at booting himself in the ankle while trying to score, needing, on one occa-sion, treatment from Gary Lewin after doing so. At Wimbledon, though, he was inspired. Banging in a late second half winner after Overmars' cut back, he performed his celebratory summersault for the first time. At the final whistle, the boys dashed to celebrate with the fans. You sensed that this vic-tory was significant; call it Gunner intuition. This was the night when Manchester United dropped two points against West Ham, and Nigel Winterburn first decided to conduct his victory dance in front of Arsenal supporters. Crucially, the bookies reluctantly reopened the book on the title race, despite one idiotic Manchester bookie already having paid out to punters who'd backed United.

With Arsenal nine points behind with three games in hand, you could now back us at 7-2. Cue nervous looks over shoulders at Old Trafford, and a torrent of excuses from Fergie. From the disasters of November, the

Gunners were now a long odds shot to complete the double. Not even the most optimistic would have predicted that outcome after the win at Selhurst Park, but one thing was certain; Arsenal would now face two shit-or-bust encounters in four days. After drawing 1-1 in the FA Cup Quarter-Final at Highbury against West Ham, we faced a tricky looking replay at Upton Park. But, first, the London press hyped our next league match as 'Arsenal's biggest game for nearly three years'. They were right; on Saturday we faced the mother of all battles at Old Trafford with Manchester United.

It is no exaggeration to say that, in Arsène Wenger, Ferguson finally met his match. For years, his team's blatant gamesmanship and his own annoying habits, like standing by the pitch with that bloody stopwatch of his, annoyed the football world at large. Although he grudgingly respected Arsenal's new style of play, the Taggart look-a-like appeared to take an instant dislike to Wenger, virtually as soon as the Frenchman arrived. Wenger dared to say what most have thought for years; that fixture lists were subtly altered at a trice to accommodate the loathsome Mancs, and being awarded a penalty at Old Trafford was as rare an occasion as the English cricket team winning the Ashes. With Arsenal now becoming a realistic title threat, a riled Fergie made a grave error of judgement. First of all, he casually dismissed the chasing pack as 'also rans'. Then he employed his old trick - claiming that other sides always raised their game against the Mancs to 'obscene levels'.

Doubtless, the sour faced Scot thought that Arsène would, in stereotypical French style, explode like Keegan had in '96. But there were no such emotional outbursts from Wenger. He simply pointed out that with the Arsenal facing London derbies by the bucket load, we knew everything about other teams raising their game. As for winning the Premiership, Arsène came out with the old English classic: 'We'll take each game as it comes'. So Fergie didn't get the reaction he wanted and was put firmly in his place by the diplomatic Frenchman. Wenger's one upmanship in verbal sparring was all well and good, but Arsène realised that another old adage rang true: 'Actions speak louder than words'. Dumping United on their smug arses at Old Trafford was the only true way to silence them.

Arsenal v Manchester United, March 14th. The game was a patchwork of drama, near misses, heroic performances and a glorious finale. Fast forward the action: man of the match Marc Overmars slicing through United's defence at will in the first half and tormenting John Curtis. Alex Manninger repelling Cole and Solksjaer. 1,500 travelling fans outsinging 57,000 Mancs.

Vieira and Petit destroying United's midfield threat, and demonstrating that they were becoming the most effective partnership in the country. And of course - the defining moment; a long ball from Petit, Anelka flicking on the ball, and Marc Overmars galloping forward to calmly strike the ball past the red nosed Dane. Finally, United throwing everything at Arsenal in the dying minutes which caused Schmeichel to tear his hamstring. Too little, too late, for the Mancs.

Arsenal won the battle of Old Trafford - the first time since '91, when that victory helped us win the title. At the final whistle, Fergie disgustedly spat out his gum and triumphant Arsenal players milked the applause from fans. Wenger's Arsenal came of age that day and, inevitably, photographs of Overmars adorned the Sunday newspapers. But it was the image of an Arsenal fan's face which truly defined the day. The rabid, frenzied features of Barry Ferst celebrating at Old Trafford remains one of *the* memories of the season. His contorted expressions neatly compounded what those of us stuck in Islington pubs now realised: 'we can do it'.

He recalls the day: 'When Marc Overmars got the goal, we all went absolutely mad. When the final whistle went, all Arsenal fans knew what it meant - it was an incredible feeling to have actually won at Old Trafford. I can't remember whether 'the moment' came when we scored or when the final whistle went. I get the feeling it was after the game - it was probably when Nigel Winterburn was going ape shit in front of all of us and dancing with delight. I was probably reacting to him. I didn't realise anything until the final credits on *Match Of The Day* that night. My wife screamed 'Oh my God, it's *you*', and very quickly the 'phone rang and people were saying: 'Is that really *you*?' I couldn't believe I'd been spotted in the crowd. I looked crazy, mad and I just thought: 'Bloody hell, did I *really* do that?'

The reaction to it amazed me. I walk to work from the station and, in the next week, I had Arsenal fans and United haters coming up to me and shaking me by the hands. The press came into work, expecting my colleagues to say I was some kind of maniac - they couldn't believe it when people said I was just a mild mannered office worker by day. The first time I went back to Highbury after the United game, my image was shown on the big screen and people around me were applauding and laughing. After that, I had Dutch fans come up to me outside the ground, and ask for a photo. I even got an e-mail from Japan saying that there was somewhere for me to stay if I ever went there. The most bizarre incident was on a trip to Las Vegas, where a bloke recognised me and said 'hello'.

The final event was when they showed the top ten images of the '97/98 season. My friends reckoned I might be on the list. But, as the list was being played on the big screen - you know, Wright's record breaking goal at number seven, Platt's header against United at number five, I thought 'I won't be on it'. Then it came to number two and there I was - screaming like an idiot. I couldn't believe that in a season with so many defining moments, only Tony Adams finished ahead of me. It still amazes me that there is so much interest but it's not a bad way to be remembered'.

Barry Ferst, Arsenal fan from Hendon

There was no time for players or fans to bask in a post orgasmic O.T. doze. Four days later, the boys travelled to West Ham for a brutal FA Cup Quarter Final replay. Our superb battling display was virtually ignored as the media focused on Dennis' elbow smash in the face on the Hammers' Lomas. Bergkamp's sending off was allowed to overshadow Anelka's net ripping goal and Alex Manninger's excellence in the penalty shoot out. The tabloids showed where their loyalties lay, by splashing Samassi Abou's pained face after missing the Hammers' vital fifth spot kick, all over their back pages.

Bergkamp's sending off was the cue for a glut of tabloid exposes on Arsenal's discipline crises, thinly veiled behind a wave of anti-French bullshit. Suddenly, every incident from the season was raked up; Manu's dismissal against Villa, and Vieira's various indiscretions. Saner fans realised that only Patrick's dismissal at Highfield Road and Dennis' gob-smashing effort on Lomas truly warranted the hype. The fact that Arsenal's stars had been subjected to sly tugs and rabbit punches in the kidneys all season wasn't going to stop the onslaught, though. Suddenly, our continental players were elevated to the 'stroppy/arrogant foreigner' guise, with several hacks betraying their true ignorance by bleating that 'salt of the earth' British players, (like Dennis Wise), wouldn't indulge in such activities.

In reality, all this meant that Bergkamp would be suspended (again) for three games at a vital stage of the season, and the whole team - including the defenders, who were all on the brink of a suspension, walked the thinnest of tightropes. Naturally, Ferguson stepped up his 'pressure' campaign by saying that Arsenal would feel overwhelming strain and that it was inevitable the Gunners would drop points before long.

Psychologically, three, tiptoeing, cautious 1-0 wins in late March and early April swung the season irrevocably in our favour. In his last game before suspension, Bergkamp ghosted in to grab the winner against Sheffield Wednesday, much to the bewilderment of dumbfounded Owls defenders

Hinchcliffe and Walker. Chris Wreh's superlative strike won the game at Bolton, where Arsenal had to fight doughty relegation-threatened opposition with ten men. Martin Keown, red carded in the first half, appeared to give away a blatant penalty, but referee Keith Burge obligingly waved away Bolton protests. Upon such narrow margins hinge league titles...

The FA Cup Semi Final against Wolves at Villa Park, Sunday April 5th. Most of us were forced to rise at dawn, all for the privilege of getting to Birmingham for a noon kick off. Anyone who regularly endures the nightmare that is the M6, knows that whatever time one leaves home, it's almost impossible to get to the intended destination on time. So it proved on this particular Sunday; Chris Wreh netted the vital early goal after just twelve minutes. Hundreds of hard core Gooners missed his trademark back flip and summersault, as they were still trying to park, or worse, negotiate the delights of the Aston Freeway. The refusal to delay kick off compounded the view that the FA's heads remained shoved in the sand. Hadn't they learnt their lesson after what happened with late crushes and stampedes at Hillsborough in '89? After Wreh's goal, latecomers witnessed a marvellously controlled display from Petit and Vieira which held Wolves at bay. Despite one pants-fillingly close call from Don Goodman, the first division team couldn't grab an equaliser. The elated faces of the grizzled old warriors in our defence at the final whistle told us exactly what this victory meant. The Double, which would have been a 118-1 shot at Christmas, was now an odds-on target.

Just as importantly, the Gunners hadn't conceded a goal for six games. Wenger talked of turning the clock back to the displays of late Summer. We hadn't quite reached those heights again, but soon we would. In the meantime, Fergie reckoned we'd need to win our next six games to realistically haul the title away from Old Trafford. 'No way will that happen', he said. But Arsenal's attacking football would soon reach the truly 'sexy' proportions of August and September and, defensively, the clock was wound back even further to the tightness of the Graham era.

By March '98, Nigel Winterburn's form suggested that he'd discovered the benefits of an age reversing elixir. Virtually written off by G.G. three years earlier, and looking jaded at the start of Wenger's reign, Nige began to regain the form he'd shown in the early '90s. With his hair becoming more cropped by the week, his tackling regained its old ferocity. Indeed, at times it actually seemed to be getting *harder*, as Wimbledon's Michael Hughes could testify. In the league game at Selhurst Park, Hughes loitered idly on the ball, unaware that Nige was hurtling towards him from the half way line. In the split second when Hughes realised what was about to hit him, he made to toe poke the ball away. It was all to no avail. Winterburn crashed into him and Hughes was almost hurled into the front row of the away fans' stand. As one, the hoards of travelling Gooners began the *'Nigel Winterburn'* chants. Winterburn, who had also been getting mysteriously quicker, smirked at the travelling Gooners and clenched his fist in triumph. Every title winning side needs a defender who tackles unnecessarily hard.

Most startling of all was his penchant for wildly celebrating Arsenal's victories towards the end of the season. Nigel, who'd always had a reputation as a fairly cool customer, choreographed his own war dances in front of our fans, later commenting in *Highbury High* that 'you reach a point in your career when you realise you should make the most of every game'. Talk of breaking up the defence had been *de rigeur* in North London for years but Winterburn realised that, at 34 years of age, time really was ticking by for him. Sheer hard work was the only way he could get through a season. He said at the time: 'we will work on the back four defensive drills. And time and again it will pay off for us in games'.

Winterburn was yet another example of Wenger finding the perfect balance within the team. The Frenchman realised that Nige's blue collar qualities - gleaned from being rejected by Birmingham, and playing with Wimbledon's Crazy Gang, complemented the continental while collar attributes. Under Arsène, he'd lost none of his defensive organisation but he'd successfully thrown off George's manacles, to maraud forward in tandem with Marc Overmars. The Dutchman clearly felt the benefits of Nige's presence, as had Anders Limpar in '91, who commented: 'My early form that season was totally down to Nigel, who allowed me to attack all the time'. History was repeating itself. Seven years earlier, teams were destroyed by attacking brilliance and defensive meanness. In 1998, strikers could burn off teams with a blast of skill, while the opposition ran into the bleakest of brick walls at the back. And in bullet headed Nigel Winterburn, they collided with the hardest competitor of them all.

Arsenal's league form now hit previously untouched heights. The power, speed, and poise within our play was astonishing, and the title run-in saw the fulfilment of all our footballing fantasies. The pre-match atmosphere before the Highbury match with Newcastle was sensational. Star of the show Nic Anelka dodged past a defender to sweep us into the lead, before Ray Parlour's marauding run helped the Frenchman gobble up a second. The Geordies' smothering defensive blanket had already been destroyed before Vieira provided the perfect *coup de grace*. Loitering on the ball from thirty yards out, he briefly looked up and unleashed the definitive rocket into Given's net. The image of Vieira's power and grace when he scored that goal will live forever, as will his insouciant celebrations which went with it. The post match vibe was simply electric. The Gunners Tavern's walls ran with sweat, as hard core Gunners jammed in to toast the young Frenchmen on their goals.

If that was the most satisfying home match of the new year thus far, we waited just two days for the best away experience of the season. A potentially tricky away match at Blackburn on Easter Monday turned into a joyous carnival. Dennis, returning after suspension, smashed in the opener within a minute and then he set up Ray Parlour for two splendid strikes. When, after half an hour, Nic Anelka roared towards the Rovers goal to make it 4-0, a record away win seemed to be on the cards. The second half blizzard, which necessitated the use of an orange ball, stopped the onslaught but, at the final whistle, away fans screamed in triumph and the likes of Andy Gray said that the Arse were about to be crowned champs. Although Gunners fans publicly subscribed to the 'We'll take each game as it comes' philosophy, you just sensed that this was going to be our year. Fergie's comments looked increasingly pathetic. Chiding us about our supposed lack of bottle, his own team lost theirs. After drawing two games on the trot, the Mancs were now just a point ahead, having played two games more.

Ironically, it wasn't the season's final two games at Villa and Liverpool which inspired nervousness in Gooners, it was the home clash with Wimbledon. Unbeaten at Highbury since '88, the Dons almost derailed the '89 challenge and pinched a point in '91 too. Speaking years later on Talk Radio, the Dons' Neal Ardley compared Arsenal's onslaught with the Roman army's assault on the brave but indisciplined Germanic tribes at the start of *Gladiator*. Ardley reckoned that Tony Adams' influence on his side was equivalent to General Maximus', in his army. To stretch the metaphor further, if Tone's presence really was similar to that of the Russell Crowe character, then it's no surprise that this Gunners team 'unleashed hell' on the Dons. Adams himself powered in a thunderbolt header to destroy Wimbledon's confidence and the two Dutchmen, who'd already grabbed a goal, each set up Petit for his first ever Arsenal goal. 5-0 to the Arsenal, and the team's performance was so faultless that Dons boss Joe Kinnear claimed: 'You can't see them as anything else but champions'.

By now, Arsenal were able to move up and down the gears at will during games. Often beginning matches cautiously, we were adept at quickly slipping into cruise control. After years of fairly predictable footie under George, Arsenal F.C. were now the most exhilarating team in the country. We'd reached a pitch which was the envy of the Premiership. Sky T.V., BBC, and assorted footie magazines analysed Arsenal's play and drooled over the aesthetics of each movement. Back in Holland, Dennis' compatriots compared him with an artist. Commenting on his slide rule passes, painter Jeroen Henneman said of Bergkamp: 'One moment the pitch is crowded and narrow. Suddenly Bergkamp makes it huge and wide'. The rest of the Premiership could only look on in awe.

If observers wanted an illustration of Arsenal's elevation to cultured performers, then the away match at Barnsley on April 25th was the only place to be. The Gunners defence soaked up Barnsley's early attacking verve, before Petit and Vieira grabbed midfield by the scruff of the neck. After 23 minutes, Dennis curled home a stunner which brought admiring gasps from the home crowd. When Marc Overmars doubled the lead, to give us a 2-0 win, the obliging Oakwell crowd sportingly chanted *'Champions, Champions'*, and formed a guard of honour as the lads departed in the team bus. How times had changed since the days when George's teams used to slink away from opposition grounds with *'boring, boring, Arsenal'* ringing in their ears.

As the title race entered its last days, we knew that two home victories in a week, over Derby and Everton, would finally clinch it. With a trip to Anfield also in the offing, it wasn't a dissimilar scenario to that in '89. And, once again, Derby were the first obstacle which had to be removed. Jim Smith's team arrived with the intention of grabbing a draw and, to achieve this, he packed midfield with a motley crew of bone heads. With their goalie in excellent form, the bad memories of Shilton's omnipotence in '89 came flooding back. Manu Petit gave possibly his best performance in an Arsenal shirt, and for good measure, fired the winner which skimmed past Poom.

Bergkamp's hamstring injury forced him to limp out of the action and, as it turned out, the rest of the season. The prime architect of our success would not be present at the prize giving and final ceremonies. It was a cruel blow for player and club - he was a star performer who now warranted a mention in the same breath as James and Brady. His injury prompted tabloids to suggest that Ian Wright would take his place and score the goals to win the Double. But the Wreh/Anelka forward line was adequate compensation for Wright/Bergkamp, though Wrighty wasn't quite finished yet.

Outside, in Avenell Road, the energy release after the Derby game was astounding. The gathering hoards realised the title was so close you could practically smell it. So, rather than a repetition of '89, this 1-0 scrap produced happier echoes of the vital 1-0 win over Stoke in April '71, which brought the Double a step closer. And for the first time in around half a century, Arsenal could win the title at Highbury in front of their own fans on the Sunday. With Howard Kendall's relegation-threatened Everton the opponents, surely the lads wouldn't let us down?

Arsenal v Everton: Sunday May 3rd. An epoch defining day in our history; the high point thus far of Wengerism. This game could have been sold out five times over and, with an estimated eighteen million watching on Sky T.V., it's no exaggeration to say that the eyes of the nation were focused on sun drenched Highbury. The Arsenal team which took the field was: Seaman, Dixon, Adams, Keown, Winterburn, Parlour, Vieira, Petit, Overmars, Wreh, Anelka. The team was poised to turn on the most brilliant of shows in a frenzied destruction of the hapless Toffees. In the process, all the old Arsenal urban myths were laid to rest, and we were given a plethora of images which will forever be logged in the memory banks.

Bilic's obligingly early own goal almost made the stadium melt in excitement, and Chris Wreh came close twice in the first half. Marc Overmars cruised past Dave Watson like an exocet missile, on several occasions and scored a well taken second goal, before he scorched in an outrageous third. Arsène, bowing to sentiment, sent on Steve Bould and Ian Wright as late subs; the thunderous ovation which greeted the latter still makes the neck hairs stand on end. The delicious finale was provided by Tony Adams. After being put through by Steve Bould, his crashing half volley made the score 4-0. Adams' glorious effort was the goal of the decade and the image of the decade - no question. As the man himself said, the previous two championship successes under George had merely been alcoholic blurs for him. With *Champions, Champions* ringing out, we all knew this was different. Style and grace, as well as grit, brought the title home.

Gunners' fan Chris Athanasi recalls the events of that day: 'We were about to see Arsenal win a Championship at home and life couldn't get much better. Everything was perfect about the day. It was a Bank Holiday Weekend, it was sunny, and the streets were filled with red and white. Thousands had turned up without tickets just hoping to be part of the celebrations after the game. Inside the ground it was carnival time, there was

red and white everywhere you looked. There were flags, giant scarves, painted faces, and it felt like everybody was wearing red. The game went like a
dream, which is unusual for Arsenal, with two first half goals and one midway through the second. The party was in full swing when that moment
arrived. That moment you know will stay with you for the rest of your life,
that moment that you will relive to your grandchildren and say, "I was
there".

With minutes remaining on the clock Steve Bould picked up the ball in
our half and floated a perfect pass into the path of a striding Tony Adams.
With a movement which was more like a belly down than a chest down,
Tony took a couple of strides, and struck a beautiful left footed half volley
into the back of the net. The whole ground now erupted as Tony walked
towards us, Christ-like, arms outstretched, embracing each and every one of
us. At that moment we were all one man, one team, one club. I have a pho-
tograph of that moment at home and you can just make me out in the
crowd, albeit fuzzy. Moments like that are why we go to football matches
year in year out, united in one thing, the love of our club.

Chris Athanasi, Arsenal fan from Finchley

With the title safely secured, the Gunners travelled to Anfield and Villa
Park for the final two games of the season. Wenger fielded a virtual reserve
team on a surreal evening at Anfield. The rookie team, given a guard of honour by Scouse players as they ran onto the pitch, was thumped 4-0. At least
it gave travelling supporters the chance to exercise vocal chords in preparation for Wembley. *'We only win when we have to'*, came the North London
mantra. A psychopathic lunge by Ince on best buddy Wrighty made him a
Cup Final doubt; *'He's supposed to be your mate'*, roared the away contingent.
Wrighty did get himself fit for the FA Cup final, and played in the last
league game at Villa Park (a 0-1 defeat), but Arsène had already decided that
Wright's late re-entry to the side was purely for nostalgic reasons.

To Wembley. Surely there's never been a travelling army of Arsenal fans
so confident of an FA Cup final victory. Even the normally vociferous
Geordies, who lined Wembley Way, seemed strangely subdued. Tabloids,
who'd hyped up Sheffield Wednesday's chances in '93, agreed that this
game should be a no contest. Newcastle boss Dalglish was in the process
of tearing apart Keegan's entertainers and replacing them with sub-stan-
dard imports. In doing so, Newcastle came close to relegation and, in
every position, Arsenal were superior, man for man. On the eve of the

final, Keith Gillespie, the only Geordie capable of providing real width in their team, became injured. So the 30,000 Arsenal fans inside Wembley expected nothing less than to emulate the '71 stars.

In ninety degrees heat at pitch level, the red and white army lapped up a Wembley cruise - almost for the first time in living memory. Newcastle fans unconvincingly chanted that they were *'gonna win the Cup'*. But even during the first three minutes, when reformed Essex man Ray Parlour crossed for Anelka to head over the bar, that clearly wasn't going to happen. Marc Overmars knocked the ball under Given to put us into the lead, and from then on, man of the match Parlour ripped into the heart of Newcastle territory.

Commentators tried to talk of 'plucky' Newcastle's comeback but, in truth, Shearer's effort which twanged Seaman's post only came about because Keown trod on the ball. The legions of face painted Geordie fans desperately chanted *'Attack, Attack, Attack'*, but all to no avail. And then the grumpy ex England captain lost it completely, shoving Adams in the back and receiving a yellow card. The Double was finally delivered when Nic Anelka shot clear of the defence and blasted a pin-point effort past Shay Given. Cue bedlam in the Arse end. Bodies flew up and down the aisles, people at the front toppled off their sawn-off plastic buckets and grown men bawled their eyes out with joy. There was even time for Parlour to rattle the post before the final whistle went.

Wenger's Arsenal had done it. The Double was ours. In just five months, we'd travelled from the despair of the Blackburn game to this joyous finale. The final, as a contest, may not have been a classic in the dramatic sense but, as Manu Petit later said, *le gloire* was all that mattered on the day. Lee Dixon commented: 'This surpasses anything we have done in the past'. Younger fans also realised that a wrong had been righted. Seven years earlier, only Gazza's monumental performance stopped George's '91 vintage from winning a Double they'd so richly deserved. Inevitably, comparisons between Wenger's double winners and Chapman and Mee's teams raged. But, taking into account the modern age of pace, power and micro-second skill, the '98 vintage was surely the greatest of all. And so - Mickey Thomas' Anfield goal aside, the memories of May '98 must also rank as the best ever. Until we win a treble Double, or the Champions League, of course.

Double Winners - Adams and Co. get their hands on the Premiership trophy

'The Terminator', Patrick Vieira lifts the Championship Trophy aloft

9

The Bigger Picture

The Gunners' exalted status was raised even further by events in the '98 World Cup; no less than seven of our Double stars helped elevate their respective nations' performances to a higher level. Bergkamp's beautifully executed goal against Argentina was an aesthetic delight in terms of his control and spellbinding finish. Dennis' strike rightly won the BBC 'goal of the tournament' title. Manu Petit performed excellently in France's midfield but Patrick Vieira played a more peripheral role in the host country's victory. He did make a spectacular late contribution to the French cause, though. With the Brazilians already beaten in the final, Vieira threaded through a glorious ball to Petit, who pushed his shot past Tafarel. Next day, the tabloids showed the Frenchmen embracing on the turf, amidst cascades of gold confetti. 'Arsenal win the World Cup', boomed *The Sun*. After the triumphs of the last few months, it certainly felt like it.

Writing in the first *One Nil Down* of the season, Tony Willis commented that the Summer of 1998 was the best time of all to be an Arsenal fan. He may well have been right - after all, the club's roll of honour was astonishing; League Champions, FA Cup winners, Wenger voted 'manager of the season', Bergkamp PFA *and* Writers 'player of the year', winner of BBC 'goal of the season' and 'goal of the World Cup'. Just as importantly, journalists queued up to pay homage to Arsenal's thrilling style of play. After all, even Gunners haters recognised top footie when they saw it. Roasting Manchester United 3-0 in the Charity Shield, also contributed to our beatific mood. Overmars, Anelka and Wreh butchered their defence all afternoon and new singing Jaap Stam was made to look a prize arse on several occasions.

By the end of the season, the quality of our football in some games actually surpassed that of the previous year. But at times, the orchestral manoeuvres on the pitch were muffled by the disquiet off it. If we believed that winning the Double had fully answered all questions about Wengerism, then season '98/99 asked rather more serious ones about the club's long and short term future. For instance, what price loyalty amongst Arsenal's foreign contingent and, crucially, how much longer would Highbury remain our home?

In reality, the dream-like pre-season period provided some clues to the knotty problems that needed addressing. Two experienced players departed and weren't immediately replaced. David Platt officially retired in order to begin his journey into footie management. Gunners fans were grateful to him for his calming presence during the Double season but, as has been well documented, he was never 'one of us'. Platt's '80s equivalent, Tony Woodcock, was much the same; after winning medals and making money elsewhere, Arsenal was the final stepping stone on the route to Woodcock's managerial targets. True Gunners fans resent such an attitude. No player should 'use' our club, and Platt's carefully planned approach to his career prevented him from being a 'full on' Arsenal man.

Ian Wright could never be accused of not possessing the Arsenal attitude. The gold-toothed one left for Upton Park (retirement home for our veterans in recent years) with a hint of bitterness in the air. In *The Sun*, he accused Wenger of reneging on his promise to give him 'a playing role in the FA Cup final'. It was inevitable that he wouldn't go quietly. Some revisionist theories on Wright are harsh. *One Nil Down* reckoned his record was 'ephemerally and flashily irrelevant rather than permanently significant'. Others believed he was more of a blockage than a catalyst in his final years at Highbury. True, Arsenal were a better all-round side without him, but the author will remember 'just done it' day, as long as he will the Double triumph. A supreme entertainer rather than a team player, perhaps, but what a brilliant seven year show he put on.

Ironically, Wrighty's name was ringing around the stadium once more by November when Arsenal fans, frustrated with the lack of goals from the forward line, chanted for their absent hero. Maybe they'd forgotten just how lacklustre his final displays were, but those who realise how unsentimental we fans can be, know that such a chant of remembrance is about the highest honour that can be bestowed upon a player. Only Liam Brady in the modern era received the same tribute as Wrighty. That just goes to show what an indelible mark Ian Wright made on the club.

Replacing the *bona fide* crowd favourite was never going to be a straightforward task. There were no ready-made London 'gangstas', poised to step into the breach, so the hot favourite to join was Patrick Kluivert. Personally recommended to Wenger by Dennis Bergkamp, there were more false sightings of Kluivert around London than of Ritchie from the Manics. The stumbling block proved to be not the reported £10m transfer fee, but the player's gargantuan wage demands - somewhere in the region of £60,000 per week, apparently. Chairman Peter Hill-Wood quashed the deal, saying: 'Books have to be balanced, and why should a club go dangerously close to financial suicide for the sake of signing a player short term?' Common sense from Pete, but the issue of players and agents holding the club to ransom would unhappily be repeated during the season.

For some, though, the failed Kluivert deal was a sign that despite the Double win, the Gunners didn't have the necessary resources to turn themselves into a European giant, to rival the Real Madrids of this world. It was becoming a prerequisite that, for a successful onslaught on the (sic) Champions League, four top quality strikers were necessary. And in Super Nic and Dennis, Arsenal had only two; Chris Wreh's five minutes of fame had come and gone. The issue of available resources, i.e. ready cash, also meant that the capacity of Highbury was under close scrutiny. Winning the Double prompted a massive demand for season tickets - to which many were told they'd need to wait over ten years for the privilege. It was at least a five year wait for a membership card; a case of slamming the temple door in eager young worshippers' faces, perhaps.

In 1997, official figures showed Arsenal's annual turnover to be £27.2 m, compared with the Mancs' £88m. By '98, Arsenal were £10 m a year behind United in gate receipts alone. To further demonstrate that Highbury was becoming too compact and *bijou*, AFC made the decision that Champions League games would be played at Wembley Stadium. In part, it was clearly a financial decision, but the fact that the old dump would be filled to bursting with around 75,000 Arsenal fans inside for each game showed the colossal support we have in the South. Clearly, we are the capital's biggest club. Chelsea FC take note - drawing crowds of less than 20,000 a few years back is insufficient qualification for the title of the Premiership's foremost London attraction. Wenger hinted that the Wembley experiment was stage one of Arsenal moving from Highbury in the long term. Attempts to redevelop and expand had already come against opposition from NIMBYs and English Heritage. The stadium debate became much more heated later in the season.

On the eve of the big kick off, a journalist wrote that the biggest threat to Arsenal repeating the previous season's success 'comes from within'. For all the tabloid hype linking us with Kluivert and the De Boer twins, only

Argentinian defender Nelson Vivas actually arrived. History shows that big Summer signings at Highbury always provide a 'cattle prod up the jacksie' effect on the rest of the team. Without this, the Gunners often start the season sluggishly - not much good when a furious Manchester United were anxious to regain their crown. The issue of 'self motivation' amongst players also raised its head. Could Manu Petit, for instance, retain the same hunger after the '97-'98 season, culminating in his World Cup triumph? Manu and Dennis Bergkamp would give us more than a few headaches during the season but the 'Anelka-gate' saga put AFC back on the front covers of the 'papers.

The season began amidst a predictable surge of optimism. A buoyed up Petit headed an excellent opening goal in the Highbury match against Nottingham Forest, and Marc Overmars blazed down the pitch to hook in a second in our 2-1 win. For the next five games, sloppy draws meant that we already had some catching up to do on leaders United. Chelsea, and newly promoted Charlton, stopped Arsenal gaining victories, though the Gunners' defence never looked in any danger. Up at Anfield, Ray Parlour was given a golden opportunity to win us our first game there for six years but, instead, he virtually blasted the ball into the Mersey from five yards out. Three goalless draws in a row hinted that all was not well with the forward line. Anelka looked listless and Bergkamp didn't seem fully fit. At times, you could be forgiven for thinking that he didn't even look interested. Sheffield Wednesday then beat us 1-0 at Hillsborough, in a game infamous for Di Canio shoving over referee Paul Durkin. It wasn't to be the last Arsenal game that season which was at the centre of a media storm.

We seemed to have lapsed into 'after the Lord Mayor's show' type displays, but the lads once more raised themselves to destroy Manchester United 3-0 in the league at Highbury. Tony Adams roared in to head the first, and Anelka scored his first goal of the season to get the second. He even smiled briefly - practically the last time he did so in an Arse shirt. The third goal came from the boot of new £3m Swedish signing Freddie Ljungberg. A dead ringer for Sid Vicious, his signing and quick impact evoked happy memories of Anders Limpar's arrival. More amusing was Fergie's fury at his team's spineless display. You could almost hear the crockery shattering in the dressing room, muffled by the season's number one chant directed at Sherringham: *'Oh Teddy, Teddy, you went to Man Utd and you won fuck all'*. It was good while it lasted, anyway.

After the 'high' of thrashing the Mancs, the next few months told a fluctuating tale of inconsistent league form and a failed Champions league debut. It was widely perceived that Arsenal's group, which contained Lens, Dynamo Kiev and Panathanaikos, was the weakest of the lot. Apparently cruising to victory in France, and at home to Kiev, we let in criminally late goals to concede draws, and in Russia, an injury ravaged side was torn apart 3-1. It wasn't as bad as the Spartak Moscow disaster in '82, but the Russians' passing and movement was still on a different level. A double win over the Greeks couldn't stop us from crashing out of the tournament.

Aside from inexperience and individual defensive mistakes, the painful truth was that Wenger's squad did not have enough quality in depth. In the Wembley defeat by Lens, Petit and Vieira were both injured, leaving Remi Garde to play in Patrick Vieira's position. Much the same problem arose in Kiev. Anelka's late withdrawal and Bergkamp's aerophobia, left a strike-force of Wreh and Boa Morte. Highbury's answer to Laurel and Hardy were hardly likely to scare the shit out of Europe's finest. Maybe they hoped to distract the opposition by making them laugh. As we'd all guessed, we were a striker light.

It is well known that the Wembley atmosphere didn't help matters, either. The thought of 75,000 Gooners inside the stadium sounded awesome. The club had decided to group season ticket holders together, which in theory sounded like a good idea. But, in practice, the 40,000 extra cheap seats on offer simply opened up the chance for dreaded 'day trippers' fans to turn up. It would have been fine if some of the terrace boys from the late '80s had re-emerged, but many of those were now lost to the club forever, having drifted away during the Bond fiasco. One of that ugly breed of 'day trippers', bedecked in red and white, sat next to me at the Panathanaikos match. I was intrigued to know that he was unaware of who 'the chappie in red boots' was. Others experienced the same thing, prompting one enraged fan to ring Five Live, and suggest that the Highbury capacity should stay at 38,000 in order to shut out the 'once a year brigade'.

Dennis Bergkamp's lacklustre form was a major cause for concern. Interestingly, his World Cup coach said of his displays in France '98: 'Dennis was mostly awful, useless in fact, for large periods. But when he scores goals like he did against Argentina, it makes up for all that'. The problem was that, during the pre-Christmas period, Dennis 'made up for it' very infrequently. He scored his first goals of the season in the 3-0 defeat of Newcastle, and grabbed a superb headed equaliser at home to Kiev in the Champions league. But, judging from his body language, he was anything but content.

Aside from various tweaks and muscle pulls, Dennis believed that players in England played too much football. He was immediately portrayed as a 'stroppy foreigner'. Earning £25,000 plus a week, critics believed he should have simply 'got on with it'. Some truth in that, maybe, but Dutch players are notoriously vocal and believe firmly in the principle of player power. It has cost them World Cups and high profile managers. History shows that the Dutch, with their history of republicanism and mercantilism, have thrived through the discussion of new ideas and challenging old practices. Marc Overmars once commented that Dutch players can be difficult and 'more susceptible to psychological blocks than others'. So, having witnessed the more illuminating side of Bergkamp over the past few years, Gunners fans now witnessed the less palatable aspects of his psyche.

The player has since said how he resents his aerophobia being turned into a 'soap opera', but this, combined with his susceptibility to colds and muscle strains, often made him a passenger in the pre-Christmas '98 period. Perhaps the best way to comprehend his state of mind is to consider that one of his heroes was Marco Van Basten. He was a player who admitted to being 'absolutely useless' if the slightest problem bothered him. His career ended due to a chronic ankle problem after years of punishment at the sharp end and 'over-playing', as he saw it. So perhaps Dennis' wish to protect his body is understandable, though this didn't make it any easier to accept at the time. Wenger showed all his managerial skills by getting Bergkamp to perform at his true level in the New Year. But by then, Arsène would have his hands full dealing with more troublesome *agents provocateurs* within the squad.

League form remained patchy by early December. Le Tissier's goal for Southampton denied us a deserved win, but Anelka's cerebral efforts plundered victories against Everton and Blackburn. Frustrating setbacks against Wimbledon and Spurs caused grumbling in the crowd, and the 0-5 defeat in the Worthington Cup by Chelsea, was just plain embarrassing, despite the fact that we sang 'we don't give a toss' all the way through. Wenger correctly viewed the Worthington Cup as the least important trophy we'd contest that season, but playing the reserves against Chelsea's first team stars, and the resulting drubbing they received, damaged fans' and players' confidence. The fiasco was part and parcel of the practice of prioritising in the modern game, but true fans are offended when domestic cup competitions are regarded simply as 'another route into Europe', rather than a chance for glory in themselves. Trophy winning was becoming less important that finishing second in the Premiership and thus gaining entry

into the 'rich man's playground'. That, along with being battered by Chelsea, is not what most of us wish to see or hear. It was another sign that top Premiership clubs like Arsenal were helpless pawns on a wider European board. By '99 therefore, it was already becoming a case of Champions League qualification, or bust.

For Blackburn '97, read Villa away in '98. In a desperate home draw with Middlesbrough a week before, some fans booed a subdued Nic Anelka, until he thumped in our late equaliser. Such muppets were clearly spoilt beyond belief with the Double victory and, presumably, history did not exist for them until George's arrival in '86, otherwise they'd have remembered the truly dark days of the mid '70s and '80s. The Boro match prompted Wenger to propound that fans couldn't accept 'sausages and mash' where, before, they'd enjoyed 'caviar'. An affront against good old English grub, maybe, but the Arse had again hit Wintry problems. Up at Villa Park, Dennis' two masterful strikes signalled his return to form and, it seemed, a comfortable away win. Villa's epic second half comeback gave them a 3-2 victory, prompting the crowd whingers to suggest a complete overhaul of the defence. It was virtually a mirror image of the previous year and, to further suggest that *Groundhog Day* was being shot again at Highbury, Wenger apparently gave up on the title race, saying : 'If you concede three goals in 45 minutes you are not title contenders'. But once again, Arsenal were about to embark on a monumental undefeated league run.

Arsenal v Leeds; the season's turning point. For the first time since slaughtering United at Highbury, the Arse actually swaggered like Champions. It helped that the team was virtually back to full strength for the first time in months. Nigel Winterburn's niggling injuries had cleared up, Vieira and Petit were mercifully suspension and injury-free, and Dennis was slowly recovering his form from the previous year. He miskicked us into the lead against Leeds, before two glorious moves allowed the French midfield duo to give us a 3-1 win. The victory was Arsenal's first in six games - our worst run under Wenger, but still we were in a far better position than a year before, lagging just four points behind leaders United. Sexy football was back, and two narrow Christmas wins over Charlton and West Ham kept us right on their tails. As well as the cerebral footie, though, another feature of Wenger's Arsenal returned; red card flashing was back in vogue.

Gilles Grimandi was idiotically sent off after coming on as substitute against Leeds, and Patrick Vieira was sent off at Charlton. TV replays proved

that Charlton's Neil Redfearn was guilty of disgusting play-acting during the incident, the whole of which bore an uncanny resemblance to that at Upton Park earlier in the year; journeymen players niggling at stars to provoke a reaction. To be honest, though, even Arsenal fans were starting to tire of Wenger's repeated excuses that he 'didn't get a full view of the incident'. But our players were being sent off for offences which would barely have warranted a yellow card five years earlier. It's partly a reflection of how football continues to mutate into a non-contact sport, and how officials have become robots. But it's also evidence of the catch-22 situations in which successful modern Arsenal teams find themselves. Our teams can be over- competitive. The crowd expected Vieira and Petit to 'rough up' other midfielders, but in the modern game this approach often meant the Arse were reduced to only ten men. This sometimes led to us actually playing better, but it would have been nice if Wenger had taught Gilles Grimandi not to headbutt opponents, or Manu Petit not to gob off at linesmen. After all, constant moaning and indiscipline on the pitch manifests itself in off-pitch whining. Not only does this cost the team points, it destabilises the whole club, as we'd soon find out.

The quest to retain the Double began in earnest on January 4th at Preston's Deepdale. The stadium literally shook with excitement when Kurt Nogan put them two goals up in the FA Cup third round. Staggeringly, Luis Boa Morte's arrival as substitute, turned the tie. His crucial goal, just before half time, meant that for the first time we were actually pleased to see him. That strike unleashed a second half avalanche which gave us a 4-2 win, thanks to Petit's midfield excellence. Overmars and Petit helped us scramble through the fourth round against Wolves and Cup form now went hand in hand with improving league displays.

Martin Keown ruined Big Ron's return from Barbados to football management at Forest, by heading the winner, and Dennis Bergkamp masterfully curled home the deciding goal against Chelsea's King's Road tarts. Due to the fact that Chelsea were actually having another decent run in the league, some suggested that they had now replaced Spurs as our main London rivals. There's some mileage in that view, but Chelsea's insistence on buying over-aged, short term fillers once again betrayed their lack of real class. Even the Totts do at least have some genuine tradition, though it's now been twenty years since they were last regarded as a decent side.

Journos eulogised about Bergkamp's display at Upton Park in early February. The *Sunday Mail's* Malcolm Folley said: 'Awesome is an overworked

adjective in the sporting lexicon, but yesterday the word awesome fitted Bergkamp like a Saville Row suit'. Arguably, the 4-0 win was the *team's* best display of the season. Anelka twisted and turned Julian Dicks to grab a goal, and Ray Parlour rapped in a ridiculously overdue first strike of the season. But the vision of Bergkamp, scampering towards goal and unleashing an unstoppable shot for the first, remained the abiding memory of the day.

New £7.5m signing Kanu demonstrated his gift for the unexpected in the 1-1 draw with the Mancs at Old Trafford. Extending one of his telescopic legs, he bamboozled Stam and laid off the ball to Anelka, who thumped it into Schmeichel's net. The Nigerian's heart by-pass operation made him an expensive gamble in many people's eyes, but, albeit belatedly, Wenger now had another class striker in his squad. With the former Inter Milan man and Vieira on the same pitch, you could be forgiven for thinking that Wenger was launching an experimental Highbury basketball team. Mind you, some of the exhibition displays the team would give was worthy of the glitzy Harlem Globetrotters themselves. Inevitably though, the forthcoming FA Cup fifth round clash with Sheffield United overshadowed everything else, and Kanu, who's always looked older than his reported age, added a few more wrinkles to his already furrowed brow.

A hitherto uneventful game seemed to be drifting towards an inevitable conclusion, after Vieira headed us into the lead. Another new Wenger signing, Kaba Diawara, missed two gilt edged chances, proving in the process that he was genetically programmed to hit the post rather than the back of the net. The guy seated next to me reckoned he was a '90s version of Ray Hankin. Suffice it to say, Diawara's Highbury stay was brief. In the second half, the United goalie booted the ball into touch in order for a team mate to receive treatment. Parlour sportingly threw the ball back into the Blades' half and poor Kanu, still apparently getting his bearings in English football, squared the ball to Overmars who scored. Both players were immediately surrounded by a bunch of furious Blades players, their features so contorted with rage they appeared to be staging an impromptu gurning competition on the pitch.

Manager Steve Bruce, whose own twisted features are capable of giving the kids nightmares, tried to pick up the ball and take his team off the pitch. How typical of an ex Manc to behave in such a petulant manner. Wenger, Dein and co. immediately offered to replay the match. The replay was unprecedented but Arsenal rightly won, with a touch of Bergkamp sorcery. Of course, Arsenal's gesture was the right thing to do, especially at a time

when the team's disciplinary record was under such close surveillance. But then Spurs and Blackburn pulled the same unsportsmanlike stunt at Highbury in recent years and got away with it. The loathsome Chris Sutton never apologised for his part in Rovers' goal, unlike Kanu, who was virtually in tears on *Match Of The Day*. Still, rules applying to the Arsenal have traditionally been different to those for other clubs.

Nicolas Anelka; a player granted several nicknames at Highbury. 'Super Nic' was the most complimentary, but, by March, he was already dubbed the 'Incredible Sulk' in some quarters. Dr Johnson once famously stated: 'when a man tires of London, he is tired of life itself'. Anelka should have been brimming with confidence and *joie de vivre* in '98/99. Instead, he was holed up in a drab Edgware flat with his brothers Claude and Didier, becoming progressively more miserable by the week. Speaking to *The Mirror's* Mike Walters, he confided that: 'I don't know anybody here and I don't want to'. Anelka found London dull, never went out, and tended to spend most of the time playing on the computer, or watching DVD movies on the team bus. The question burning in most fans' minds and, in his team mates' heads was; Nic Anelka - footballing genius, or petulant, nerdy teenager, who needed to be sold at the first opportunity.

On the pitch, Anelka seemed a worthy successor to Wrighty. Indeed, despite his rawness during the '97/98 season, he actually appeared to be a better all round player than the gold toothed one. His searing pace, excellent touch on the ball, and peripheral vision seemed set to make him a crowd hero for years to come. Yet pockets in the crowd, concerned by his lack of passion, were lukewarm towards him. Anelka later told *Four Four Two* magazine that ideally Arsenal fans wanted another Wright type persona and that, basically, he never stood a chance at Highbury. That's a little too simplistic and we knew that Wright was a one off. It wouldn't have hurt Anelka to have smiled or kissed his shirt a bit more, though. Wright's approach was the epitome of how we'd like all players to play the game, whereas Nic appeared spiky, aloof and temperamental. This trait was certainly reflected in his brothers.

Considering they had such a tight rein on him, they allowed him to make some dreadful public *faux pas*, like not turning up to collect his young PFA 'player of the year' award, for instance. (Nic 'wasn't aware that this is an important event'). Or blurting to the press that Marc Overmars 'doesn't pass to me'. Or claiming he'd be 'better in a team with Weah and Ronaldo'. Wenger skilfully sorted out these little episodes but it was clear that, in a dressing room as tight as Arsenal's, there was no place for a player who felt himself to be above the collective.

Back in November, he'd scored some decent goals but he often seemed totally disaffected during games. Martin Keown famously screamed at him: 'look like you *want* to play for the Arsenal', in front of astonished away fans at Blackburn. Nic just walked away, head bowed. Then, on the weekend when he scored a sublime first half hat-trick in the 5-0 defeat of Leicester at Highbury, (and looked bloody miserable in the process), the tabloids picked up that a host of top foreign clubs were sniffing around him. Moves to Real Madrid, Lazio or Inter Milan all seemed distinct possibilities. Conventional wisdom held that he was worth around £10m. It didn't take a genius to deduce that Claude and Didier were basically acting as pimps - offering their kid brother's footballing services to the highest bidder, and at the best price for them.

In a French footie magazine, Anelka commented that: 'I don't think I'll see it (his contract) through. I love Spain and, after that, I can see myself going to Italy'. Not only was that hurtful to true Gooners, it meant that he was 'using' Arsenal as a stepping stone in order to hop to a 'bigger' European team. It was a sobering thought that the mighty Arse were not only at the mercy of the 'ten percenters', but that in the grand scheme of things, we weren't regarded as part of the European elite.

The Frenchman's belief that he would leave before his contract expired, became a self fulfilling prophecy. Every sulk and shoulder shrug made him more vilified with passing weeks. It's not nice to hear boos for your own players, especially one as talented as Anelka, but no player is bigger than AFC. Arsène Wenger later defended his young protégé by saying that he was badly advised, and easily led by his brothers. It's also important to remember that the Anelka clan, which hailed from Martinique, was penniless, so young Nic was virtually breadwinner for the entire family. None of this, though, can excuse his comment that: 'They should stop telling stories about love of the shirt and loyalty. All that, apart from the national team, no longer exists'. Anelka's chilling view of late '90s football undermined everything which fans hold dear and, after a drawn out saga worthy of a US Presidential election, he inevitably moved on in a mega-bucks deal, to Real Madrid, during the summer. But for now, we were more concerned about whether he would find it within himself, at least, to *pretend* that he wanted to stay, and score the goals which would retain the Double.

The arrival of Kanu had injected a freshness into Arsenal's attacking panache. Baffled defenders found him impossible to play against. He had the ability to play up front as an orthodox striker, despatching shots and volleys at will, or in a deeper position, roving between midfield and the front line. In either position, he revealed his dazzling ability to side step defenders, backheel balls away, and nutmeg the opposition. How we could have done with Kanu in the opening part of the season, when the attack looked so stunted and predictable. But, now that he was finally here, it gave Wenger the opportunity to play Marc Overmars solely as a winger. Arsène could also rotate his strikers, in yet another nod towards new age footie. An early example of Kanu's impact was seen in the FA Cup Quarter Final with Derby, where his net busting swivel and smash took us into the Semi Final. In his early days, he was used mainly as a substitute, where his unorthodox thinking destroyed several tired defences.

If teams were having a hard time containing Kanu's exuberant play, commentators were having more difficulty pronouncing his first name. Political correctness ruled on *Five Live* and *Capital Gold*, until transmissions on both radio stations temporarily ceased after correspondents were unable to pronounce Nwankwo without descending into hysterics. From then on he became straightforward Kanu. The guffawers also reckoned we were booing him while he warmed up, whereas, in fact, we were shouting *'Kanuuu'* at top volume. It was a slightly more suitable chant than Manchester United fans': *'He's tall, he's black, he's had a heart attack'*, which never quite caught on at politically correct Highbury. The Nigerian's super-sub role was in evidence again at home to Sheffield Wednesday. Goalless with fifteen minutes to go, he set up Dennis for a majestic double and side stepped Peter Atherton before slamming in a third in a 3-0 home win.

League form yet again hit the perfect pitch by Spring time. All components within the team clicked into place; the attack was rejuvenated, the defence regained its meanness and midfield was a rampaging success again. Example: Everton away in mid March. Patrick Vieira controlled and tormented the Scousers all afternoon, leaving Ray Parlour free to fire in the opener, and Manu Petit to maraud around Goodison Park, trying to pick out Bergkamp with inch perfect passes. Unfortunately, Manu also set out to smash Toffees' Olivier Dacourt's legs. Why does French *bonhomie* always disappear when they play against each other? Manu was inevitably sent off in the second half, and the fall out totally overshadowed our excellent 2-0 win, sealed by Bergkamp's penalty.

Stomping off the pitch, Petit offered referee Uriah Rennie his shin pads, and announced to a stunned press that he was quitting English football. Along with Anelka, Petit was rapidly becoming Highbury's problem child.

His excellent on-field displays, despite regular disruptions due to injuries and suspensions, put him in the frame for the 'Player of the Year' awards. Yet the Highbury grapevine quivered with news that, in the dressing room, team mates were regularly party to his storming around in a foul mood. The root causes of Petit's problems were that he believed English referees had a vendetta against him, and that in general, Premiership performers played too much footie.

Amazingly, Petit had called for a player's strike earlier that season, displaying a distinctly early '80s attitude to industrial relations. The thought of the Frenchman as a late '90s Arthur Scargill requires a great deal of imagination, especially as he earned around £25,000 a week and his livelihood certainly wasn't under threat. The 'stroppy Frenchman' card was again played by the press. This time, there was little that could be said to defend Petit. His three sendings off were deserved and, in the next game, there was even sporadic booing of him from pockets of the crowd. Most urged him not to go - arguably another case of pandering to late '90s superstars. In *One Nil Down*, Tony Willis reckoned the episode highlighted just how out-of-touch modern players were with the lives of everyday fans - people for whom Manu's weekly wages would be, in some cases, more than they'd earn in a year or even two.

Just to show what suckers we were, Manu was quickly forgiven, even by the grumblers. Wenger talked him out of leaving and claimed that Petit was simply frustrated, rather than permanently unhappy. And many of us could never hate a player who'd signed for us in such glorious circumstances. Originally, he seemed bound for Spurs, but once he'd spoken to mullet-head Gerry Francis, and Alan Sugar, at the Amstrad chief's house, he decided that wouldn't be a prudent decision. Petit temporarily kept his thoughts to himself. He asked Sugar if he could 'sleep on it' and if he could borrow some money for the taxi fare to his hotel. Sugar agreed to both requests; when the cab arrived, Manu left for Highbury with all due haste, and signed for Wenger. The story becomes more embellished with passing years, but it's a neat metaphor which aptly summed up North London rivalry in the late '90s. Frumpy Spurs courted Europe's top talent, but always lost out to the stylish hunk who lived down the road.

Miraculously, Petit did cool down within a few days, behaved himself for the rest of the season, and decided to stay at Highbury for a while longer. We were thrilled. After all, Wenger was set to lose Anelka - but to have lost two Frenchmen would have seemed positively careless. With the FA Cup Semi Final looming, it was as well to remember Fergie's opinion that, along with Tony Adams, it was Petit whom the Mancs feared most of all.

Routine wins over Coventry and Blackburn kept title chances bubbling. In *The Times*, Oliver Holt described Kanu's style in those games as 'a joy to watch. He has that wonderfully instinctive gift bestowed on only a few..... He makes room for himself effortlessly...' We'd now entered the 'death or glory' stretch of the season, fully aware that United were still slight favourites to win the league. But the titanic FA Cup Semi Final with the Mancs gave the Gunners a perfect chance to derail the quest for an unprecedented treble. The first game, played at Villa Park, saw Arsenal roared on by the most passionate away following in years. Red and white balloons were released in their thousands, and chants of *'Who the fuck are Man Utd?'* filled the air. The game ended goalless, despite the frenzied vocal support. Roy Keane had a good goal struck off, and Freddie Ljungberg missed a last minute sitter which would have put us through.

The replay has passed into FA Cup folklore, not that that is any consolation. Hundreds of Gooners were missing due to travel problems and high ticket prices. The game, contested between the country's two best sides, was pulsating. Beckham's swirling drive put them ahead but the Arse roared back in the second half. Dennis' deflected shot flicked past Schmeichel to bring us level, and from them on, we were subjected to a decade's worth of 'what ifs'?

What if Schmeichel hadn't tipped away Bergkamp's late second half shot? What if the linesman hadn't spotted that Anelka was a yard offside, when he seemed to have put us into the lead? The ten second delay between Nic's strike and the realisation that the flag was up was worth it though. Anelka went mental, jumping into the posse of Arsenal fans in the Trinity Road end. He did enjoy scoring against United, at least. And finally, what if Schmeichel hadn't made the penalty save of his life to push Dennis' kick away. Instead, the abiding memory is of Ryan Giggs' carpet chest and shirt twirling after he'd scored *that* goal. Only a strike of such quality could have beaten us. So, heart breakingly, a back to back Double wasn't going to become reality, despite the team's passion on the night.

The Gunners' response was to bury the next two Premiership opponents under an avalanche of goals. Ray Parlour opened the floodgates against Wimbledon, leaving Kanu to provide a delicious dessert, by slicing open the Dons' defence and teasing in a couple of goals himself in a 5-1 win. Some reckoned that the Kanu - Anelka partnership orchestrated the decade's most awesome attacking display up at the Riverside Stadium. Middlesbrough didn't play badly - it was a simple case that the attacking duo were on a different plane that day. A video of that match provides conclusive evidence of why Wenger's sides were such compelling viewing in the late '90s. Take your pick from Anelka's rapier thrust for the first and Kanu's side-step and smash for the second. Surely, topping the list was the Nigerian's mid-air back heel, which beat Schwarzer for Arsenal's fifth. That 6-1 away win even had the locals applauding. Nicolas Anelka steered in the winner against Derby at a tense Highbury on Bank Holiday weekend, to finally put us a point clear in the title race, having played a game more.

U nbeaten in twenty games, the boys faced three matches in ten days, which would decide whether or not we retained the title. How ironic that George Graham would play a major role in deciding our fate. Back in November, he'd accepted Sugar's invitation to try to restore Tottenham's glory days. Not even a Worthington Cup triumph, though, would ever convince Spurs die hards that he was anything but an Arsenal man. The reaction from Arsenal fans to his appointment was one of bewilderment and, in some quarters, anger. How could a man with such passion for AFC do such a thing? In the background, there was always the nagging fear that George would turn Spurs around and transform them into a leading force once again. We needn't have worried, though. GG tried to repeat his old trick of buying doughty Wimbledon players and midfield scrappers.

The Arse torched Spurs' defensive blanket with an inferno of attacking brilliance. Anelka rammed in the first and clattered the post a minute later. Manu Petit spectacularly lobbed a second and Kanu once again provided the fulminating climax. Flicking the ball over Luke Young's head, he volleyed in an unstoppable third in our 3-1 win. When the stadium announcer filtered through the news that Paul Ince had grabbed Liverpool's equaliser at home to the Mancs, it seemed that, once again, we would be getting high from the smell of silver polish. Three points ahead of United, with two games left; it felt that we were within touching distance of retaining the title.

With David O'Leary's Leeds opposing us in the final away game at Elland Road, we secretly hoped that our record appearance holder might encourage his team to 'ease up'. After all, Leeds hate United as much as us, right? Quickly, the Yorkshire side proved they had no intention of helping us out. They were their usual over-physical selves, booting the likes of Vieira up in the air at every opportunity. No matter that desperate goal line clearances by Woodgate kept out Vieira and Diawara efforts, or that Tony Adams' performance was superb. Leeds held firm. Late on in the game, Nigel Winterburn sickeningly collided with Ian Harte's knee. Bruised and bleeding, Nige was replaced by Nelson Vivas, who'd never looked too comfortable in the left back position. After eighty minutes, the Argentinian pressed too far forward, and allowed Hasselbaink to cut loose in the area. He headed the winner. For the first time, Wenger publicly blamed one of his players. Vivas, said the Frenchman, had made 'a huge tactical error' at the back post. Tabloids labelled the full-back a 'fool Nelson'. Their reports were harsh, implying that a reckless foreigner had probably cost us the title, through a mistake which an English defender wouldn't have made.

This gave further substance to the lobby which held that foreign stars didn't quite have the necessary steely edge required for dramatic show-downs. The likes of Henry Winter were already suggesting that Arsenal's 'foreign cavaliers' were beginning to undermine the fabric woven by 'English roundheads'. Maybe it's as well to remember that in the mid '80s we had an entire team stuffed with Brits who used to pootle about in mid table all season. But the incident did prove what a huge task Wenger had in replacing Europe's finest back line. In the meantime, Arsenal's title hopes hung by a thread.

Quite simply, the Gunners had to win against Villa on the final Saturday, and hope that Graham's Spurs could draw, or win, at Old Trafford. Kanu's goal secured our victory but naturally, Spurs lost at Old Trafford. They'd even scored first, causing us to celebrate a Spurs goal - a once a century event. But, as even their fans now realised, the Totts are no more than a tease; leading on their supporters before the realisation that an eternity of ineptness beckons. The Gunners had failed to retain the title by a single point, and United had completed the first leg of their treble.

Naturally, the players did a lap of honour after the final whistle. It was a low key affair, but Rob Williams recalls one aspect of it: 'As the players trooped off the pitch, I noticed that Tony Adams was one of the last to come off. I was watching him closely, and just as he went down the tunnel, he looked up and stared me in the face. I grinned at him, turned around and showed him the letters A-D-A-M-S on my back. He put his thumbs up and pointed to the canon on his shirt. Then he mouthed 'thanks', and dis-appeared. I saw in those few seconds just what Arsenal means to Tony Adams, and what he means to this club. We were crap and we were brilliant at different times in the '90s - but he was a rock through all of it.

Rob Williams, Arsenal fan from Watford

Unquestionably, Tony Adams was our Player of the '90s. He wins by virtue of his performances as captain, and because he embodies not only the spirit of Arsenal, but also the extent of change which the club underwent during the decade. Ten years earlier, Tone was a boozy lager lout whose on-pitch heroics couldn't disguise the fact that, off the field, he was headed for the abyss. By the end of the '90s, the remodelled Adams, like his club, was considered 'cool'. Presumably, his new found interests in poetry and the piano impressed Caprice, whom he met on Wrighty's chat show. Football and showbiz had well and truly merged. It was impossible not to look at the captain without a wistful glance. A staunch one-club man, many of us had grown up with him in the team since the dark days of Howe and Neill. When he made his debut in '83, none of us could have predicted that he'd still be at the club more than sixteen years later, or that the term 'boring Arsenal' would finally be consigned to the dustbin of history. The captain's brand of loyalty, as Anelka commented with all the tact of Ann Robinson, was dying out. The great defence was about to disintegrate; Bouldy would be given a free transfer to Sunderland that Summer.

But not everything had altered by the end of the '90s. Four years after he'd left the club, we still expected George's defence to bail us out on the big occasion - a legacy of the Scot's lasting impact at Highbury. And although Manchester United had now replaced Liverpool as 'the yardstick' in the '90s, we were still moaning about having to chase 'those arrogant Northern bastards who play in red'. If George and the board had got their transfer policy right in the early '90s, it could have been Arsenal's decade. But, although we hadn't created a Chapmanesque dynasty, six trophies, including a Double, is a good return.

If the end was in sight for Arsenal's defence, the bell seemed to be tolling loudly for the future of Highbury Stadium. In the *Sunday Times*, Brian Glanville stated that our 38,000 capacity was 'a bad joke'. The club's preferred option had been to stay at Highbury and increase the capacity to 50,000. This was confirmed at the '97 AGM when the board announced that a feasibility study was being launched into the redevelopment of Highbury. A myriad of problems made this target almost impossible. The East Stand is a listed building and, therefore, couldn't be demolished.

To demolish the West Stand, and rebuild it, would have required a compulsory purchase order for the houses behind the stand on Highbury Hill. This would have resulted in a minefield of legal wrangling, NIMBY whinging (a quintessential British trait), and prevarication by the Department of the Environment. There was little chance of the club negotiating a way past the Highbury Hill Resident's Association, either. While they were understandably concerned about their houses, their complaints about disruption on match days seemed strange. What do you expect if you move next to a foot-ball ground? It's like going swimming, and moaning about getting wet. And, of course, even if Highbury's capacity had been raised to 50,000, it would still lag some 18,000 behind United's capacity.

In May '99, an Islington Council spokesman confirmed that the club had halted the feasibility study. Other options were now being considered. A site near Kings' Cross station had long been discussed, though local res-idents had recently gone ape-shit over plans for a proposed new McDonalds. If they couldn't stand the thought of a few acne-ridden teenagers munching on a Big Mac, what chance was there for 60,000 Arsenal fans every two weeks?

Shockingly, Wembley Stadium was the club's preferred second option. In late '97, Arsenal tabled a £125m bid to buy the slum. In a neat parallel with the Labour party, rumours suggested that Arsenal's board was split into the modernisers (Dein, Fiszman) and the traditionalists (Hillwood and the Carr brothers. The modernisers were supposedly keen to move on, and finance the bid by a share flotation. For the club to be restricted, *a la* Newcastle, in the transfer market, was an even more horrifying vision than facing the over zealous Wembley stewards every two weeks. Fans who went to the '98 Cup Final realised that the heinous crime of carrying a plastic water bottle *with a lid* was virtually a capital offence in those parts. Thankfully, the bid fell through, due to the Wembley licence limiting the number of games which could be held there each year. As yet, the Ashburton Grove site hadn't even been mentioned as an option.

The stadium debate split fans into two broad churches of opinion. The argument has since moved on, but for the purposes of this book, several fans voiced their opinions in '99 on the issue. The two fans who put for-ward the following conflicting arguments had to be restrained from doing each other physical damage.

'The thought of leaving Highbury is like dicing with death. So many peo-ple have jumped on the football bandwagon, they've forgotten about Arsenal before '93. 50,000 fans wanting tickets for every game is a modern phenome-non - because the sport is currently booming. But in '88/89 and '90/91 we won the title, and our crowds averaged out at around 35,000. Who's to say that in a few years, things won't go back to that level? It would be much better to demolish the Clock End, rebuild it with a few thousand extra seats and fill in the corners. Let's get beyond all this bollocks about 'oh, we have to have open corners or our pitch won't get enough air'. No other club has that problem.

If we did fill them in, our capacity would be about 48,000 which is fine.

They talk about United's crowds at 60,000 but as Liverpool found in the '80s, interest does wane. Booms and busts happen, and great new stadia will look like ridiculous white elephants in a few years. I don't want to sit in a half empty dump somewhere else in London.

Highbury is the soul of the club. It's our spiritual home; all those memories, Chapman's bust, '30s art deco stands, all ringed by Victorian houses. Christ, I sound like Ron the manager off the *Fast Show*!! But Highbury is the club's heart. Tear it out and you'll kill us.

Chris Driver, Arsenal fan from Highgate

'Highbury is now becoming harder than ever to get into. Even if you're a registration scheme member, you can get balloted out. My brother, whose 15, can't even get a membership card and if things carried on as they were, he won't get in for about another six years. Staying put means we're losing our future fans. They'll go and support Man Utd instead. Do we really want that?

I read somewhere the other day that we're lagging £500,000 a game behind United on gate receipts alone. Football will get bigger all the time. More Champions league games and more cash coming in. Everyone deserves a chance to see Arsenal in the 21st century. Forget the grim mid '70s and '80s - they don't exist anymore. Highbury's a good stadium but those who talk of historical roots are talking shit. We've already moved from Woolwich to here. So our roots aren't here at all. And if you want to keep a monument, the East Stand will always be here, won't it?

People who want to stay at Highbury are living in the past. Have you ever actually sat in the East or West stands? The view is crap, actually. The old place holds some great memories for me, like the two Doubles. But if we stay, we'll turn into a medium sized club. Even Sunderland's capacity is 10,000 more than ours. Highbury is out of date and even if it could be redeveloped, to say 45,000, it's not enough. The *fans* are Arsenal and we deserve the best. So let's give *everyone* a chance to see the team in a new era.

Robbie King, Arsenal fan from Tilehurst

Events during the last couple of years prove that due to financial considerations, the tide irrevocably turned in favour of moving away from Highbury. With Old Trafford growing ever larger, the Mancs are virtually out of sight, regarding their financial muscle. The JCBs are likely to move in over the next few years, and Highbury will become just another snapshot in a photo album - a coliseum from a by-gone age, where players performed epic deeds.

The '90s were the most exciting era in which to be an Arsenal fan, but the rapid rate of change which the game underwent proved that virtually nothing lasts forever. As other clubs were discovering, bricks and mortar are only temporary. And fans were susceptible to changing outlooks too. Example: David Dein, once a vilified figure during the Bond crisis, was now regarded far more favourably by a sizeable number in the crowd after bringing Wenger to Highbury. We no longer 'marched' with George's army, an unthinkable change at one stage. Instead, many were simply content simply to 'follow' Arsène's Arsenal. The modern breed of supporter is less feisty and raw than his or her early '90s counterpart but, rest assured that, 38,000 or more guardians of the faith will always want to watch the Arsenal. And that's some consolation, isn't it?

'Cheerful Nic' celebrates a goal against Southampton - October '98

Kanuuuuu!!!

Appendices

Summary of Arsenal's playing record: August 1990 – May 1999

Arsenal's League results: August 1990 – May 1999

Arsenal's Cup results: August 1990 – May 1999

Players' appearances and goals, season by season: 1990 – 1999

Arsenal in the transfer market: 1990 – 1999

Arsenal's attendances: 1990 – 1999

Summary of Arsenal's Playing Record: August 1990 – May 1999

Season	Pld	W	D	L	F	A	GD	Pts	Pos	FA	L.Cup	Europe
90/91	38	24	13	1	74	18	+56	83	1st	SF	R4	-
91/92	42	19	15	8	81	46	+35	72	4th	R3	R3	ECR2
92/93	42	15	11	16	40	38	+2	56	10th	W	W	-
93/94	42	18	17	7	53	28	+25	71	4th	R4	R4	CWCW
94/95	42	13	12	17	52	49	+3	51	12th	R3	QF	CWCLF
95/96	38	17	12	9	49	32	+17	63	5th	R3	SF	-
96/97	38	19	11	8	62	32	+30	68	3rd	R4	R4	UEFAR1
97/98	38	23	9	6	68	33	+35	78	1st	W	SF	UEFAR1
98/99	38	22	12	4	59	17	+42	78	2nd	SF	R4	CLR1

R	=	Round
QF	=	Quarter Final
SF	=	Semi-Final
W	=	Winners
LF	=	Losing Finalists

EC	=	European Cup
CWC	=	Cup Winners Cup
UEFA	=	UEFA Cup
CL	=	Champions League

Arsenal's League Results: August 1990 – May 1999

	90-91	91-92	92-93	93-94	94-95	95-96	96-97	97-98	98-99
AstonVilla	5-0 0-0	0-0 1-3	0-1 0-1	1-2 2-1	0-0 4-0	2-0 1-1	2-2 2-2	0-0 0-1	1-0 2-3
Barnsley								5-0 2-0	
Blackburn			0-1 0-1	1-0 1-1	0-0 1-3	0-0 1-1	1-1 2-0	1-3 4-1	1-0 2-1
Bolton						2-1 0-1		4-1 1-0	
Charlton									0-0 1-0
Chelsea	4-1 1-2	3-2 1-1	2-1 0-1	1-0 2-0	3-1 1-2	1-1 0-1	3-3 3-0	2-0 3-2	1-0 0-0
Coventry	6-1 2-0	1-2 1-0	3-0 2-0	0-3 0-1	2-1 1-0	1-1 0-0	0-0 1-1	2-0 2-2	2-0 1-0
Crystal Palace	4-0 0-0	4-1 4-1	3-0 2-1		1-2 3-0			1-0 0-0	
Derby	3-0 2-0						2-2 3-1	1-0 0-3	1-0 0-0
Everton	1-0 1-1	4-2 1-3	2-0 0-0	2-0 1-1	1-1 1-1	1-2 2-0	3-1 2-0	4-0 2-2	1-0 2-0
Ipswich			0-0 2-1	4-0 5-1	4-1 2-0				
Leeds	2-0 2-2	1-1 2-2	0-0 0-3	2-1 1-2	1-3 0-1	2-1 3-0	3-0 0-0	2-1 1-1	3-1 0-1
Leicester					1-1 1-2		2-0 2-0	2-1 3-3	5-0 1-1
Liverpool	3-0 1-0	4-0 0-2	0-1 2-0	1-0 0-0	0-1 0-3	0-0 1-3	1-2 0-2	0-1 0-4	0-0 0-0
Luton	2-1 1-1	2-0 0-1							
Man City	2-2 1-0	2-1 0-1	1-0 1-0	0-0 0-0	3-0 2-1	3-1 1-0			
Man Utd	3-1 1-0	1-1 1-1	0-1 0-0	2-2 0-1	0-0 0-3	1-0 0-1	1-2 0-1	3-2 1-0	3-0 1-1
Middlesbro			1-1 0-1			1-1 3-2	2-0 2-0		1-1 6-1
Newcastle				2-1 0-2	2-3 0-1	2-0 0-2	0-1 2-1	3-1 1-0	3-0 1-1
Norwich	2-0 0-0	1-1 3-1	2-4 1-1	0-1 1-1	5-1 0-0				
Notts County		2-0 1-0							

Arsenal's League Results: August 1990 – May 1999 (continued)

	90-91	91-92	92-93	93-94	94-95	95-96	96-97	97-98	98-99
Notts Forest	2-0 1-1	3-3 2-3	1-1 1-0		1-0 2-2	1-1 1-0	2-0 1-2		2-1 1-0
Oldham		2-1 1-1	2-0 1-0	1-1 0-0					
QPR	2-0 3-1	1-1 0-0	0-0 0-0	0-0 1-1	1-3 1-3	3-0 1-1			
Sheff Utd	4-1 2-0	5-2 1-1	1-1 1-1	3-0 1-1					
Sheff Wed		7-1 1-1	2-1 0-1	1-0 1-0	0-0 1-3	4-2 0-1	4-1 0-0	1-0 0-2	3-0 0-1
Southampton	4-0 1-1	5-1 4-1	4-3 0-2	1-0 4-0	1-1 0-1	4-2 0-0	3-1 2-0	3-0 3-1	1-1 0-0
Sunderland	1-0 0-0						2-0 0-1		
Swindon				1-1 4-0					
Tottenham	0-0 0-0	2-0 1-1	1-3 1-1	1-1 1-0	1-1 0-1	0-0 0-1	3-1 0-0	0-0 1-1	0-0 3-1
West Ham		0-1 2-0		0-2 0-0	0-1 2-0	1-0 1-0	2-0 2-1	4-0 0-0	1-0 4-0
Wimbledon	2-2 3-0	1-1 3-1	0-1 2-3	1-1 3-0	0-0 3-1	1-3 3-0	0-1 2-2	5-0 1-0	5-1 0-1

Arsenal's home results always first

Arsenal's Cup results: August 1990 – May 1999

	90-91	91-92	92-93	93-94	94-95	95-96	96-97	97-98	98-99
AstonVilla				0-1(L4)		2-2 0-0 (LSF)			
Austria Vienna		6-1 0-1 (EC1)							
Auxerre					1-1 1-0 (CWC3)				
Barnsley						3-0 (L3)			
Benfica		1-3 1-1 (EC2)							
Birmingham									
Bolton			2-2 1-3 (F4)					4-1 (L3)	
Borussia M									
Brondby							2-3 2-3 (UEFA1)		
Cambridge Utd	2-1 (F6)								
Chelsea					2-2 2-1 (CWC2)			2-1 1-3 (LSF)	0-5 (L4)
Chester	5-0 1-0 (L2)								
Coventry		0-1 (L3)						1-0 (L4)	
Crystal Palace			2-0 3-1 (LSF)					1-1 2-1 (F5)	
Derby			1-1 2-1 (L3)					1-0 (F6)	2-1 (L3)
Dynamo Kiev									1-1 1-3 (CL)
Hartlepool				1-1 5-0 (L2)					
Huddersfield					2-0 5-0 (L2) 5-0 3-0 (L2)				
Ipswich			4-2 (F6) 2-2 3-2 (F4)				0-1 (F4)		
Leeds	0-0 1-1 0-0 2-1 (F4)	2-0 1-1 (L2)							
Leicester					0-1 (L5)				
Lens							2-4 (L4)		
Liverpool									0-1 1-1 (CL)

Arsenal's Cup results: August 1990 – May 1999 (continued)

	90-91	91-92	92-93	93-94	94-95	95-96	96-97	97-98	98-99
Man City	2-1 (L3)								0-0 1-2 (FSF)
Man Utd	2-6 (L4)							2-1 (F4)	
Middlesbro			1-1 1-1 (**) L2					2-0 (FFi)	
Millwall				1-0 (F3)	0-0 0-2 (F3)				
Newcastle				1-1 3-0 (L3)		2-0 (L5)			
Norwich			2-0 (L5)						
N. Forest			2-0 (F5)						
Odense				1-1 2-1 (CWC1)					
Oldham					0-0 2-0 (L3)				
Omonia Nicosia					3-0 3-1 (CWC1)				
Panathanaikos									2-1 3-1 (CL)
PAOK Salonika								1-1 0-1 (UEFA1)	
Parma				1-0 (CWCFi)					
Paris S.G.				1-0 1-1 (CWCSF)					
Port Vale								0-0 1-1 (**) (F3)	
Preston NE									
Real Zaragosa					1-2 (CWCFi)				4-2 (F3)
Sampdoria					3-2 2-3 (**) CWCSF				

Arsenal's Cup results: August 1990 – May 1999 (continued)

	90-91	91-92	92-93	93-94	94-95	95-96	96-97	97-98	98-99
Scarboro									
Sheff U			1-0 (L4)						
Sheff W			2-1 (LFi) 1-1 2-1 (FFi)		2-0 (L4)	1-1 0-1 (F3) 2-1 (L4)			
Shrewsbury	1-0 (F5)								
Standard Liege				3-0 7-0 (CWC2)					
Stoke									
Sunderland	2-1 (F3)						1-1 5-2 (L3)		
Torino				1-0 0-0 (CWC3)			1-1 2-0 (F3)		
Tottenham	1-3 (FSF)		1-0 (FSF)					2-1 (L5) 1-1 1-1(**) (F6)	
West Ham								1-0 (FSF)	2-1 (F4)
Wolves									
Wrexham		1-2 (F3)							
Yeovil			3-1 (F3)						

F = FA Cup
SF = Semi Final
L = League Cup (in all its guises)
EC = European Cup

L = League, Milk or Littlewoods Cup
Fi = Final
UEFA = UEFA Cup
CL = Champions League

E = UEFA/Cup Winners Cup
F = FA Cup
CWC = Cup Winners Cup
** = Arsenal won on penalties

Number always denotes round Arsenal reached.
In European ties, and league Cup 3rd round ties, Arsenal's home result is always first.

Players' appearances and goals season by season

	90-91	91-92	92-93	93-94	94-95	95-96	96-97	97-98	98-99
T. Adams	37/4	44/2	50/2	49/4	39/1	28/3	34/3	36/3	36/2
N.Anelka								28/9	45/19
V. Bartram					11				
D. Bergkamp						39/16	33/14	40/22	39/16
L. Boa Morte								6/2	7/2
S. Bould	50	24/1	30/1	34/1	41/2	24/1	40	32	19
K. Campbell	19/10	30/14	41/9	40/19	26/5				
J. Carter		6	13/2		2				
A. Clarke						5			
P. Davis	46/3	18	11	32	5/1				
K. Diawara									3
P. Dickov			1/2		6/3	1/1			
L. Dixon	50/6	47/4	44	48	55/1	47/2	36/2	38	47
M. Flatts			7	2	1				
R. Garde							7	7	13
G. Grimandi								23/1	7
D. Grondin									4
P. Groves	20/6								
L. Harper							1		
J. Hartson					18/8	17/5	18/4		
N. Heaney			3	1					
G. Helder					12	21/1			

Players' appearances and goals season by season (continued)

	90-91	91-92	92-93	93-94	94-95	95-96	96-97	97-98	98-99
D. Hillier	14	28/1	38/1	16	11	5			
S. Hughes					1				
J. Jensen			36	41	32/1	20	11/2	13/3	10/2
S. Jonsson	2								
Kanu									5/7
M. Keown			15	32	33/1	41/1	41/1	25	44/2
C. Kiwomya					6/3				
A. Limpar	39/13	27/5	18/2	12					
A. Linighan	10	18/1	30/4	26	20/2	19	12/1		
F. Ljungberg									14/1
J. Lukic							17		
P. Lydersen		5	8						
A. Manninger									10
S. Marshall			2			10/1	6	16	
E. McGoldrick				31/1	13		1	2	
G. McGowan					1	2			
A. Mendez								3/1	3/1
P. Merson	48/16	50/13	49/8	39/12	34/7	47/5	40/9		
A. Miller			3	3					
S. Morrow		14	19/1	9	13/2	4	7		
D. O'Leary	16/1		9						
M. Overmars								45/16	48/12

Players' appearances and goals season by season (continued)

	90-91	91-92	92-93	93-94	94-95	95-96	96-97	97-98	98-99
R. Parlour		2/1	23/2	29/2	36	23	21/2	47/6	47/6
C. Pates		12/1	2						
E. Petit								44/2	33/6
D. Platt						30/5	33/5	14/4	
D. Rocastle	15/2	44/4							
M. Rose						1	1		
S. Schwarz					47/4				
D. Seaman	50	51	56	57	48	47	28	38	44
I. Selley			13	22/1	14/1				
P. Shaw							1/2		
A. Smith	47/27	41/17	39/6	33/7	25/4				
M. Thomas	37/3	9/1							
M. Upson								8	4
P. Vernazza								2	1
P. Vieira							37/2	43/2	43/4
N. Vivas									18/1
N. Winterburn	50	49/1	44/2	51	55	44/2	45	48/1	42
C. Wreh								10/4	8/1
I. Wright		33/26	45/30	53/35	44/30	40/23	36/30	26/11	

Appearances comprise League, FA and League Cups and European competitions. Substitute appearances are not included.

ARSENAL IN THE TRANSFER MARKET – JUNE 1990 – AUG 1999

INCOMING		OUTGOING	
June 1990 – May 1991			
David Seaman (QPR)	£1.3 m	Martin Hayes (Celtic)	£600,000
Andy Linighan (Norwich)	£1.2 m	John Lukic (Leeds)	£1 m
Anders Limpar (Cremonese)	£1 m	Kevin Richardson	
		(Real Sociedad)	£750,000
		Brian Marwood (Sheffield Utd)	
			£350,000
		Pat Scully (Southend)	£100,000
		Kwame Ampadu (WBA)	£50,000
Total in :	**£3.5 m**	**Total out :**	**£2.85 m**

INCOMING		OUTGOING	
June 1991 – May 1992			
Ian Wright (C. Palace)	£2.5 m	Michael Thomas (Liverpool)	£1.5 m
Jimmy Carter (Liverpool)	£500,000		
Pal Lydersen (I.K. Start)	£500,000		
Total in :	**£3.5 m**	**Total out :**	**£1.5 m**

INCOMING		OUTGOING	
June 1992 – May 1993			
John Jensen (Brondby)	£1.1 m	David O'Leary (Leeds)	free
Martin Keown (Everton)	£2 m	Andy Cole (Bristol City)	£500,000
		Perry Groves (Southampton)	£750,000
		David Rocastle (Leeds)	£2 m
Total in :	**£3.1 m**	**Total out :**	**£3.25 m**

INCOMING		OUTGOING	
June 1993 – May 1994			
Eddie McGoldrick (C. Palace)	£1 m	Anders Limpar (Everton)	£1.6 m
		Neil Heaney (Southampton)	£300,000
		Alan Miller (Middlesbro)	£500,000
Total in :	**£1 m**	**Total out :**	**£2.4 m**

INCOMING		OUTGOING	
June 1994 – May 1995			
Stefan Schwarz (Benfica)	£1.8 m	none	
John Hartson (Luton)	£2.4 m		
Chris Kiwomya (Ipswich)	£1.25 m		
Glenn Helder (Arnhem)	£2.3 m		
Total in :	**£7.75 m**	**Total out :**	**£0**

INCOMING

June 1995 – May 1996
David Platt (Sampdoria)   £4.5 m
Dennis Bergkamp (Inter Milan) £7.5 m
John Lukic (Leeds)   free

Total in :   **£12 m**

OUTGOING

Paul Davis (Brentford)   free
Alan Smith   retired
Jimmy Carter (Portsmouth)   free
Kevin Campbell (N. Forest)   £2.5 m
Stefan Schwarz (Fiorentina)   £2.5 m
John Jensen (Brondby)   free
Total out :   **£5 m**

INCOMING

June 1996 – May 1997
Patrick Vieira (A.C. Milan)   £3.5 m
Remi Garde (Strasbourg)   free
Nicolas Anelka
(Paris St Germain)   £500,000

Total in :   **£4 m**

OUTGOING

Paul Dickov (Man City)   £1 m
David Hillier (Portsmouth) £250,000

Andy Linighan (C. Palace)   £1 m
Steve Morrow (QPR)   £500,000
Eddie McGoldrick
(Man City)   £300,000
John Hartson (West Ham)   £5 m
Total out :   **£8.05 m**

INCOMING

June 1997 – May 1998
Alex Manninger   £500,000
(Casino Salzburg)
Gilles Grimandi (Monaco)   £1.5 m

Chris Wreh (Monaco)   unknown
Marc Overmars (Ajax)   £5 m
Matthew Upson (Luton)   £2 m
Luis Boa Morte   £1.8 m
(Sporting Lisbon)
Emmanuel Petit (Monaco)   £3.5 m
Total in :   **£14.3 m**

OUTGOING

Paul Merson (Middlesbro)   £4.5 m

Glenn Helder   undisclosed fee
(Benfica)
Paul Shaw (Millwall)   £250,000
Ian Selley (Fulham)   £500,000

Total out :   **£5.25 m**

INCOMING

June 1998 – May 1999
Nelson Vivas (Boca Juniors) unknown
David Grondin (St Etienne) £500,000
Frederik Ljungberg (Halmstads) £3 m
Kanu (Inter Milan)   £4.5 m

Total in :   **£8 m**

OUTGOING

David Platt   retired
Ian Wright (West Ham)   £750,000
Scott Marshall (Southampton)   free
Matthew Wicks (Crewe)   £100,000
Vince Bartram (Gillingham)   free
Gavin McGowan (Luton)   free
Total out :   **£850,000**

Season	Av home attendance	Av away attendance	Highest home attendance	Highest away attendance
90/91	36,907	25,520	42,512 (C.Pal)	47,232 (Man U)
91/92	31,909	24,037	41,703 (Man U)	46,594 (Man U)
92/93	24,404	22,119	29,739 (Man U)	37,301 (Man U)
93/94	30,576	23,448	36,203 (Man U)	44,009 (Man U)
94/95	35,325	24,197	38,377 (Tottenham)	43,623 (Man U)
95/96	37,568	29,038	38,323 (L'pool)	50,028 (Man U)
96/97	37,821	28,934	38,264 (Tottenham)	55,210 (Man U)
97/98	38,053	30,635	38,269 (Everton)	55,174 (Man U)
98/99	38,023	31,632	38,302 (Aston V)	55,171 (Man U)

Note

Throughout '92/'93, the North Bank was demolished and subsequently rebuilt, which accounts for the low average home attendance.

In the early part of '93/'94, the Clock end was closed until mid October, which also affected the average home attendance.

The highest away attendances demonstrate the increasing gulf in capacity between Highbury and Old Trafford.

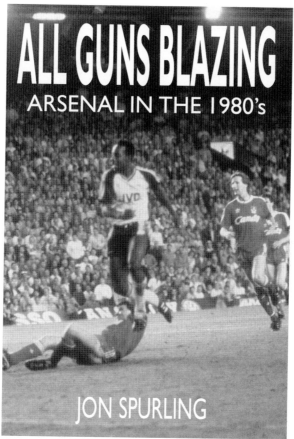

Title: All Guns Blazing   Subtitle: Arsenal in the 1980's
Author : Jon Spurling   ISBN : 1-899750-08-8
Price: £9.99

All Guns Blazing documents the highs and lows of Arsenal Football Club during the 1980's, a decade of drama, controversy and glory for one of Europe's most successful clubs.

Many of Arsenal's major personalities speak frankly about the club for the first time. Charlie Nicholas tells the real story behind his Highbury career and Paul Davis recounts the impact of George Graham on Arsenal.

Uncompromising and opinionated, All Guns Blazing is an indispensable guide to the origins of the modern Arsenal, beginning with the club's cup exploits of 1980 and ending with George Graham's boys' heroics at Anfield in 1989.

Jon Spurling is a lifelong fan of Arsenal and shares the unforgettable blend of tragedy and triumph experienced by Arsenal fans in the 1980's.

Available now: Aureus Publishing Limited, 24 Mafeking Road, Cardiff, CF23 5DQ.
Tel/Fax: (029) 2045 5200. email: sales@aureus.co.uk

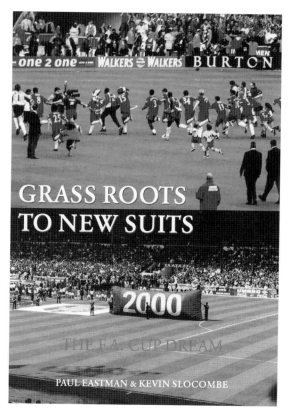

GRASS ROOTS
TO NEW SUITS

2000

THE FA CUP DREAM

PAUL EASTMAN & KEVIN SLOCOMBE

Title: Grass Roots to New Suits

ISBN : 1-899750-11-8

No. pages: 224

Authors : Paul Eastman & Kevin Slocombe

Price: £8.99

Size: A5 Paperback

Grass Roots to New Suits is a humorous in-depth journey through the 1999-2000 FA Cup knockout competition. The story meanders through each round of the world's oldest football cup competition, from the earliest qualifying rounds to the pomp and ceremony of the last Wembley Final.

Grass Roots to New Suits takes the reader inside the areas that matter. Revel in the highs and lows of minnows Mangotsfield United and the millionaire lifestyle of Chelsea FC. The efforts of the few men who keep the semi-professional clubs going are vividly depicted, so too is the high-life of the chosen few at the top. Self-effacing and full of laughs Grass Roots to New Suits captures the electric atmosphere of football dressing rooms, the pressure and formality of the boardrooms and the opposite ends of the emotional scale in the post-match players' bar.

Paul Eastman and Kevin Slocombe have had complete freedom to gallop through the sacred areas of football reserved for the select few. Their perceptive and intelligent analysis is an insight to the football world at all levels. If you are a terrace wit, a Sunday league player, or a millionaire director Grass Roots to New Suits is an essential read.

Available now: Aureus Publishing Limited, 24 Mafeking Road, Cardiff, CF23 5DQ.
Tel/Fax: (029) 2045 5200. email: sales@aureus.co.uk

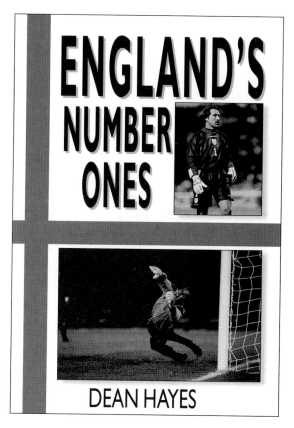

DEAN HAYES

Title: England's Number Ones
ISBN : 1-899750-57-6
No. pages: 156

Author : Dean Hayes
Price: £7.99
Size: Royal Octavo Paperback

Goals are what football is all about. And the great ones, like great occasions, live long in the memory, stored away in the mind to be re-lived and re-told again and again. But if there is one facet of the game which captivates the onlooker as much, it is 'the great save'. The ball speeds goalwards but in the very moment that the roar reaches a crescendo, a palm or a finger tip stretches to divert it away. And in that moment, one hero replaces another.

Every goalkeeper has his day and since their first official international match in 1872, England have had 97 custodians. They form an extremely varied gallery ranging from leading figures in politics, church and the armed forces to the more unusual, the British High Jump champion, a blacksmith's apprentice and a coffee planter from Sri Lanka!

This book captures the flavour of those players who have been England's Number Ones.

Available now: Aureus Publishing Limited, 24 Mafeking Road, Cardiff, CF23 5DQ.
Tel/Fax: (029) 2045 5200. email: sales@aureus.co.uk

Other sports titles published by Aureus Publishing

Title	Author	ISBN	Price
Cardiff City FC - An A-Z	Dean Hayes	1 899750 03 7	£7.99
Swansea City FC - An A-Z	Dean Hayes	1 899750 04 5	£7.99
Swindon Town FC - An A-Z	Dean Hayes	1 899750 06 1	£7.99
Bristol City FC - An A-Z	Dean Hayes	1 899750 07 X	£7.99
All Guns Blazing			
- Arsenal in the 1980's	Jon Spurling	1 899750 08 8	£9.99
Grass Roots to New Suits	Eastman/Slocombe	1 899750 11 8	£8.99
Sunderland FC - An A-Z	Dean Hayes	1 899750 14 2	£7.99
Middlesbrough FC - An A-Z	Dean Hayes	1 899750 17 7	£8.99
Queens Park Rangers FC - An A-Z	Dean Hayes	1 899750 18 5	£8.99
Blackpool FC - An A-Z	Dean Hayes	1 899750 20 7	£7.99
Famous Footballers of Wales	Dean Hayes	1 899750 21 5	£7.99
Scotland's Number Ones	Dean Hayes	1 899750 22 3	£7.99
Top Guns			
- Arsenal in the 1990's	Jon Spurling	1 899750 23 1	£9.99
Liverpool's Number Ones	Darren Phillips	1 899750 24 X	£8.99
With Hope In Their Hearts	Darren Phillips	1 899750 25 8	£9.99
- Liverpool in the 1960's			
Liverpool FC An A-Z	Darren Phillips	1 899750 26 6	£8.99
England's Number Ones	Dean Hayes	1 899750 57 6	£7.99
Supermac	McCallen, Phillip	1 899750 63 0	£15.99
We Will Be Back	Kerr, Ian	1 899750 68 1	£6.99
Scarborough FC's Farewell To			
The Football League			

Available now: Aureus Publishing Limited, 24 Mafeking Road, Cardiff, CF23 5DQ.
Tel/Fax: (029) 2045 5200. email: sales@aureus.co.uk

www.aureus.co.uk